EXPERT TEACHERS

Expert Teachers is a compelling book that explores issues surrounding the concept of the expert teacher from a truly international perspective. Expert teaching, a global phenomenon that exerts significant influence on education policy and practice, has developed rapidly since the 1980s and significantly impacted many teachers' careers. As a result, this book poses pertinent and important questions scrutinising the topic as well as considering possibilities for future models. The book reviews and expands upon issues such as:

- What does it mean to be an 'expert' teacher?
- What have been the most successful models of expert teaching?
- Is rewarding a minority of the 'best' teachers a sustainable method of raising standards?
- What is the role of expertise in furthering the aim to make teaching a 'top tier' career?
- What are the dominant and emerging models of expert teaching globally?
- In what ways can we expect models of expert teaching to develop in the future?

With case studies of specific systems, and analyses of the issues and context therein, this book offers an exceptional insight into the effects of expert teaching models – their effects on the teacher as an individual as well as standards and education policy internationally. The book argues that the current focus on pursuing misleading high-stakes test scores is underserving the teaching profession and that instead the focus for expert teaching should be grounded in issues of social justice and community wellbeing.

This book will appeal greatly to current teachers, those currently undertaking teacher training and students or academics carrying out research in the field of teacher education, professional development and expertise.

Andrew Goodwyn is Professor of Education at the University of Reading, UK.

EXPERT TEACHERS

An international perspective

Andrew Goodwyn

Routledge
Taylor & Francis Group
LONDON AND NEW YORK

First published 2017
by Routledge
2 Park Square, Milton Park, Abingdon, Oxon OX14 4RN

and by Routledge
711 Third Avenue, New York, NY 10017

Routledge is an imprint of the Taylor & Francis Group, an informa business

British Library Cataloguing in Publication Data
A catalogue record for this book is available from the British Library

Library of Congress Cataloging in Publication Data
A catalog record for this book has been requested

ISBN: 978-0-415-81220-7 (hbk)
ISBN: 978-0-415-81221-4 (pbk)
ISBN: 978-0-203-06957-8 (ebk)

Typeset in Bembo
by Apex CoVantage, LLC

I should like to dedicate this book to my wife, Linda Fitzsimons, for her love and support throughout the time of writing this book and for her patience whenever my enthusiasm for the cause of teachers became too strident or loudly passionate, especially in the kitchen.

. . . you and I are old;
Old age hath yet his honour and his toil;
Death closes all: but something ere the end,
Some work of noble note, may yet be done,

Tho' much is taken, much abides; and tho'
We are not now that strength which in old days
Moved earth and heaven, that which we are, we are;
One equal temper of heroic hearts,
Made weak by time and fate, but strong in will
To strive, to seek, to find, and not to yield.

From 'Ulysees' by Alfred, Lord Tennyson

CONTENTS

ACKNOWLEDGEMENTS

I should like to thank Carol Fuller for her chapter on ASTs in England and Ellie Francis-Brophy for hers on ASTs and HATs in Australia. The very great majority of the book was therefore written by me and its shortcomings are therefore mine.

I should also like to thank the many teacher educators and teachers who I have worked with over 40 years and who have helped me to understand just how complex and extraordinary teaching is as a profession and also just how remarkable are the expert teachers who exemplify everything about what we mean by 'great teachers'.

Andrew Goodwyn

INTRODUCTION

This text is, to our knowledge, the first book-length discussion of the concept of the expert teacher from a truly international perspective. The concept itself is much disputed from many perspectives, not least by teachers themselves but also, rather more powerfully, by policymakers and politicians. However, what cannot be disputed is that what we call 'models of expert teaching' are a global phenomenon and have sufficient importance to exert global influence. The Advanced Skills Teacher (AST) model – really more a title – developed in Australia in the 1980s, was 'borrowed' by England in 1997 as a designation; the AST attribution in Australia is being replaced by Highly Accomplished Teacher (HAT) as part of career structure, a model developed in the US in the 1980s as a form of teacher certification: it is now one of the longest-running success stories of such models. However, the AST model in England was summarily abolished in 2013, as was the short-lived Chartered Teacher model in Scotland in 2011. These abolitions were political, not educational, decisions.

What do these examples tell us about models of expert teaching around the world? They tell us several important things that link to some of the key questions whose answers lead to themes explored in this book:

What do you call an 'expert teacher' and who chooses the name?

How do you credibly identify such expert teachers and how long does that status remain current?

What do you 'do' with these teachers? Just give them a title like the original ASTs in Australia or give them a job to do, as associated with the AST designation in England?

Is this job and/or title meant to show comparability with advanced levels in other professions? For instance, has the term Chartered Teacher in Scotland been chosen because 'chartered' is a term with commonly understood meaning across professions?

Is the recognition also a reward? If it is, is it intrinsic (i.e. indicating status) or extrinsic (i.e. to do with pay and career)?

What is the main purpose of such categorisation? Is it, for example, to keep the best teachers in the classroom rather than have them tempted out of it to become managers?

Who 'controls' such categorisation? Is it ministries of education, which means it can be politically established and then abolished like the AST in England and the Chartered Teacher in Scotland? Or is it under the auspices of a genuinely independent entity like the National Board for Professional Teaching Standards (NBPTS) in the US?

How do the teachers themselves participate in the design and maintenance of such models?

What difference do these teachers make? Supposing you can accurately define expert teaching and then select the appropriate teachers, how will you know they are 'making a difference'?

This last point also raises the question of economics: who pays for what?

Does having expert teachers have a value in elevating the status of the teaching profession? 'Chartered' would appear to be an aspirational term suggesting comparison with other 'top' professions. Does Advanced Skills Teacher sound rather like a superior technician?

Is the expert teaching model quite deliberately elitist, with only a proportion of teachers achieving 'expert' status? For example, ASTs in England never made up more than 2 per cent of the workforce. Or should it be more of an *aspiration*? For instance, the Chartered Teacher model in Scotland was predicated on most teachers reaching the level.

Can having these exemplary expert teachers not only raise the status of the profession but also have a value in improving public understanding of teaching, give teachers a stronger role in the community and, perhaps most importantly, have an impact on politicians and policies?

We believe these are very important questions and only partly answered at this stage of the emergence of the global phenomenon. We began to think in depth about these questions when we embarked on a major research project in 2009 to try to understand the experiences of Advanced Skills Teachers in England. We have subsequently undertaken further research, which this book draws on.

The research work was a team effort and the book was conceived by the team; for this reason the term 'we' is used throughout the text. However, while the book was being written, people's careers moved on, so two, very important, chapters have been contributed by individuals from that team: Carol Fuller (ASTs in England) and Ellie Francis-Brophy (ASTs and HATs in Australia).

As national education systems develop around these models, we argue for an adaptive approach – that is, there is no 'one size fits all' super model; rather, there should be intelligent local developments informed by good international examples. We argue this not only at the deep level of Darwinian theory about human adaptation but also at the much more practical level of working within highly structured but individually distinctive school systems, however flawed they might be. We do argue that teachers everywhere can learn from others about expert practice and that developing models around the world will lead to more knowledge of what expert teaching 'is' and, perhaps more importantly, how it can be developed. At the same time we try to demonstrate that what appear to be the best models are highly locally inflected.

Certainly we believe that the decade 2010–20 will be a period of attention paid to teachers both as a profession and as individuals and that this is a shift from the previous paradigm, which focused on school improvement. It is not that school improvement has stopped being an issue: what has happened is that a number of different voices from a range of speakers has now become a chorus agreeing that any system can only ever be as good as its actual teachers. So, school leadership is crucial, learning environments are increasingly sophisticated, more technology can help, but *teachers* really are what make the difference in the classroom and to the lives of students.

A very significant element, which we see as part of the greater focus on teacher quality, is the focus on developing descriptors of teacher competence, most of which are called 'standards'. Some of these have evolved as part of a national system (as in England in the early twenty-first century) or federal system (as in Australia in the 1980s), some are entirely associated with expert teacher categories such as the US Highly Accomplished Teacher (HAT). The latter are highly subject and age-phase related; others are either generic or hierarchical, or, sometimes, both. Some are holistic and about much more than classroom performance – for example, those connected to Chartered Teacher models. These models and their various standards and descriptors form a great deal of the substance of this book. As the basis for analysis and discussion we have chosen to quote extensively from their documentation; this can mean quite lengthy extracts, but we prefer this specific approach to many pages of appendices and always sending the reader off to the back of the book. Much of this material principally exists on websites, often accompanied by booklets for teachers and others; almost always the standards have no author as such: they have been produced, it appears, by the agency that sponsors or operates them.

This latter point raises two issues discussed at length in the book: first, what is the status and governance of such standards, and second, who 'owns' them – by which we mean in part, what is their credibility with the teachers themselves? Such documentation can also be extremely ephemeral, disappearing as policy changes: for example, models of expert teaching, such as the AST in England, have been peremptorily abolished, raising issues of sustainability. The US HAT model has now survived – and, in our view, thrived – for over 25 years, not least because the National Board for Professional Teaching Standards, which developed and operated the HAT model, is truly independent and not subject to direct political interference. Politics and policy will inevitably feature throughout this book.

Chapter 1 considers some of the key questions above, its main focus being what we mean by *expert*. Close attention is paid to the general concept of expertise, explored principally from a Darwinian perspective. Expertise is thus considered as a profoundly human phenomenon, and the chapter explores some of its implications for professions in general, as well as those specific to teaching.

Teaching has a long history, but its attempts to become a profession are more recent, and its ambition to have parity with 'top tier' professions such as medicine and law is much disputed. In Chapter 2 we explore the interrelationship between teaching as a second-tier profession and the role of teacher expertise in furthering the aim to become 'top tier'. Using the English example, this includes analysing the difference between the rhetoric of governments extolling the virtues of the teaching profession and parading its importance, and the reality of how teachers are controlled and treated. Part of the negative treatment of the profession is about the balance between autonomy and accountability, so much weight being placed on the latter element. We know that expert teaching flourishes in an atmosphere of public trust and self-regulation, as in countries like Finland. In England, the General Teaching Council was created to be the key body in the lives of teachers but swiftly 'failed' and was summarily abolished, a perfect example of how not to elevate the profession – indeed, how to diminish the view that teachers are expert and effective professionals. We consider influential concepts such as 'effective' teaching and 'reflective teaching', both of which have contributed to increasing recognition of what makes 'expert teaching'. The chapter also reviews the role of inspection in accountability and, more importantly, the increase and ubiquity of teacher standards around the world. We argue that standards are highly problematic but on balance can be seen as a potentially positive development for teaching as a profession and particularly for creating descriptors of best teaching practice that have external validity and credibility.

Chapter 3 considers Hattie's seminal meta-analysis of expert teaching and reviews in detail both the five dimensions and the 16 attributes that he identified. It then reviews the emergence of models of expert teaching in relation to the growing field of teacher expertise in general. One element in these fields has been the consideration of stages of expertise and we examine the influential model developed by the Dreyfus brothers, whose hypothesis came from their work in artificial intelligence (AI). They concluded that the human mind has unique powers that AI will never match, fundamentally because in skilled domains, human beings learn from a combination of practice, experience and mental focus. Their five-stage model, from *novice to expert*, has been extremely influential across many skilled domains, from highly structured ones such as chess playing, to relatively weak ones such as nursing and teaching, and we devote some space to illustrating how the stages were used in a significant study of nursing. This consideration of stages leads on to a discussion about the most common and extant names for expert teachers. The chapter concludes with a consideration of the AST model in England and the appearance but failure of the Excellent Teacher (ET) model, which was intended to complement but not replace AST (looked at in detail in its case study chapter). The discussion considers the standards used to define AST and how teachers in England felt about the titles AST and ET, seeking to explain why the ET model failed to become accepted and viable.

The next three chapters offer case studies of three of the most significant developments in the history of expert teaching, Chapter 4 focusing on the AST in England, Chapter 5 on the AST in Australia and Chapter 6 on the Highly Accomplished Teacher model in the USA. Each case attempts to consider in depth the matrix of issues that surround both the creation of such models and what makes them sustainable or, in a sense, fragile. This matrix includes aspects of the education system and the culture within which it operates, matters of governance and political control and/or independence and economics. Together they demonstrate the complexity of such developments and illustrate both similarities and differences in nation states. This leads on to the discussions in the final chapters that focus on what lessons might be learnt from these three examples for the longer-term development of such models in an increasingly global context.

The final two chapters, 7 and 8, develop a discussion of the various models around the world and offer some speculation about the future. Chapter 7 looks closely at rather different territory, exploring the much more holistic and ethically charged Chartered Teacher concept, both as a national focus, for example in Scotland, and also in more specific and distinct institutional forms such as subject associations and the very unusual city model, the London Chartered Teacher. The other focus in this chapter is on the highly contrasting models developed in two small nation states: one is the teaching profession in Finland, which has no expert model but rather a flexible and distributed but overarching approach to teacher expertise, and the other is the highly centralised and hierarchically structured model in Singapore. We argue that these two national systems are fascinating examples of the global phenomenon of expert teaching, even though neither approach would be replicable elsewhere, certainly not in large and highly diverse nation states or federal systems.

Finally, Chapter 8 brings together the major themes of the book in considering future possibilities. It reasserts that models of expert teaching are a global phenomenon and clearly here to stay and that they have much in common, many differences and also much to learn from each other. It is clear that political policies will always have a place in forming the direction of the education systems of nation states but that they rarely help to elevate the teaching profession and have often interfered disastrously with the expert teacher element. Research into teacher expertise develops nationally and internationally at a good pace and we can now begin to see teacher expertise becoming a recognised part of the many domains of expertise that stretch from chess playing to flying jumbo jets. One significant development is increasing attention paid to expert teaching from an international perspective and the chapter looks at some success stories such as the advocacy work of the NBPTS and the relatively new and intelligent model being developed by the Australian Institute for Teaching and School Leadership. We conclude that there is need for much more research, especially into the affective dimensions of great teaching, and less pursuit of simplistic measures such as the attempt to judge all teachers by high stakes test scores. Equally, there is a significant opportunity for real improvements in student achievement if the principles of social justice are applied; for example, having recognised and certified expert teachers they can, where relevant, be deployed to schools where students have the greatest needs. We believe that this is a very positive time for models for expert teaching to develop and flourish around the world, learning from each other but always adapting to the local environment and celebrating the success of the teaching profession where it matters, in the schools and communities where the students live and grow.

1

WHAT DOES IT MEAN TO BE AN EXPERT?

Exploring the concept of expertise in (and out) of the classroom from an international perspective

Andrew Goodwyn

Introduction

There has been a steady growth in the knowledge base about expertise in a range of skill-based domains, often generated by novice-to-expert comparisons. This chapter provides a section on defining the nature of expertise, before applying this understanding to teacher expertise. As this is an international book it includes contrasting models of expertise generated over time through cultural and historical influences. It identifies different paradigms (for example, in China expert teachers must demonstrate a passionate love of their country). How is the concept of expertise used in worldwide educational policy and teaching scholarship? Whose interests are served by such definitions and whose might be ignored? How does this focus on expertise relate to more marketised, neo-liberal changes in education over the same time period? Is expert teacher status the desired 'end state' for all teachers or simply something to be aspired to?

It is important to stress that there are a number of models emerging around the world, some – like the US Highly Accomplished Teacher, in existence for over 25 years – can be considered fully established. Developed systems are sharing an interest in how to identify expert teachers and experimenting with what you 'do' with them. For example, is the purpose of recognising such teachers to enhance the status of the teaching profession (like the Chartered Teacher in Scotland) or is it to require them to undertake special activities (as with the Advanced Skills Teacher in England). As yet there is no international consensus and there may never be, but there is most certainly strong international influence – for example, the Advanced Skills Teacher title originated in Australia before being exported to England in 1997, where it may be replaced in the future by Master Teacher, a term commonly used in the US. More examples of this international 'borrowing' or adapting will be discussed later in the book. While this book was being written, the government decided to terminate the designation Advanced Skills Teacher in England with effect from September 2013 and, as mentioned, has considered a recommendation to replace it with 'Master Teacher'.

The key point to note here is that this appears to be a purely political decision, an illustration of how the teaching profession in many countries is subject to the whims of ministers who come through the political turnstyle, make their mark and then move on. No evidence was provided to justify this decision to abolish the AST and there was no government-funded evaluation of the effectiveness or otherwise of the AST – our research (see Chapter 4) remains the most comprehensive review of recent years. Recent research in England (Goodwyn and Roberts, 2015; Goodwyn 2015a, 2015b, 2014) finds that head teachers and other senior management staff profoundly regret the passing of the AST, and while a minority had some reservations about the effectiveness of the role, the great majority consider a national scheme necessary to benefit the teaching profession and assist with raising standards.

Another universal issue is that no country (to our knowledge) uses the term 'expert teacher' and our research indicates clearly that teachers themselves do not like the term. For example, in England, the creation of the 'Excellent Teacher' (ET) grade in 2006 seemed illustrative of increasing recognition of the importance of expert teaching. However, the establishment of the Advanced Skills Teacher role in 1998, some ten years before, points to real uncertainty around what to call 'expert teachers' and equally complex issues around role definition: what do you do with expert teachers once you are sure you have correctly identified them? The establishment of these two categories also demonstrates how reluctant teachers and policymakers are to use the term 'expert' when applied to teaching. In the end the Excellent Teacher category was a complete failure in terms of teacher interest (see Hutchings, Mansaray, Minty and Smart, 2009). Although it was designed to complement the Advanced Skills Teacher role, not replace it – the AST emphasis had been on 'outreach' (see Chapter 4), the Excellent Teacher would concentrate on 'inreach' – by 2011 only 57 ETs had been appointed and our research suggests that there was little or no further interest; like the AST, this role has now been abolished.

What is expertise?

However, the very first concern is to examine the term *expert* and its derivative, *expertise*.

There has been a remarkable focus on the term 'expert' during the twentieth century, but its historical development reminds us how long it has been central to our lives – so much so that its application to teaching may be considered to have come about surprisingly late. However, from expert comes expertise, a much less divisive notion. What all the major professions (law, medicine, etc.) have in common is a powerful focus on identifying what characterises expertise in their particular field and ensuring that they 'control' and develop those features.

The term 'expert' has enjoyed a much simpler history than 'profession'. Deriving originally from the Latin meaning 'experienced' and 'practiced in', the term has been rather consistently defined and understood. There is the occasional mention in English literature – for example, in Chaucer's *General Prologue to The Canterbury Tales*, in introducing the Mancible and his learned advisors, there occurs the line, 'That were of lawe expert and curious', and in Shakespeare's *Othello*, Cassio says of Othello's ship: 'his Pylot Of verie expert, and approu'd Allowance'. In the nineteenth century, expert becomes more about having both specialised knowledge and being a specialist, but this was already implicit in both Chaucer and Shakespeare's usage. Late in the nineteenth century the definition included having an expert opinion, implying that others would want to access such an opinion and also pointing to the later development of the 'expert witness'.

Expertise is variously defined but there is fundamental agreement. *The Cambridge Handbook of Expertise and Expert Performance* (see Ericsson *et al.*, 2006, pp. 1–17) is an authoritative place to begin and we have adapted their comments to add some additional points about teaching:

> First, it is the characteristics, skills and knowledge that distinguish the experts from novices and less experienced people. For example, it is very easy to hear differences in musical performance, even without having musical expertise.
>
> Second, experts are able consistently (though not perfectly) to reproduce high levels of performance. For example, experienced and expert doctors typically make correct diagnoses. This aspect of expertise is often called 'superior reproducible performance of representative tasks'; this is a very clear distinguisher in teaching between the novice and the expert teacher.
>
> Third, although the notion of the 'precocious' is powerful and especially impresses the general public in certain domains, particularly in musical performance, chess playing, various sporting domains, etc., experts are highly experienced in their domain. This can be simplistically quantified: e.g. 'she has been teaching for 40 years'.
>
> Fourth, being experienced does not guarantee expertise. Experts have mental organisations of their experience that make them vastly superior to equally experienced peers. However, although there is increasingly a body of evidence to support this point, it is, by its mental nature, not easily susceptible to 'proof'. At a pragmatic level most teachers do develop a sense of who, amongst their colleagues, is open to maintaining a developmental perspective on their teaching, however experienced they are. There is a danger here of mere 'folk lore' conceptualisations, one argument, therefore, in favour of more professional attention to identifying and studying true teacher expertise.
>
> Fifth, and less certainly, expertise is acquired through *deliberate* training and practice, rather than through merely *repetitive* practice. This point seems very obvious, but it is more complex than it seems at first. It might imply that if one practised a skill in isolation for long enough one would become

> expert, for example in playing the violin. And expert violinists spend huge amounts of time doing just that. However, they also learn from watching others, from direct instruction and from indirect means such as reading about the lives of musicians. For teachers, all these elements are also important – that is, observing other teachers, engaging in professional development and absorbing knowledge through 'indirect' means, using everything from a book like this one to a conversation in the staff room.

Historically, the idea of the expert, whether the term is used or not, is an aspect of all cultures and civilisations and this will be considered below. However, when going deeper into human history, Darwinian theory is fundamentally important. This is not the place for a full explanation of Darwin's and subsequent thinkers' views on evolutionary development: there are numerous examples in many disciplines, with psychology dominating – see, for example, *The Oxford Handbook of Evolutionary Psychology* (Dunbar and Barrett, 2007). The last 30 years have seen a quantum leap in Darwinian studies, with these ideas applied to many current forms of human activity. The chief shift in intellectual emphasis has been to apply Darwinian concepts to the humanities and social sciences and generally to develop interdisciplinary models of investigation such as sociobiology. The key development of modern versions of Darwinian theory, and most relevant to thinking about professions such as teaching, is the concept of the adaptive mind. This argues that adaptation is not just physiological (as in the first humans becoming upright) or just about creating physical objects (such as tools which are more fit for a specific function than the human body) but extends to the mind evolving psychological mechanisms. The seminal work *The Adapted Mind: Evolutionary Psychology and the Generation of Culture* (Barkow, Cosmides and Tooby, 1992) began a revolution in thinking about psychological evolutionary changes that could explain fundamental aspects of human development and, for want of a better term, our increasing 'civilisation'.

For example, a crude view of Darwinian theory would argue that our only real concern is survival – our own and that of our immediate family: we are endlessly focused on mating, food and shelter. While it is important to recognise that these are strong and fundamental urges, most of the time human beings do not behave as if this is all they are focusing on. What we have developed is self-regulation, allowing us to override such urges and see their limitations. Modern theory also puts forward the idea of 'inclusive fitness' – not just the survival of the fittest, but a desire to support others to survive. This begins with offspring but moves on to include other relatives and then on again to 'similar individuals' – the tribe, perhaps, or other type of bonded social group. This is the beginning of cooperative social behaviour. More recent theorists have argued that we could not live in cities without this being a fundamental part of our adapted minds. For all the problems associated with life in cities, we seem to choose to live in them and, remarkably, get along most of the time, creating highly elaborate systems of support.

It might be speculated that education systems are an example of this inclusive fitness. That is, that they are systems designed to help the survival of the species generally but also a particular 'tribe': this might be a national system (England, France, etc.) or a federal one (US, Canada Australia). There may also be an intellectual link to the biological fact that human beings produce remarkably helpless offspring needing several years of intensive care before they can achieve any real independence. Education might be conceptualised as an extension of this parenting function, i.e. a system that ensures the survival of the knowledge base and provides offspring with the time they need to achieve maturity. Whatever else, we know that, in most countries, teachers are expected to act in 'locus parentis', to behave like a 'reasonable parent' would behave. This point has clear implications for expert teachers, not least because 'caring' for children does not have an obviously measurable outcome. The degree to which the test results for schemes such as PISA (Programme for International Student Assessment, controlled by the Organisation for Economic Cooperation and Development; see www.oecd.org/pisa/) dominate certain nation states' educational policies reveals the importance attached to international league tables.

For our purpose here, the key focus is human *adaptiveness* and skill acquisition. Whether adopting a Darwinian perspective or not, one can see a common pattern in human history, the essential principle of which is specialisation. Once humans lived in groups, especially once a certain degree of stability was achieved, the group could undertake a far wider range of activities than just foraging for food and raising young. Our increasing understanding of human development through, for example, archaeology provides a rapidly expanding evidence base for human specialisation: a seminal text is Mithen's *The Prehistory of the Mind: A Search for the Origins of Art, Religion and Science* (1998).

Modern specialisation

What follows is a summary of what seems to be accepted as key developments in what we now call expertise. This book on expert teachers is not the first (see, for example: Loughran, 2010; Goodwyn, 2010; Bisset-Turner, 2001) but it can claim to be the first with such an international reach. Ericsson *et al.*'s *Handbook of Expertise and Expert Performance* was only published in 2006 and the editors comment:

> A significant milestone is reached when a field of scientific research matures to a point warranting the publication of its first handbook. A substantial body of empirical findings, distinctive theoretical concepts and frameworks, and a new set of adapted methods justifying a unifying volume.
>
> *(p. 4)*

The editors go on to cite many other publications which focus on specific fields, but an examination of its 901 pages of densely printed text reveal very little directly related to expertise in teaching – although there is an interesting chapter on educators and expertise, which will be discussed below. Suffice it to say that while there has been a much more scientific focus on expert teaching over the last 25 years, this has not yet generated a consensus or a unifying volume.

Despite the point made above about education systems being a universal feature of almost every society, there is absolutely no general agreement about the exact purpose of education and even less about how it should be organised and regulated. The pattern seems to be that formal education in the shape of schooling begins in an ad hoc way but at some point the state takes some or complete control and then creates or regulates a 'system'. This book can only acknowledge the extraordinary debates about education that were a dominant feature of the twentieth century and seem very unlikely to diminish in the twenty-first. Governments in general are obsessed with the outcomes of education, and this leads – certainly in democratic states – to endless 'reform', which educators themselves see more as interference and change for change's sake.

A number of points emerge from this brief reference to debates about education. There is universal acceptance of the vital importance of an education system and very deep differences regarding what it is for. Many systems tolerate significant differences within the system at school level, and many countries have different names for different types of school. In England, for example, one can contrast 'faith' and 'state' schools, 'grammar' and 'vocational' schools, more recently 'free schools' and 'academies'. All systems need teachers and there is much shared rhetoric about the fundamental importance of recruiting and retaining good teachers, as any government website will attest. Again, that is where agreement ends: how good teachers should be recruited and retained, what do we mean by 'good', what should teachers actually do, for example 'love' children, or 'discipline' them – these remain topics of fierce debate. Barber and Mourshed's (2007) *The McKinsey Report: How the World's Best Performing Education Systems Come out on Top* and Mourshed, Chijioke and Barber's (2010) *How the World's Most Improved School Systems Keep Getting Better* both look at how very different 'successful' systems (successful in their terms) recruit and retain teachers.

So, while models comparing educational systems began to emerge in the late twentieth century – the best known being PISA (see above) and PIRLS (Progress in International Reading Literacy Study) and TIMMS (Trends in International Mathematics and Science Study) – heightening political neuroses about national systems, there is as yet no consensus regarding what good teachers 'are'. The Teaching and Learning International Survey (TALIS) is a relatively new development by the OECD, as is its Education Today series, an attempt to summarise some of its main findings. In the edition for 2013, for example, it states:

> Teachers have a key role to play in delivering quality education, and feedback is increasingly important to help them cope with changing demands and curricula. The quality of programmes is driven by the need for foundation skills plus adaptability and ability to learn going forward; increasingly too education is not just a matter of national standards but ensuring quality in cross-border offerings.
>
> *(OECD, 2012, p. 9)*

Here the OECD is much in tune with the contributors to this book, also stating:

> Shared patterns exist alongside notable differences such as in teacher beliefs (as charted with the Teaching and Learning International Survey (TALIS) and in school time use. OECD work has analysed the characteristics of learners and learning, teachers, and how to improve school leadership.
>
> *(p. 27)*

Thus, there is sufficient evidence and emerging research to justify some universalising judgements about teachers and also to show where local differences are explicable in terms of culture and traditions. This is the precise approach this book takes – discussing and analysing what we know about 'good' teachers and looking at specific examples of 'expert teaching' in real, usually national, contexts. This book does not claim the same status as Ericsson *et al.*'s *Handbook* and there is not a unified field from which to draw definitive conclusions. Indeed, in education this may never be possible. Our endeavours thus focus on what we can say we 'know' about the best teachers and, very often, what we 'feel' is important about them; there is a necessary degree of speculation. In this way we aim to contribute to an internationally shared understanding of 'great teachers' without claiming that any national model has achieved a definitive status; see further discussion of international comparisons below.

Returning to the concept of expertise and its historical development, societies generally begin with the creation of cultural structures that create mutually recognisable identity. Such structures may be visible in the form of religion, ways of producing food, similar clothing, etc. Such developments usefully reveal the interrelated nature of cultural and physical change. The development of religion leads to the origins of the religious figure or leader. Such a figure will be distinguished by garments and physical symbols and someone has to make these artefacts.

A good example is the development of a highly skilled physical domain like jewellery making. Jewellery was designed to be long lasting and some very old jewellery has survived; it appears to satisfy a universal human need for display and for indicating status and power. It also seems to be one of the earliest forms of highly skilled specialist domain. It is also representative because it needs craft knowledge, passed on by others, yet also innovation and individual imagination. Such physically skilled domains become established over time as recognisable bodies of knowledge, with customs and traditions that manifest themselves in part through the creation of institutions – for example, the craft guilds formed in England (and many other societies). Such bodies typically devised regulatory functions, models of training and codes of conduct and became powerful interest groups. They even developed hierarchies of expertise, from the lowly apprentice to the master builder and so on.

There would seem to have been a parallel development in the emergence of skilled mental domains: the example of religion was cited above. Early civilisations very quickly found they had a need for doctors, merchants, lawyers, accountants – whatever they were then called, we recognise their universality. These domains are by no means purely intellectual: doctors need physical skills as well as mental ones. However, these groups tended to form themselves into the institutions that have become our professions, with the emphasis on higher-order knowledge and societal status often linked to financial reward.

The emergence of these skilled domains reminds us, at a simple level, of our need for very specific expertise and our human adaptiveness in longer-term development. Whether physical or mental or both, the expertise resides not only in the individual during their life span but also in a body of knowledge that can be passed on. However, the very term 'expertise' reminds us that whatever our potential to become expert, very few of us become truly expert in any specific domain: most of us become modestly good at a whole range of skills because life, and survival, requires them.

Some characteristics of human expertise

What follows is a summary of our current understanding of human expertise. The thinking in this area continues to progress and certain points below are especially pertinent to still controversial aspects of teacher development.

Individual differences in mental capacities

Whatever else we might not agree about, we have all come to recognise that the brain is the control box for everything we do, whether 'mental' or 'physical'. We also appreciate that humans have very different individual mental capacities. This is not the same as notions of 'intelligence'. In passing it is worth noting that the debate over whether IQ (intelligence quotient) can measure one overarching capacity called 'intelligence' has preoccupied much educational and political debate since at least the 1950s. Indeed, the reaction against this simplifying view of the human mind has generated many alternative views, a spectacular example being Gardner's development of 'multiple intelligences' (see Gardner, 1983, 1993, 2000). For education systems this debate works at the structural level, as indicated above: if you believe that some children are 'good with their hands' and others are 'good with their heads' then you create a system based on this distinction, with very clear implications for what expert teachers should be able to teach. Either you take that approach or you organise different learning routes within your school.

What matters for this summary is that mental capacity differences are a real feature of human life, in every society and every culture, and therefore some people will have better capacity than others for the skilled domain of teaching. They will also have better long-term potential to become increasingly good as that capacity is exercised and challenged; this is especially important for the notion of expert teachers – that is, those who move from 'novice' to 'expert', the central theme of this book. It is important to stress that the recognition of these mental capacity differences is a clear feature of the expertise of teachers in understanding their own expertise and an absolute divider of novices and experts. This is not elitism per se, although systems may themselves deliberately foster elites. As teachers work, essentially, with more and more capacity to understand individual minds, they become remarkably astute at differentiation; there will be more discussion about this and teacher expertise later on.

Inherent or genetic?

If we accept that individuals display significant differences in mental (and even more obviously physical) capacity, how do we explain it? Are these capacities inherent – that is, do we all have the same human capabilities present in our brains but only some develop? A simple example is music. It appears that the enjoyment of music can be considered a human universal; however, as always there are some humans who do not, or cannot, enjoy music. We also know that some music listeners become more sophisticated as listeners over time.

For our purpose here, the more important issue is making music – that is, writing or producing/performing it. It appears that we are almost all capable of making some form of music, singing being the most obvious example, but there are huge differences in individual skill. Indeed, the virtuoso musician is a supreme example of an inherent, universal capacity developed as a true specialism, particularly as instruments are so different from each other (compare the trumpet and the piano . . .). Again, for teachers the recognition of capacity, such as musical aptitude, is a key element of their expertise. Schools are, in a sense, structures that display our view that humans have a range of inherent capabilities: why else would we teach everyone a range of subjects? Or in Gardner's view, address the range of our multiple intelligences?

Most human activity, especially skilled activity, cannot be reduced to a single mental capacity. Even the act of making music is not drawing solely on one mental element. We would argue in this book that teaching is not a distinctive mental capability, even though it is reasonably accepted that all humans 'teach', indicative of something inherent in our species. We can return to Darwinian theory here because our understanding of most animal species is that the young have to learn and they learn mostly from the adults around them. It is also clear that certain species have adopted a more deliberate teaching mode and show young ones what to do. As touched on above, humans have adapted this capacity to a particularly high level and created social structures within which to maximise the learner's inherent potential. Thus, teaching is a form of *capability* that almost all humans recognise and, in various ways, undertake, but it is not the same as more obviously narrow specialisms such as music or art. The general human capability to teach creates a societal issue for teachers, in that the 'public' do not always see teaching as a high-order profession compared to, say, medicine or law. This matter will be considered further in Chapter 2.

Finally, we must address the old adage, 'Teachers are born not made'. Most developed societies decided long ago that, whether or not this is true, the main question is how to create effective and knowledgeable teachers. What evidence there is indicates that some humans have more aptitude for becoming good teachers than others, and this is one theme of the book: what do you do to ensure that aptitude turns into expertise? Perhaps more fundamentally, the question might be how genetic is the capacity to teach? Anecdotally, most humans know families where there is more than one teacher – where, for instance, the offspring of teachers enter the teaching profession; this is equally true of doctors and lawyers. As regards the teaching population, this factor is probably inconsequential. We would suggest that direct familial influence, linked to status and 'insider' knowledge of the profession, is much more powerful. What is more speculative, but part of our view, is that the higher-order teaching with which we are concerned has become part of the adapted mind, making the capability to teach part of a genetic structure – that is, we do all inherit such capacity, it is not just learnt from other humans. However, this point is very much open to debate.

Education and/or environment?

A final conundrum in expertise is more contextual. In the literature on expertise (see Ericsson *et al.*, 2006), one area for discussion is '*elite achievement from superior learning environments*'. It is clear that education makes a difference to the development of expertise, and the environment in which learning skills takes place also makes a difference. Humans have developed a very high degree of environmental control in some areas, the most obvious being the home. The kind of home we grow up in is unquestionably a major factor for most people in how their human capabilities begin to be developed. The continuation of such development then depends to some extent on educational opportunity in specific institutions; in the most developed systems this usually means primary, then secondary school, followed by higher or further education or training establishments. Much educational policy is focused on creating such settings, with different ideologies hugely influencing what is adopted. In most systems there is a tension between breadth and depth, centred around the question, 'How soon should we specialise?' So, even if a child is a musical prodigy, we tend to favour a balance between ensuring this extraordinary ability is developed and maintaining their broader development of other capabilities.

There are plenty of anecdotes about children showing a capability to teach from an early age; certainly, prospective teachers often say something about how others – it might be parents, siblings or friends – have said, 'You would make a good teacher'. However, most developed systems do not begin selecting teachers until they are at least 18, and a number of countries begin later, when candidates have completed a non-teaching-related degree and are typically at least 21 (see Barber and Mourshed, 2007). Teaching is also a profession which many much older adults join, even as late as mid-life; this is much less common in other established professions such as medicine and law. There is a school of thought, typically from a right-wing perspective, that considers teacher training essentially an irrelevance.

This view posits the notion that a combination of deep subject knowledge and love of the said subject is the only requirement for a successful teacher. Although it is a powerful lobby in many countries, real research, such as the seminal work of Shulman (1986, 1987), suggests that these are, indeed, key ingredients of successful teaching, perhaps especially beyond the primary years, but there is no systematic evidence that these elements are, by themselves, truly sufficient.

Looking specifically at becoming a teacher from a novice scenario, this would mean that the nature of the initial training matters and that the place where the training occurs also makes a significant difference. More detail will follow in Chapter 2, but for the summary, the main issue is the degree of situatedness of teacher training: because it is an experiential and practical activity, you need – to put it crudely – 'to do it to understand it'. This is true of any skilled domain, from playing chess to flying aeroplanes, even though a mistake in chess only injures the player's pride, while a mistake flying a plane may have tragic consequences. In teaching there is real debate around how best to learn teaching practically and in what environment. There is a 'get in the deep end' school of thought that sees teaching as following an apprentice model (see Goodwyn, 2010, ch. 2) – i.e. training should be entirely school based, watching others (even some expert teachers) and trying it yourself until you start to get it right. However, most developed systems attempt to integrate preparation, often based in higher education institutions, into a gradual and staged introduction to practice.

It would require a separate book to consider the range of learning environments created around the globe, and organisations exist – for example, the OECD – to describe and evaluate education systems and, within them, school systems, modes of assessment, student outcomes and so on. Teachers are, of course, products of the system in their own country before they (usually) pass through some form of environment that trains or educates them to become teachers. This raises one of the universal themes of the book: how do different systems recruit and retain teachers and then develop them, even perhaps into 'expert teachers'?

What characterises experts?

Research across a wide range of domains (Ericsson *et al.*, 2006) shows very clearly that experts demonstrate reliably superior performance on representative tasks. In many domains it is relatively easy to assess both superior performance and what is achieved consistently. With teaching, however, it is more problematic. First, we may have to consider whether teaching can be broken down into representative tasks. Second, there may be subjectivity issues around judgements of 'superior performance' if they are undertaken by one observer (such as an inspector) on only one occasion. There will be more discussion of these matters in Chapter 2 and elsewhere in the book; it is where the various models of expert teaching – notably the Highly Accomplished model from the US – are beginning to establish a more objectified evidence base. However, an area where teachers reveal the depth of their knowledge when presented with the challenge of a 'problem' rather than something as simple as a task is indicated in the next area of expertise, which explains their highly organised mental representation system.

It is established that experts have remarkably organised minds that allow them to demonstrate qualitatively different representation and organisation of knowledge. Typically, this is revealed when comparing novices and experts either doing, or talking about, skill-related problems and tasks. Hattie's hugely influential list of the characteristics of expert teachers (Hattie, 2003, ch. 2) closely matches the following features. Experts are 'more automatic' – that is, when in the skilled domain they do not have to 'stop and think' and are not conscious of deliberate thinking; this also matches Schon's equally influential concept of the reflective practitioner (Schon, 1983, 1987) who is highly reliant on intuition (see Chapter 2). In a very grounded way, teachers learn to read the classroom and see patterns. Novice teachers are overwhelmed with the intensity of the classroom and are often quite incapable of even recalling what happened in a lesson, so a skilled observer can describe the lesson much better than the novice teacher. Experts are also reliably able to problem solve – indeed, because of their fluent practice based on automaticity, it is problems that get their attention and they use their available mental space to define what the problem is and review possible solutions. They are also highly anticipatory, solving problems even before they occur. For novice teachers this means watching lessons where everything appears to go effortlessly right, though the teacher has been trouble shooting in invisible ways (Goodwyn, 1997). A great deal of this capability to solve problems comes from case knowledge – that is, a deep understanding of the domain and what can happen within it. In a domain like medicine, this element clearly comes into play when a patient is diagnosed. The doctor generally (not in emergencies) has the advantage of being able to seek the advice of senior expert colleagues and refer to the latest research. Teachers also demonstrate case knowledge, especially when talking about classroom issues such as behaviour or trying to teach an aspect of their subject. They can seek the opinion of expert colleagues and look at what research or the professional literature may have to offer. We would argue that this is an area for development in teaching (see Chapter 8).

Even more challenging in teaching is 'theory creation'. Research on experts suggests that they are not merely highly skilled in their domain, they are also innovative and ground-breaking: they try new things based on a hypothesis that must come from a theory about the domain. It is recognised that all humans are theoretical: again, with experts we are considering where theory reaches a level at which established practice can be challenged. Such capability is not always appreciated by non-experts (the public, politicians, civil servants, etc.) as it can seem to come from arrogance, justified simply by being an expert's opinion – which may be contradicted by another expert.

Experts are *self-monitoring* – that is, they are aware of what they are doing when they need to be. Automaticity provides the mental space for this, and self-monitoring is a classic novice-to-expert difference (Hattie, 2003). In teaching this is quite easy to demonstrate: beginner teachers constantly feel 'out of their depth' in the classroom, while most experienced teachers feel at ease and in control and can recognise whether their performance is succeeding (or not), the classic element in reflective practice for reflection 'in action'. They can also reflect on the 'action', considering how to improve a classroom element that has been ineffective, which might be as microscopic as the relationship with one child.

Achieving expertise is a long process and a feature of experts is their capacity to take on challenges that not only challenge them (obviously) but also take them to a new level, either specifically (trying out a new teaching technique) or more generally (moving schools to achieve promotion). It also appears to be the case that experts do not just learn from their mistakes, they learn from their desire to constantly improve, regularly working at the limit of their competence to stretch it. Perhaps this is part of the adapted mind. Why risk failure when you are doing well and things are comfortable? This drive appears to be about the higher-order need to satisfy a desire for self-improvement, in teachers focused on better learning outcomes for their students. It is notable that a number of the expert teacher designations both celebrate and demand this quality, albeit in different ways.

Deliberated practice is a feature of how experts develop and then deepen their capabilities. The literature on expertise is unanimous on skill development. Put crudely, you have to 'do it' (play chess games) in order to do it better over time. Teaching also has this model, but it is contentious because, as discussed above, there is a view that this is the fundamental mode of learning to teach: just do it. If it *were* the core mode then teachers would not need much in the way of refinement apart from updating (using new technology, for example) or retraining in the wake of new government policy (the National Literacy Strategy in England is a classic example of this; see Goodwyn and Fuller, 2011): why would you waste resources on something as woolly as a master's programme?

Deliberated practice is unquestionably a feature of expert skill development. It is that kind of practice where the individual is knowingly practising. This is easiest to understand in physical domains – say, golf, practising that swing, or tennis, working on that serve. Here, conscious repetition and expert advice (the coach) lead to improved technique and confidence in 'getting it right'. There are strong similarities between physical and artistic areas in these respects – not only the value of repetition (scales on the piano/strokes) but also the part played by demonstration, by having an expert (musician, sportsperson) who says 'Watch me do it, then you try'. This is not a straightforward area in teaching but it is where the case for developing expert teachers is especially strong. Teaching is an isolating activity, mostly done (in most cultures) by one person and a crowd of students. There has been a great deal of research on the need to change this into a more collegiate and developmental environment and some progress has been made (see Chapter 8).

Whatever strides might be made in making teaching a less *isolated* activity, it seems unlikely that the essential nature of the teaching act will change. So teachers everywhere in the world will be 'practising' constantly in the sense that they will be using teaching skills all day and every day. However, this is not usually deliberated practice but practice without deliberation; it is perhaps merely repetition.

First of all, teachers are working in real time with real students whose motives and reactions on that day are particular to that day. One can never say with a real class, 'Sorry, can I try that again?' Even an expert coach in the room would either have to interrupt the teacher and say, humiliatingly, 'That could be done much better so I am taking over to demonstrate how it should be done' or wait until the teaching episode was over and give feedback to be used another time. Airline pilots make use of simulations where real time and challenging issues can be dealt with experientially but with no risk to passengers. At present teaching generally lacks the means of creating opportunities for deliberated practice. Certain kinds of activity, especially focused observations, lesson study and increasingly sophisticated recording of teaching episodes which can provide *stimulated recall*, offer ways forward to an equivalent, if not exact, way to engage in deliberated practice.

It would be a fascinating research project to provide expert teachers from different countries with materials that would invite them to engage with each other's expertise. When this happens currently it tends to be in the form of short-term visits, which unquestionably can be powerful learning experiences. Such a model can never be feasible for the millions of teachers around the world but technology, used intelligently, may provide significant opportunities.

Domains of expertise

Expertise by its nature is *highly situated*. Even playing chess is not the same as playing drafts, lawn tennis is not the same as the hard court, no one imagines that football and volleyball have much in common apart from a ball. Talented sportspeople do move between different sports and reach a high standard but there is almost no example, in the last 50 years, of someone excelling at more than one distinctive sport. Interestingly, athletes in something like the pentathlon do not reach levels that would allow them to compete in the single disciplines, although they have clear strengths and limitations across the varied activities required. Perhaps uniquely, cricket has the term 'all rounder', someone who can bowl and bat, or wicket keep and bat, and there have been (and are) top international cricketers who do both well enough to be in the international team. This is far rarer than batsmen who can 'bowl a bit' and vice versa, and all of it is in *one domain*. Essentially, expertise is highly situated and as overall performance improves (take the Olympic 100 metres or the marathon, records continue to fall) it gets more intensely situated and clearer that gold medal winners are expert and intelligent runners, not just fast animals: they understand what they are doing to be the fastest.

All of this is something of a problem for teaching. Teaching is clearly situated and, usually, very literally in a physical space and time-limited period. However, its varieties and complexities are infinite, at least as teaching is currently constituted. Expertise domains are broadly categorised into 'highly structured' (chess being the perfect example) and unstructured domains. There is another domain, 'weakly structured', which is where we put teaching. At first glance teaching might appear almost obsessively structured given the way typical schools are timetabled, with bells ringing to signal mass changes and the year dominated by examinations and holidays. However, this should be considered to be the *school* domain, not the *teaching* domain.

Exceptional performers and novice–expert contrasts

By definition, the word 'expert' implies both the non-expert and the novice. The expert might be characterised as able to demonstrate high levels of expertise in a reliable (relatively, world champions often lose) way. Teaching across the globe has developed terms for its exceptional performers and, as will be discussed later, designations and modes of recognition. They could not be considered robust and suffer endlessly from selectively motivated definitions of what being a 'great' teacher means. Fortunately, useful work has been done on novice–expert comparisons in other domains. Here there is a sufficient body of research to be robust (Ericsson *et al.*, 2006). Novice teachers cannot do what even competent teachers can do and their performance is unreliable. A substantial number of teachers who make it through the novice stage do not progress far enough to stay in the profession. There is also no empirical evidence of how many make it to 'expert'. In England the AST model seems never to have employed more than about 5,000 teachers at any given time (there are no definitive figures) so this figure represents about 1 per cent of the active teaching population (see Fuller, Goodwyn and Francis-Brophy, 2012). The Chartered Teacher model from Scotland was predicated on the idea that any suitably developed teacher could achieve the status; it would have been interesting to see what proportion of teachers achieved the status had the scheme survived (see Chapter 8). So, an unanswered question for any system is how many expert teachers (excellent, outstanding, master – whatever the local term might be) are practising at any given time. The other, much deeper, question is how many there might be if the conditions fostered expertise and constantly supported its development; in other words, a system that consciously developed expert teachers and knew what to do with them. Later we discuss Finland and Singapore as potentially demonstrating such a system-wide approach.

Experts and expert development: recognition, stages of development and the possibility of 'accelerated development'

Peer recognition

Who can judge the capability of an expert? One of the simplest approaches is using the judgement of a sufficiently recognised authority – the definition in the opening of the chapter was clear about the idea of authority as part of expert status. There is the danger of an endless circle here, beginning with 'who gets to be this authority?' but there is enough agreement in most domains for some form of peer recognition to be operable. Clearly, in very physical domains, results speak for themselves: who is fastest is not in dispute as long as the technology is accurate. But even here there is potential for cheating, so there needs to be some expert scrutiny of performance. Equally, when it comes to questions such as who is the greatest runner of all time, taking into account chronological and other contexts, the typical approach is to put together a panel of experts – who will then, usually (see below), disagree.

There are positives and negatives here for teachers. We would argue that teaching, like medicine, is an ethical profession. The prime goal in medicine is to be an excellent doctor for the patients' benefit. Professions have hierarchies and reward systems and, increasingly, performance-related pay, so identifying the outstanding performer is highly charged, often ideologically, and certainly it can be highly competitive. We would argue that teachers are fundamentally not highly competitive with each other. However, in many countries they are increasingly in *situations* that are competitive – for example, school league tables in England, or systems outcomes judged by PISA. They are increasingly being judged. The Ofsted system of inspection in England, which began with Her Majesty's Inspectors back in Queen Victoria's reign in the 1870s, is a prime example. In the current Ofsted system, teachers' classrooms are visited briefly by an inspector who rates the performance they observe; the aggregate of these performances is then used to judge a whole school. This is an astonishingly high-risk strategy, completely dependent on the individual judgement of inspectors who cannot be considered 'peer reviewers' because they are not open to scrutiny by the teacher, who, of course, may be a far more expert teacher than the inspector. To overcome this risk, a great deal is written about what inspectors are looking for and, indeed, the production of written standards is having a very significant impact on concepts of teacher expertise around the world (see Chapter 2). For inspection purposes, this written description of, say, 'outstanding teaching' is a double-edged sword. It appears like a benchmark, trialled and made credible across many different contexts so a teacher would recognise the descriptors. At the same time this becomes a 'one size fits all' tautology: to be outstanding you have to do what the template says and so you help to confirm the template. It might be best to argue that expert judgement is important, that written criteria, produced by appropriate authorities, are important, but also that peer review is more about sharing expertise in order to develop it and less about consigning it to a grade.

Issues with experts

There are many different sorts of issue with expertise status and what it is *for* (what should be done with experts when you know who they are). It is a cliché that 'experts do not agree', but it is also a valuable point in reminding us that knowledge is in a dynamic of change at all times and expertise is a vulnerable concept because it is dependent on numerous variables and pressures and, ultimately, human judgement. It is also important to stress that experts are able to disagree in democracies and that disagreement generates new knowledge. Even if computers can beat chess experts there is no likelihood that they will improve the playing of chess: only humans 'play chess' – machines do not have 'off days', but they have no motivation either. To be an expert is a difficult and responsible position (consider the 'expert witness'); it can be an exposed and vulnerable position, especially when challenging ideologies. Politicians are very fond of dismissing the evidence of 'so-called experts' – that is, the ones who disagree with their profoundly novice opinions. Some suspicion about experts is valid, but we also need honest recognition of our dependence on human judgement and the importance of trying to identify the best experts and develop the associated body of knowledge. Teaching has a long way to go in this respect and this may undermine some of its status as a profession (see Chapter 2).

Experts are often confused with elitist models because of a false assumption that identifying the 'best' somehow devalues all the rest. Head teachers want to claim that all their teachers are outstanding, as Hattie (2003) argues. This is palpable nonsense, however well intentioned: simply having a novice invalidates the claim, however 'outstanding' they may be as a novice. However, there is a philosophical issue: the teaching profession's core values tend to be about students and their treatment. There was a policy in England in the early twenty-first century called 'Every child matters', which would appear unarguable. But what about 'Every teacher matters', or should it be 'Every good teacher matters and some of those matter more than others'? In this sense there is an elitism dilemma in teaching (and other professions): does identifying and, usually, rewarding the 'best' mean that not all teachers are capable of being the best? The honest answer is yes, but a more profound issue will be whether the body of teachers support and approve of any such designation. For example, the AST model (brought in by the government in 1997) was hotly opposed by the teacher unions in England for many years on just those grounds (see Goodwyn and Fidler 2002; Goodwyn, 2001b). There will not be an elitism issue if the values and purpose of expert teachers are shared and co-constructed.

Accelerated development?

One of the fundamental components of this book is its exploration of the 'expert teacher' and how that teacher acquired such expertise. Given the clear evidence from so many skilled domains that development 'happens' but also, importantly, that it can be accelerated and, less certainly, continuously enhanced, then surely teaching capability can be accelerated? This is one of the most cogent arguments for initial teacher training, a relatively short period of intense learning about teaching preparing an individual for a whole career. The 'intense period' varies in length and structure around the world, from as long as four years in some contexts to nothing at all (you just go in the classroom and get on with it) (Barber and Mourshed, 2007). In relatively poor countries this may be due to simple economics, although the same would not happen to a novice doctor. Darwinian theory would remind us that 'the medicine man' was an early specialism in emergent tribal structures.

Most societies have learnt that reliance on such (untrained and unaccountable) specialists is rather too risky.

However, to return to teaching, the apprentice model is still much favoured and is also, of course, a very cheap model of learning. The term 'apprentice' is not used here in any derogatory sense. In the areas of primarily physical skill, for example the medieval trades of wheel making, blacksmithing, making pottery or jewellery and so on, the apprentice model was a tried and tested means of creating the next generation of skilled workers. Over time, highly complex and legally defined models of apprenticeship developed and this mode remains hugely important around the globe. To say that it is essentially dependent on imitation i.e. *watch what I do, now you try it and practise while I advise you*, is to oversimplify the process, but nevertheless this is the key mode of learning. It is also obviously a form of 'accelerated development'.

Novice teachers all across the globe clearly learn a very great deal through observation and can certainly be seen as comparable to apprentices when other teachers are showing them their practice (Goodwyn, 1997). Novices have plenty of opportunities to imitate other teachers and 'try out' their more tried and tested approaches. They tend not to be very successful if they rely too much on imitation and relatively quickly understand that they need to assimilate others' practice and find their own style. We would argue this is the beginning of teacher expertise and a sign that the novice stage is ending. Most developed countries have gatekeeping systems such as initial teacher training, to ensure that those who cannot get beyond poor imitation are not allowed to join the profession.

This is a very important point for the book. First, it demonstrates conclusively that a high level of motivation is not sufficient to make someone become a good teacher in a formal setting: some individuals are unable to reach even a basic standard and are deemed not to be suitable for the profession of teaching. It might be debated how fair such a judgement is or whether different circumstances would have produced a different outcome, but teaching, like most professions, operates a minimum standard as the 'gate'. Second, in most education systems, some form of standards are set to evaluate how well the teacher is performing in case they fall below the minimum standard. Politicians are obsessed with 'failing teachers'. The main point is that teachers can deteriorate. At a biological level we simply age and our powers, both physical and mental, diminish. It is very obvious that the most intensely physical domains such as sport are characterised by short careers 'at the top'; only the young can compete with each other. Teaching is intense but nevertheless there are biologically old teachers whose work is still excellent, especially in societies where life expectancy is steadily increasing.

There is much debate about initial training, its gatekeeping function and its weaknesses. Certainly, some individuals qualify but then struggle to achieve competence and removing them from the profession is a highly charged business. We would argue that this is best treated as part of the professional structure of teaching because it is not, by its nature, about expertise but the opposite – that is, a failure to acquire any significant level of expertise. The more important elements of deterioration in relation to teaching would appear to have two dimensions.

The first is motivational, and the expression 'burn out' or equivalent is well recognised: the question is whether this is a temporary phase or a life change. Teaching is a profession that people choose to leave for a whole variety of reasons. At the same time, many teachers choose to move out of the stressful classroom and into a different part of the system, such as management; this will be discussed in Chapter 2.

The second deterioration is much more complex because it is essentially about moral behaviour and perhaps should be distinguished from anything physical. All teachers are placed in relationships with the young and we expect them to act responsibly, especially sexually. Thus, if teachers act irresponsibly they are punished by society. In certain instances they may be pardoned and given another chance, but in more serious cases they are banned from teaching. It would be interesting to examine whether teacher expertise includes the accelerated development of moral knowledge. It seems credible to argue that teachers not only mature as humans ('older and wiser') but learn more about the vulnerability of young people and also to read the signs of a young person becoming too close to a teacher, understanding that this intensifies their responsibility even when accompanied by quite natural temptation.

The teaching profession in most countries has developed a number of models that are intended to accelerate development. The list below is by no means comprehensive:

- School-based continuing professional development (CPD) programmes, usually provided by members of the school staff.
- 'Short courses' or workshops provided by 'experts' (often commercial companies) or school support systems (e.g. local education authorities, school districts, etc.) – tend to focus on just one topic, often an externally imposed policy change.
- Study visits, sometimes to other countries – as mentioned above, these might be especially valuable for expert teachers.
- Coaching and mentoring by experienced staff – a feature of the AST model in England through 'outreach'.
- Specific models of ongoing development in a school or across schools – Lesson Study is a good example.
- Expert teacher developments – these (the AST, the Chartered Teacher, the Highly Accomplished Teacher and so on) will be discussed in depth later on.
- 'Long courses' – these might be professionally oriented or academic (e.g. master's programmes).

There is now a great deal of relevant material on websites around the world produced by a variety of actors that include government agencies, research projects, commercial operations, even unusual set-ups like 'Teachers TV' in England. All these provide individual teachers with opportunities for development.

The list is indicative of the somewhat eclectic approaches to accelerating teacher development or the simple updating that is much more about external policy change than any genuine attempt at teacher development. The list also reveals how much of such work is 'practical' and short term, with master's programmes and expert teacher programmes the exceptions to the rule. For example, to qualify as a Highly Accomplished Teacher in the US takes a minimum of a year.

This obsession with the 'practical' is especially important when considering more systematic development and the sharing of expertise in teaching, whether nationally or internationally. One reason for it is the persistent folklore belief in teaching that 'you can only learn by doing it', which extends to the idea that a teacher is only credible if they have taught for many years and still regularly teaches. This affects perceptions of head teachers and other senior staff who no longer teach; similarly, teacher educators who are no longer in the classroom can be perceived as too 'theoretical'. We would argue strongly that this is one of the myths that keeps teaching in second-tier mode in many countries (Goodwyn, 2001a) as a profession and tends to make competence (i.e. a reasonable level of practice) a dominating paradigm.

The second reason for seriously addressing this 'obsession with the practical' is the important notion of *deliberated practice*, which will be elaborated on in Chapter 7. At this stage it is sufficient to summarise what is a complex issue by an example. Teacher questioning is increasingly identified as one of the key skills in any subject domain or age phase. What might be the best way to move, as rapidly as possible, from novice to expert application of this skill? We do not have a definitive answer, partly because it is very difficult to create a domain in which to study teacher questioning, the real classroom being such a complex arena. Similarly, how might we create a practice environment for teachers that reasonably approximates to a classroom? The difficulties these challenges pose mean that the individual teacher tends to be left to reflect on their practice in isolation.

Models and stages of expertise

An important starting point for identifying an operationally useful definition of expertise for teachers is the Dreyfus model (Dreyfus and Dreyfus, 1986). This is a model that fits well with the research evidence about the stages of teachers' long-term development, and its genesis is also interesting. The Dreyfus brothers worked in the emerging field of artificial intelligence in the 1970s. Their hypothesis was not that robots and AI would come to be more significant than human beings, but quite the reverse. They considered that human beings' capacity to learn, especially from experience, made them infinitely adaptable and capable of improvement (Dreyfus and Dreyfus, 1986).

They first put forward a six-stage model and then revised the sequence to become: Novice, Advanced Beginner, Competent, Proficient, Expert. Interestingly, their first outline did not include Advanced Beginner but had 'Master' above Expert. This is a very challenging element and will be discussed below in relation to what we should call 'Expert teachers'; the term 'Master Teacher' has had some currency in the US, for example, as indicated by the University of Georgia Master Teacher programme. The Dreyfus model has been widely interpreted and adapted but the stages may be broadly and simply expressed as follows:

Novice

Minimal, or 'textbook' knowledge without connection to practice
Unlikely to be satisfactory unless closely supervised
Needs close supervision or instruction
Little or no conception of dealing with complexity
Tends to see actions in isolation

Advanced Beginner

Working knowledge of key aspects of practice
Straightforward tasks likely to be completed to an acceptable standard
Able to achieve some steps using own judgement, but supervision needed for overall task
Appreciates complex situations but only able to achieve partial resolution
Sees actions as a series of steps

Competent

Good working and background knowledge of area of practice
Fit for purpose, though may lack refinement
Able to achieve most tasks using own judgement
Copes with complex situations through deliberate analysis and planning
Sees actions at least partly in terms of longer-term goals

Proficient

Depth of understanding of discipline and area of practice
Fully acceptable standard achieved routinely
Able to take full responsibility for own work (and that of others where applicable)
Deals with complex situations holistically, decision-making more confident
Sees overall 'picture' and how individual actions fit within it

Expert

Authoritative knowledge of discipline and deep tacit understanding across area of practice
Excellence achieved with relative ease

Able to take responsibility for going beyond existing standards and creating own interpretations
Holistic grasp of complex situations, moves between intuitive and analytical approaches with ease
Sees overall 'picture' and alternative approaches; vision of what may be possible

The five-stage model, including Advanced Beginner, fits well in broad terms with our understanding of teacher development and is helpful in that it identifies the necessity of going through stages to become an expert teacher. We would argue that the Novice description is the least suited to describing teaching. It certainly captures the limitations of many novice teachers but such teachers do manage reasonable levels of performance and certainly carry out independent teaching without constant supervision. They are also not confined to what are called 'textbook' approaches as even at this stage teachers draw on numerous sources for their teaching, not just textbooks.

The concepts embedded in the model help to characterise the five stages with evidence from teaching, making observers and assessors more able to plan development and training opportunities and teachers more aware of the stages so they can have more relevant and intelligent expectations. Practically speaking, in England, Novice might be equated to a trainee seeking qualified teacher status (QTS) and Advanced Beginner to a newly qualified teacher (NQT). However, individual professional development should never be overly tied to simplistic notions of a training year.

It is also important to recognise that these five stages may be distinguished in a number of professions, a comparative point that helps establish teaching as an equivalent profession and not just an apprenticeship vocation. For example, Benner's seminal work, *From Novice to Expert: Excellence and Power in Clinical Nursing Practice* (1984), applied the Dreyfus model to nursing, developing it into a much more grounded and usefully detailed modus operandi. The following extracts come from Chapter 1.

> The Dreyfus model posits that in the acquisition and development of a skill, a student passes through five levels of proficiency: novice, advanced beginner, competent, proficient, and expert. These different levels reflect changes in three general aspects of skilled performance:
>
> 1 One is a movement from reliance on abstract principles to the use of past concrete experience as paradigms.
> 2 The second is a change in the learner's perception of the demand situation, in which the situation is seen less and less as a compilation of equally relevant bits, and more and more as a complete whole in which only certain parts are relevant.
> 3 The third is a passage from detached observation to involved performer. The performer no longer stands outside the situation but is now engaged in the situation.

Benner's interpretation closely aligns with that of Schon, especially point 3, and highlights how experts retain, as Hattie notes, that passion and enthusiasm for their teaching. Benner elaborates on each stage; here we will just review the novice and the expert stages:

> **Stage 1: Novice**
>
> Beginners have had no experience of the situations in which they are expected to perform. Novices are taught rules to help them perform. The rules are context-free and independent of specific cases; hence the rules tend to be applied universally. The rule-governed behavior typical of the novice is extremely limited and inflexible. As such, novices have no 'life experience' in the application of rules.
>
> 'Just tell me what I need to do and I'll do it.'

These descriptors are certainly the characteristics of the 'beginning' teacher and usefully highlight that experience of living – i.e. being a mature student is not the same as the lived experience of the role as a teacher.

> **Stage 5: The Expert**
>
> The expert performer no longer relies on an analytic principle (rule, guideline, maxim) to connect her or his understanding of the situation to an appropriate action. The expert nurse, with an enormous background of experience, now has an intuitive grasp of each situation and zeroes in on the accurate region of the problem without wasteful consideration of a large range of unfruitful, alternative diagnoses and solutions. The expert operates from a deep understanding of the total situation. The chess master, for instance, when asked why he or she made a particularly masterful move, will just say: 'Because it felt right; it looked good.' The performer is no longer aware of features and rules; his/her performance becomes fluid and flexible and highly proficient. This is not to say that the expert never uses analytic tools. Highly skilled analytic ability is necessary for those situations with which the nurse has had no previous experience. Analytic tools are also necessary for those times when the expert gets a wrong grasp of the situation and then finds that events and behaviours are not occurring as expected. When alternative perspectives are not available to the clinician, the only way out of a wrong grasp of the problem is by using analytic problem solving.

There are powerful echoes here of both Schon and Hattie and of the paradox of unconscious competence: the expert teacher is highly automatic and works intuitively at such a speed that even recalling decisions may be difficult, making the explanation of expertise and expert performance hard to articulate. This description of stage 5 also highlights the point that deliberate thought will slow down any decision-making process and may therefore hamper the quality of the problem solving. This is thoughtfully explored in *The Intuitive Practitioner* (Atkinson and Claxton, 2000), the subtitle of which is *On the Value of Not Always Knowing What One is Doing*. . . .

We would argue that if the word 'teacher' is substituted for 'nurse' in Benner's characterisations, most highly effective teachers recognise themselves immediately. However, the fact that Benner's detailed account of the model relates to a very different domain from teaching is not only interesting in itself but also striking because, although nursing is also perceived as a second-tier profession, Benner is clearly positing a very high level of expertise, the kind normally associated with a top profession. We would add that teaching, like nursing, is an overly modest profession and that its reticence is part of the problem: in our view, status is not arrogance and confidence is not complacency.

The Dreyfus model has been influential in the caring professions but it is not the only one. For example, Hoffman, Ward, Feltovich, DiBello, Fiore and Andrews (2013) conceptualise a 'proficiency scale', beginning with 'naive' ('one who is totally ignorant of a domain') and then calibrates novice, initiate, apprentice, journeyman, expert and finally master (the experts' preferred expert); this model could be also used to analyse expertise in teaching. Schyns, Goldstone and Medin's (1997) finer-grained model of 'perceptual learning' offers some insights into teaching as it 'happens' in the classroom. They suggest that five 'mechanisms' operate together to produce an expert reading of a situation: 1) attention weighting (knowing what to pay attention to), 2) detector creation (working out what the various components are in a situation), 3) dimensionalisation (knowing what matters most within a situation), 4) unitisation (by knowing individual components in a situation, developing control over the whole situation), and 5) contingency detection (realising that the situation is changing). One fundamental teaching skill is summed up as 'reading the classroom', i.e. the classroom being a very complex, multi-variant situation happening in real time, understanding its dynamics is vital for effective teaching and learning.

There are numerous models of expertise and/or skill acquisition that can help analyse and understand teaching expertise either holistically (like Dreyfus) and in parts (like Schyns, Goldstone and Medin, 1997).

Adaptive expertise

A constant theme of this chapter has been to review expertise from a twentieth century Darwinian perspective. The concept of adaptive expertise, developed from the concept of the adapted mind, is an especially powerful notion in relation to expert teaching. It is now a sub-field of expertise, with its own literature and a good deal of empirical evidence (e.g. Feltovich, Ford and Hoffman, 1997 and Ericsson and Smith, 1991), but, considering the term generally, a key element concerns the relationship between what might be called routine expertise – that is, efficiently solving the same kind of problem many times – and the capacity to solve new problems and create new models of problem solving for novel situations.

The term was first used by Hatano and Inagaki in 1986 to distinguish between 'classic' expertise and the adaptive mode, which may be at a deeper conceptual level. There is plenty of evidence that new situations challenge experts and bring their full knowledge to the active use of the mind. It might be argued that, in Darwinian terms, this is true for all humans. However, while all humans use routines to lighten the cognitive load, experts are exceptionally able to do this. Where experts are adaptive it may be in seeing the limits of the routine and risking experimental approaches to improve problem solving or procedures and so on. There is now some research examining whether adaptive expertise can be taught in schools to help develop the experts of the future (for example, Hatano and Oura, 2003 and Mercier and Higgins, 2013).

For expert teachers, adaptive expertise would seem a very good way to describe the restless improvisation and flexibility of the best teachers, who both know and value routines but recognise that they are potentially, in themselves, a kind of limitation. This concept also fits very well with Schon's ideas of 'reflection in action' and 'reflection on action' (Schon, 1983). Adaptive expertise has special value from an international perspective since it appears to be a universal human capacity and one that may work in any cultural context and therefore local education system. As argued throughout this book, this means that a local example remains local, it works in a situated way, but the way of making it work illustrates how expert teachers, or any capable teacher, can adopt such an approach to innovation. Sharing examples internationally of where adaptive expertise has been used successfully, perhaps especially in breaking through the limitations of routines, could be of enormous value in developing expertise at local levels.

In summary, we have explored concepts of expertise and examined them from a historical and indeed sociobiological perspective with the idea of 'adaptive expertise' bringing history and biology together. The notion of the expert teacher remains problematic in a way that 'expert chess player' has never been, teaching is a weakly structured domain and there are vastly differing interpretations of what an expert teacher might be or even whether such a level is achievable. We are clear that teaching can be expert and that much work is needed to demonstrate and evidence this, both within and outside the profession. The next chapter tackles this issue directly in seeking to define teacher expertise.

References

Atkinson, T. and Claxton, G. (2000) *The Intuitive Practitioner: On the Value of Not Always Knowing What One is Doing*. Buckingham: Open University Press.

Barber, M. and Mourshed, M. (2007) *The McKinsey Report: How the World's Best Performing Education Systems Come Out on Top*. New York: McKinsey & Co.

Barkow, J., Cosmides, L. and Tooby, J. (1992) *The Adapted Mind: Evolutionary Psychology and the Generation of Culture*. Oxford: Oxford University Press.

Benner, P. (1984) *From Novice to Expert: Excellence and Power in Clinical Nursing Practice.* Menlo Park: Addison-Wesley.
Bisset Turner, R. (2001) *Expert Teaching: Knowledge and Pedagogy to Lead the Profession.* London: David Fulton.
Dreyfus, S.L. and Dreyfus, H.L. (1986) *Mind over Machine: The Power of Human Intuition and Expertise in the Era of the Computer.* New York: Simon & Schuster.
Dunbar, R. and Barret, L. (eds) (2007) *The Oxford Handbook of Evolutionary Psychology.* Oxford: Oxford University Press.
Ericsson, K., Charness, N., Feltovitch, P. and Hoffman, R. (eds) (2006) *The Cambridge Handbook of Expertise and Expert Performance.* Cambridge: Cambridge University Press.
Ericsson, K.A. and Smith, J. (eds) (1991) *Toward a General Theory of Expertise: Prospects and Limits.* New York: Cambridge University Press.
Feltovich, P.J., Ford, K.M. and Hoffman, R.R. (eds) (1997) *Expertise In Context.* Menlo Park: AAAI Press/MIT Press.
Fuller, C., Goodwyn, A. and Francis-Brophy, E. (2012) 'Being an advanced skills teacher: Professional identity and status', *Teachers and Teaching: Theory and Practice*, 19(4): 463–474.
Gardner, H. (1983) *Frames of Mind: The Theory of Multiple Intelligences.* New York: Basic Books.
Gardner, H. (1993) *Multiple Intelligences: The Theory of in Practice.* New York: Basic Books.
Gardner, H. (2000) *Intelligence Reframed: Multiple Intelligences for the 21st Century.* New York: Basic Books.
Goodwyn, A. (1997) *Developing English Teachers: The Role of Mentorship in a Reflective Profession.* Milton Keynes: Open University Press.
Goodwyn, A. (2001a) 'Second-tier professionals: English teachers in England', *L1-Educational Studies in Language and Literature*, 1(2): 149–161.
Goodwyn, A. (2001b) 'Who wants to be a super teacher? The perils and pleasures of recognising expertise in English teaching, *English in Australia*, 129/130, Dec 2000/Feb 2001: 39–50.
Goodwyn, A. (2010) *The Expert Teacher of English.* London: Routledge.
Goodwyn, A. (2012) 'One size fits all: the increasing standardisation of English teachers' work in England', *English Teaching Practice and Critique*, 11(4): 36–53.
Goodwyn, A. (2014) 'Head teachers view of expert teachers: Do they see the Advanced Skills Teacher as an innovation benefitting the profession?' Paper presented at the British Educational Research Association, University of London, London.
Goodwyn, A. (2015a) 'English teachers in England: What is their identity in a time of deprofessionalisation?' Paper presented at the International Federation for the Teaching of English, Fordham University, New York.
Goodwyn, A. (2015b) 'Has the Advanced Skills Teacher role been an advance for the profession? The views of principals and other senior leaders'. Paper presented at The American Educational Research Association Conference, Chicago.
Goodwyn, A. and Fidler, B. (2002) *Advanced Skills Teachers: The emergence of the role.* Paper presented at the BERA annual conference, Exeter.
Goodwyn, A. and Fuller, C. (eds) (2011) *The Great Literacy Debate.* London: Routledge.
Goodwyn, A. and Roberts, R. (2015) 'Emerging models of expert teaching in the era of performance-related pay in England: The views of experienced head teachers and deputies'. British Educational Research Association, Queens University, Belfast.
Hatano, G. and Inagaki, K. (1986) 'Two courses of expertise', in Stevenson, H., Azuma, J. and Hakuta, K. (eds), *Child Development and Education in Japan* (pp. 262–272). New York: W.H. Freeman & Co.
Hatano, G. and Oura, Y. (2003) 'Reconceptualizing school learning using insight from expertise research', *Educational Researcher*, 32(8): 26–29.

Hattie, J. (2003) *Teachers Make a Difference: What is the Research Evidence?* Auckland: University of Auckland.

Hoffman, R., Ward, P., Feltovich, P.J., DiBello, L., Fiore, S.M. and Andrews, D.H. (2013) *Accelerated Learning: Training for Proficiency in a Complex World.* New York: Psychology Press.

Hutchings, M., Mansaray, A., Minty, M. and Smart, S. (2009) *Excellent Teacher Scheme Review.* London: DCSF.

Loughran, J. (2010) *What Expert Teachers Do: Enhancing Professional Knowledge for Classroom Practice.* London: Routledge.

Mercier, E.M. and Higgins, S.E. (2013) 'Collaborative learning with multi-touch technology: Developing adaptive expertise', *Learning and Instruction*, 25: 13–23.

Mithen, S. (1998) *The Prehistory of the Mind: A Search for the Origins of Art, Religion and Science.* London: Phoenix.

Mourshed, M., Chijioke, C. and Barber, M. (2010) *How the World's Most Improved School Systems Keep Getting Better.* New York: McKinsey & Co.

OECD (Organisation for Economic Cooperation and Development) (2012) *Education Today 2013: The OECD Perspective.* OECD Publishing. http://dx.doi.org/10.1787/edu_today-2013-en

Schon, D. (1983) *The Reflective Practitioner: How Professionals Think in Action.* London: Temple Smith.

Schon, D. (1987) *Educating the Reflective Practitioner.* San Francisco: Jossey Bass.

Schyns, P., Goldstone, R. and Medin, D. (eds) (1997) *Perceptual Learning: Advances in Research and Theory.* San Diego: Academic Press.

Shulman, L. (1986) Those who understand: Knowledge growth in teaching, *Educational Researcher*, 15(2): 4–31.

Shulman, L. (1987) Knowledge and teaching: Foundations of the new reform, *Harvard Educational Review*, 57(1): 1–22.

2

THE GLOBAL RISE OF THE TEACHER'S ROLE, BUT IN A PROBLEMATIC PROFESSION

A case study of England's professional context

Andrew Goodwyn

Although teacher expertise has been studied for over a hundred years, the concept of the expert teacher is much more recent. Arguably stemming from Dewey's work in the 1920s and 1930s, refined by Schon in the 1970s and 1980s, then refined again by Shulman and others in the 1980s and 1990s, the prevalence and importance of teacher expertise in educational theory and policy development is really a feature of the last 25 years. This chapter reviews theoretical underpinnings of the concept of the expert teacher from several perspectives: cultural (i.e. societal values and public perceptions), political (i.e. policy) and educational (i.e. teacher as professional and carer/developer). The first appearance of a formal role, the Advanced Skills Teacher in Australia in the 1980s, marks a significant moment of expertise recognition. New ways of describing expert teaching emerged at a time when complex issues of teacher retention and related status were having an impact on educational systems around the world. These expert teacher models were attempts to keep the best teaching practitioners in the classroom and halt the rapid departure into management or advisory roles, partly for status and partly for pay. The AST, for example, was sold as a solution to both issues.

From effective to expert (but only in a second-tier profession?)

This book is not a history of teaching but chiefly concerned with the period from about 1980 to the present, with some evidence-based speculation beyond that. However, this section will attempt to explain why models of expert teaching began to appear at government policy level in the last quarter of the twentieth century in several countries; some of these models are explored in more detail in subsequent chapters. Certainly one factor in the emergence of the 'expert teacher' is related to the long struggle for teaching to become a true profession, comparable to those great professional bastions, medicine and law. These two colossi have long had the status of top professions in almost all countries, although teaching arguably enjoys a high level of respect in certain countries, for example Singapore and China, and some level of respect in all developed systems, including England, the USA and Australia, where it is perhaps best described as persistently second tier (Goodwyn, 2001). Government rhetoric in many countries from the 1980s onwards is shot through with grand claims about the vital importance of teachers and schools and how crucial it is to raise the status of the profession and attract the brightest and best. For example, a 2015 official UK government report states:

> Evidence from around the world consistently arrives at the same simple conclusion: the quality of teaching is the single most important school-based factor determining how well children achieve. That is why the Government's plan for education has put a world-class teaching profession at the very heart of driving up standards in schools. In 2010 we published our White Paper, The Importance of Teaching; since then we have made great progress – working in partnership with teachers and school leaders – to raise the quality of teaching in our schools.
>
> *(DfE, 2015, p. 5)*

This is typical of such rhetoric, found in many countries but especially in England over the last few years, where the gap between rhetoric and the reality of the teaching profession may be considered exceptionally wide. It must be noted at this point that there is increasing diversity between the four parts of the UK in all manner of respects and most certainly in relation to their systems of education, a good example being the contrast between the Chartered Teacher model in Scotland and the AST in England and, to some extent, Wales.

> We are firm in our belief that England's teachers are already world-class; we are proud to have many thousands of dedicated, hard-working professionals in classrooms across the country. We also believe that it is our responsibility, as Government, to do whatever we can to support the teaching profession to go even further as it strives for development and improvement.
>
> We believe that, to achieve high-quality teaching, it is essential to put more powers in the hands of an increasingly self-improving teaching profession, whilst continuing to support and nurture our teachers' commitment to their own continuous learning and development.
>
> *(Ibid.)*

These grand claims have not been matched by the reality of what it is to be a teacher. However, one concrete outcome of these claims in many countries has been the tentative establishment of models of expert teaching, the earliest probably being the Advanced Skills Teacher in Australia (see Chapter 5) and the Highly Accomplished Teacher in the USA (see Chapter 6). One of the key arguments about establishing such models is the need to raise the status of the profession, so these models can be seen as partly a recognition that teaching lacks status, compared to other professions, but also that some teachers can be recognised as at the 'top' of the teaching profession. This mixed message remains a dilemma. Put simply, the expertise of law and medicine as professions is almost never fundamentally questioned. Of course, and quite rightly, there are many questions raised about such professions and especially individual practitioners, but the public and most politicians demonstrate a trust in their expertise. The DfE document makes this explicit, commenting:

> It is remarkable that teaching remains one of the only professions in this country whose members cannot benefit from being part of a professional body promoting high standards of practice and development. We, along with many teachers and school leaders, believe that this situation should be rectified – by teachers for teachers, but with Government support where appropriate.
>
> *(Ibid, p. 3)*

It continues with a further suggestion that teaching needs its own professional body:

> The opportunity to do so will give teachers the professional recognition and status that teaching should rightly command. In the longer term, a new professional body could play a leading role in the promotion of high-quality professional development for teachers. Such opportunities are one of the defining hallmarks of all established and respected professions.
>
> *(Ibid.)*

The idea of a professional body will receive further discussion throughout the book, especially in relation to such a body being independent of political interference.

Expertise is associated with knowledge and skill but also with value: some forms of expertise are highly valued and highly rewarded, others much less so, and those two elements, value and reward, exist in a creative tension. A concept like expert teaching cannot be understood in a vacuum and this book is addressed to readers who want to understand such expertise in its context. Comparisons with other forms of professional expertise are illuminating and the term 'professional' is essential in defining the context in which teaching takes place. All kinds of teaching take place in all sorts of 'amateur' settings, and these are of interest. We would argue that the image of law and medicine, reinforced to an extent by media imagery, is of professional activities taking place in highly specialised settings – the court room, the operating theatre and so on. The image of teaching, in almost any part of the world, can only be described as a lot more homely. It is often remarked that a time-travelling doctor from the nineteenth century would be amazed at the twenty-first century hospital, whereas the equivalent teacher would not just recognise the school and the classroom but might be deeply disappointed by how little has changed. There would seem to be an important truth in this image of teaching; it is not merely perception. The teaching profession, certainly in England and the USA, is frequently attacked in the media and by politicians (as is social work in England). There is a persistent sense that it is *almost* a real profession but cannot quite reach the top tier.

However, the kind of teaching we are focused on has developed within a professionalised environment. Even the term 'teaching' needs some scrutiny, partly because it does not begin to capture the multiplicity of roles and functions that every teacher makes use of to develop students' learning. We also need to examine what is considered *effective teaching*, as this term has been widely used in many national systems; only after that will it be reasonable to look at what may be called *expert teaching*. We argue in our conclusions that the establishment of models of teaching expertise is the right step for moving the teaching profession into the top tier but we insist that such models must be separated from political control and interference, as is the case with law and medicine, at least in the UK. In the next section we consider some of the residual issues that continue to hinder the profession of teaching from becoming 'top tier' and the pervasive sense in developed systems that most teachers are pretty competent but not better than that.

Being a professional

The teaching profession has had a long struggle with defining itself, especially in relation to other professions (Eraut, 1994). What follows is a critical examination of this issue, with two limitations. One is that it focuses principally on England, to allow for in-depth treatment. The other is that it considers a conceptualisation of teachers and teaching within a broadly Western paradigm of the notion of a profession. There are a number of important references in this book to teaching in different cultures, but it is beyond its scope to examine the cultural differences in great depth – again, in order to permit an in-depth examination of models that have emerged in the English-speaking world: this is not a claim for their *superiority*. Finally, it is striking that certain cultural traditions, notably, for example, in China, seem to be imbued with much deeper respect towards teachers; however, at the same time they position teaching as an honourable vocation and expect its practitioners to accept very modest pay compared to other professions. So, although these cultural differences are fascinating and important, they do not undermine the basic assertion in this chapter that the profession of teaching, however ennobled in culture or political rhetoric, remains in reality weak in relation to many others.

Although the teaching profession in England has always wished to be taken seriously, especially by the public, it has often rather undermined its own status. 'Everyone knows about teaching' is an obvious point but it is all the more important to state because of that loose generalisation. Every parent, politician and media commentator has experienced school, so they have a genuine, if extremely limited, knowledge base from which to pass opinions on teachers and teaching. This knowledge is chiefly based on what we call 'the passenger perspective' – that is, the views of a passenger in the car who has been present while a great deal of driving has taken place, but has neither experienced the challenge of driving nor observed it closely. It is also reasonable to say that everyone has done some teaching if you define teaching as helping someone else learn how to do something new (learning to ride a bike) or to improve (learning how to avoid falling off a bike).

Another highly defining element is that teachers themselves are driven by an intrinsic concern for their students rather than themselves. They thus share with other caring professions such as nursing, counselling and social work a tendency to describe what they do in terms of the benefits to students rather than the extraordinary difficulty of their daily work. We argue throughout this book that we need a great deal more research evidence about how expert teachers work with their students, not just cognitively in relation to test scores but also affectively – for example, how they motivate and inspire students to make them resilient, even if they score a low grade.

These factors combine at times to produce a curious but powerful paradox. There is a consensus, even among politicians, that teaching really is important; at the same time it is taken for granted and, especially given the passenger perspective, seen as rather an easy job: the old cliché, 'think of the holidays', is never far away. There is evidence (Goodwyn, 2004a) that the last 20 years has seen some shift in this perspective but it is not yet fundamental. The phrases 'top lawyer' or 'expert financial adviser' are commonplace and have an immediate credibility that 'top teacher' simply does not. What we actually call a 'top teacher' will be much discussed in this book. However, here we are initially concerned with the status of teaching and how that may, or may not, add kudos to expert teaching.

When teaching is compared to other well-established professions it shares only some of their characteristics (Eraut, 1994). Any term as general as 'profession' is bound to have many and often competing definitions and, given rapid change in the workplace, a necessarily evolving definition. For example, teaching assistant (TA) and the higher level version (HLTA) are in use in England for adults working in the classroom to literally assist the teacher; is this a straightforwardly professional role, or is it, as seems more currently accurate, a paraprofessional role like a paramedic? Is Higher Level Teaching Assistant a more professional role than TA? The answer seems, almost certainly, 'yes'. Finally on this point, it may well be that the establishment of a well-defined paraprofessional role such as teaching assistant raises the status of teaching per se by implication. For example, how do expert teachers work productively with another trained adult in the classroom? Might there be an implication that such teachers do not need assistance?

This short section is devoted to the linguistic and semantic origin of the term 'professional', in England and in English so that we may reflect on the notion of 'expert' within this semantic field. There are many sources to draw on but any decent dictionary will do (for example, *The Shorter Oxford English Dictionary*) and this analysis draws on some key points. An interesting text, a key sociological study of English teachers by Margaret Mathieson (1975), called the English teachers of the 1970s 'preachers of culture'. This has a specific resonance in a subject like English but also fundamental relevance for our argument because the origins of professional come from the medieval religious notion of 'professing' – that is, professing, or 'declaring', the vows of religion (1510). These origins are also relevant in the countries that adopted both English as their language and developed education systems modelled on England, such as Australia, New Zealand, Canada and the USA.

The act of *professing* was crucial to being accepted into the community of the preferred religion and, by implication, a particular 'order'. By the late 1500s the term had already extended to mean both laying claim to some particular knowledge and expertise in art or science and *teaching some subject as a 'professor'*. Simultaneously, the idea of a profession as a vocation, a chosen calling, developed, still tending to be associated with religion but also extending to medicine, the law and the military.

In the late 1700s the term 'professional' appears as pertaining to or being proper behaviour in relation to a chosen occupation; taking on the sense of having values and a moral code, i.e. not just about having knowledge but being concerned with *how that knowledge is used*. By the mid-nineteenth century, professionalism had come to mean having a professional quality, the stamp of a profession, and by the 1880s the distinction in sport emerges between amateur and professional, bringing in the inevitable question of financial reward. Thus, what can be considered the ideological underpinnings of the modern understanding of 'professional' were established by the end of the nineteenth century. For example, the first use of the term 'unprofessional,' meaning contravening what is expected of a professional, was in 1899.

In the twentieth century the notion of the professional has become absolutely established as a normative role within a highly structured economy and with defined characteristics. However, these defining features (see below) must be seen as contested and contestable. For example, with the idea of professional status may come accountability, but to what extent is a true professional autonomous and to what degree accountable – and if accountable, to whom? This latter point has been a particular issue for teachers, especially highly effective ones, in the late twentieth and early twenty-first century. A serious question for teachers is whether having experts diminishes the authority of the other teachers or, conversely, raises the status of the whole profession.

Therefore, although particular professions will set out lists of skills, as does teaching, these can fragment into microscopic items that become almost pedantic. All professions, then, are skilled, and they debate, principally internally, exactly what the skill set is at any one time. As Michael Eraut puts it, the professions are best understood, 'as an occupational ideology' (Eraut, 1995, p. 227). In his excellent discussion in *Developing a Knowledge Base within a Client-centred Orientation* he argues that the debate about professional characteristics has become sterile and that 'professionalization can . . . be viewed as a strategy for gaining status and privileges in accordance with that ideology – the three central features of the ideology of professionalism are a specialist knowledge base, autonomy and service' (ibid., p. 227). But, Eraut points out, teaching struggles to be a 'full' profession, especially as politics exerts increasing influence down to classroom level and there is an ever-increasing number of stakeholders who demand influence. It is not surprising that teachers are sometimes confused: as Eraut asks, 'Are they meant to be serving the pupils, the parents, the local community, the school district, or the whole nation?' (ibid., p. 228). Eraut's analysis, now more than 20 years old, remains as accurate today as it was then.

In 'top tier' professions there is a very strong element of client service and a highly distinctive knowledge base, so distinctive in fact that most lay people describe themselves as completely lacking that knowledge. As discussed above, that is not quite the case with teaching (Goodwyn, 2004b), about which lay people definitely believe they can express a view and should be entitled to do so. On these grounds, 'old' professions such as medicine (which still means doctors rather than nurses, though that is changing in an interesting way), law, architecture, etc., are 'top'. Teaching has enough of the characteristics of these established professions to be *almost* a top-tier profession.

Although Eraut defines the professions as principally having in common an ideological stance, it is reasonable to note what are relatively common features associated with professional status, certainly in the English-speaking world. For example, the knowledge base usually comes from an initial period of graduate-level study in the key subject or a related one. In top professions there is then a period of further study, possibly vocational, very often postgraduate. At some point the novice actually enters the profession – gets, as it were, *through the gate*. As the individual professional becomes established this tends to be through developing a specialism that demands further study and ongoing upskilling (continuing professional development, or CPD). Such specialists then have students and novices of their own whom they induct into the profession. Most professions of this kind also have a strong, sometimes direct, relationship to a discipline studied in higher education; this academic subject (say mathematics) may have a very long history. The top professions of medicine and law are perfect examples of all these characteristics.

Education as a discipline still struggles to hold its own in the academic world and Furlong (2013) makes a cogent case for why this has a long history and why more recent changes to universities across the globe have made it even more difficult for education to be 'accepted' into academia, not least because populist views cluster around it but also because teachers themselves frequently undermine it as a theoretical subject. Much of this view comes from the experience of the academic study of education during initial teacher training (ITT); other professions insist on much more post-initial training study. It must be said that in most models of expert teaching, further study in an academic sense is not required, the Chartered Teacher model in Scotland being an exception (this will be explored later on). Certainly, a feature of the turbulence in teaching professions across the world is the endless changes made to ITT and the, in our view, fruitless debate about whether such training should be *academic* or *practical*, when it clearly needs to be both. In England even the precise number of weeks of the different stages of university ITT has been dictated by government, a perfect example of political, not educational, control weakening the independence of the profession to determine what it thinks is the best model of training.

Professions are marked also by their very particular language and technical vocabulary. They have a regulatory body of some kind and the ability to practice is dependent on belonging to that body. As well as having codes of practice set down in great detail, they tend to have ways of behaving that are much less defined but are part of the culture of the group. In England, 'Never smile until Christmas' is not a technical term, it is more of a folklore phrase, but it carries meaning within the professional group that is teachers. Teachers do not wear uniforms (unlike nurses) or particular gowns (think of barristers), but each setting tends to have a strong dress code, even if it is not written down. Teaching has most of the markers of a top profession: it has, in England for example, the appropriate level of esteemed qualification (it is almost entirely a graduate-level group), an appropriate initial training period with a strong gatekeeping function, and a certification of practice that can be revoked.

It does now require teachers to continue their professional development (see the Standards section of the Department of Education's website), although the lack of any real system persists and teacher in-service development is haphazard at best. There is a well-defined, although constantly changing, career structure. Perceptions of teaching as a career alter over time and international comparisons are very interesting. The McKinsey report (Barber and Mourshead, 2007) discusses how vital the status of the teaching profession has become to attracting the best graduates; this is linked to history and culture but the report stresses how influential teachers themselves can be and how, in synergy with positive government policy, status can quickly (over five years) be raised.

The importance of a regulatory body: a case study of the General Teaching Council for England

Expert teachers thus work in a profession that is clearly service-orientated, and respected for that dimension, but which also has some persistent issues about its status and its knowledge base. Before 1998 in England there had never been a single body dedicated to both the regulation and the development of teaching as a profession. Many other bodies existed, for example unions, teacher subject associations and various other interested parties such as charities and examination bodies, all of whom had views about the profession and a measure of authority.

So – given the eminence of a body such as the General Medical Council – the establishment of a single regulatory body had the potential to be a very significant step up for the profession. The 1998 Act that set up the General Teaching Council for England (GTCE) gave it two aims: 'to contribute to improving standards of teaching and the quality of learning, and to maintain and improve standards of professional conduct among teachers, in the interests of the public'. In other words, '[t]he General Teaching Council exists to support teachers' professional efforts to offer children and young people high quality teaching that meets their needs and enables them to learn and thrive' (GTCE website, 2009).

However, the GTCE was abolished in 2010 and has not been replaced, although this may change, perhaps between 2016 and 2020 (see discussions later in the book). It is a theme of this book that there should be no political interference in expert teacher development. Because the Council was established by a political decision it could legally be abolished by another such decision – in other words, it never had autonomy or freedom and was not created by the will of teachers.

The GTCE had the power to strike a teacher off the official list of practitioners and did exercise this power. Despite being a body that fulfilled this function, the perception among teachers was that the GTCE was without much influence in relation to the more significant function of being an advocate for the profession. It was also not seen as a threat to the autonomy of teachers: that comes from other sources. Put simply, the GTCE was not perceived as a serious body of self-regulation, the mark of a top profession, but rather a bureaucratic and remote entity. It was never seen as the authoritative voice of the profession, a role that is still more associated with the unions. This can be contrasted, within the UK, with the equivalent body in Scotland (the General Teaching Council for Scotland), which has much recognition and influence among teachers and carries out some of the functions of government agencies such as England's Training and Development Agency for Schools (TDA) (see below). Later we discuss in detail the US National Board for Professional Teaching Standards and the Australian equivalent, which, we argue, are more credible examples of independent bodies that advocate for the profession.

It might be argued that the GTCE was a relatively young body in comparison with those of other professions, and this is a reasonable point. However, there is little evidence that it ever matured or gained authority; it was more to be tolerated than respected. A significant reason for this is that the most powerful bodies in relation to teaching in England were the Training and Development Agency for Schools (now called the National College for Teaching and Leadership) and the Office for Standards in Education (known as Ofsted). The GTCE had no obvious influence compared to these hugely important agencies, more discussion of which will follow.

The role of the unions

The unions can also be significant for teaching and its status, although there is considerable variation internationally. For example, Canada's teacher union has substantial power and is assertive about the status of teaching. In the UK, unions have generally focused on pay first and conditions second. How well teachers are paid is always contentious, especially in relation to *what it is they are being paid for* (remember 'the holidays'?). The unions have been very influential in bargaining and, at some points, in uniting the profession to take industrial action. They have had considerable influence, especially in more recent years, in defining the actual conditions of teaching. In England, the National Union for Teachers (NUT) was formed in 1870 and remains a powerful influence on policy and teachers' career possibilities. For example, in the last decade the NUT (and other unions) have helped to challenge the testing regime set up in the 1990s, leading to the abolition of a highly contested test in England known as the Key Stage 3 test.

However, the unions in England are not perceived as raising the *status* of teaching. One reason is that there are several and they publically squabble with each other. Another is that collective bargaining is often seen as a sign of the weakness of the individual practitioner's position (hence needing to be collective). Architects, doctors and lawyers very rarely make a desperate public display of their negotiations with employers. Equally, teachers do not have to belong to a union – though the advantages are obvious, especially in terms of professional indemnity. A teacher is much better protected in a union than in the GTCE or equivalent. It must also be said that despite some specific historical episodes, teachers in the UK are not generally militant, although the media frequently portrays them as such.

It is worth noting that the GTCE appeared to have no opinion regarding the concept or status of expert teaching. The unions, especially the NUT, have generally been negative about the establishment of any kind of formal recognition. The advent of Advanced Skills Teachers (ASTs) was not supported by the unions (Goodwyn and Fidler, 2002): their prevalent view still seems to be that such a role is more divisive than positive. There will be further discussion of ASTs below.

To sum up, the unions are powerful and important but do not add status to the profession. The GTCE was tolerated but seen as insignificant, recent research (Goodwyn, 2015, 2014) demonstrates emphatically that the GTCE was never valued by teachers and its demise was mostly welcomed. It might well be argued that it is the culture of teaching itself which undermined the GTCE. If teachers were more concerned about their public status it seems probable that they would demand to have a more assertive regulatory body. So, teachers, certainly in England, do have a degree of self-regulation, and continue to have a modest level of autonomy, but they work within a very dominant accountability regime that, it can be argued, does not encourage innovation or genuine expertise.

The tension between autonomy and accountability and the use of standards

As Eraut argues, a genuine professional must be reasonably accountable but must also retain a significant degree of autonomy and be able to exercise reasoned professional judgement (Eraut, 1994). What degree of accountability is reasonable for teaching as a profession? Do differing degrees of accountability act as a developmental pressure on improving teaching or can they produce a compliance culture that restricts innovation and nullifies expertise? This is an especially challenging question in relation to expert teaching: should not such teachers, if they are agreed to be expert, have a great deal of *additional* autonomy as leaders within the profession?

This book is not a history of the teaching profession but, on occasion, the longer perspective is valuable. It is also a fact that most English-speaking countries have some model of inspection; we define this as, literally, the inspection of teachers in the classroom. While the inspector may also examine many other artefacts (plans, students' books) and activities (assemblies, teacher meetings, interviewing senior leaders), a prime function will be to observe teachers in action.

In the 1990s, teaching in England became, we would argue, a highly accountable, punitively observed activity. That is to say, in England (specifically), the Ofsted regime has been perceived by teachers as essentially negative and obsessively judgemental. The Office for Standards in Education is defined as an independent body, funded by government, whose purpose is to maintain and raise standards in a number of areas. For the purpose of this book, we are concerned with its relationship to schools and therefore teachers. It is ironic that, in a period when teaching across the world has been subject to more professional observation than ever before, teachers themselves feel that they have learnt very little from this potentially rich database of observation. Ofsted was initially given the power to rate teaching on a scale that includes the terms 'good' and 'outstanding' (there has been modification over time). This recognition of the quality of teaching per se might have been a major stimulus to the profession, especially as the observers were recording their observations in a systematic way. However, Ofsted adopted a secretive model in the literal sense that only reports and summaries were ever made public. At the same time, Ofsted inspectors were made unaccountable to the profession, which means that the accumulated evidence of good teaching could never be discussed.

It might be argued that teaching had been too unaccountable pre-Ofsted, and that teachers could get away with poor teaching very easily. However, there is no evidence to support this view, and no evidence, apart from Ofsted's own claims, that teaching has improved as a direct result of inspection. An extraordinary opportunity was missed. The essential conceptualisation of Ofsted as a body charged with hunting down bad practice and failing schools meant that the gaining of a positive report was seen as a happy escape. It also engendered a culture of compliance towards Ofsted descriptors. Research during this period (Cullingford, 1999) has shown that schools, and individual teachers, learnt how to 'play the game', even though they found the effects of an inspection highly unproductive. The three-step formulation of building up to the inspection, coping with the inspection period and recovering from the inspection, led to huge amounts of time and effort being diverted from teaching and from students' learning.

Had Ofsted been conceptualised as employing a sampling, best-practice model, teachers might have welcomed inspections as a chance to demonstrate what they were genuinely doing and to receive professional feedback from highly qualified and widely experienced colleagues. The benefits for expert teaching could have been substantial. Not only might there have been a publically accessible database of descriptions of expert teaching but this might have been refined and developed over time and fed back to the profession.

The emerging (at the time of writing) more self-evaluative model may well be a step forward on a number of dimensions, and the reduction of direct observations of teaching is not a loss on the basis of the old, negative, model. However, it means that there will no longer be the trusted independent observations of teaching that ASTs undertook, except from minor players such as, perhaps, the replacement for the ASTs as part of an outreach role. The one very positive development, certainly in relation to developing expertise in teaching, has been the acceptance throughout the profession that observation, per se, is an essential part of teacher development. In simple terms, teachers' doors are generally 'open' rather than 'closed' and both teachers and students are entirely used to observers in the classroom.

This acceptance of the open door is a cultural change stemming from several complementary sources, all contributing to a better-developed knowledge base in schools in relation to teacher expertise. One key but contentious and problematic development has been performance management for teachers. The original introduction of performance management in 1997 required head teachers to justify their recommendations for teacher reward. Whatever the complications of such a system, it meant that teachers had to be observed and the basis on which they were being observed had to be explicitly stated. This was equally the case for the initial assessment of Advanced Skills Teachers (see below).

From the perspective of developing a knowledge base for increasingly expert teaching, the performance management initiative offers great potential. Although it is designed to attribute relatively simplistic quality indicators to individual teacher performance, it is an annual entitlement and linked to, for instance, a portfolio of evidence including professional development work undertaken since the last assessment. It does, therefore, offer a developmental perspective. The setting of targets, if used imaginatively, also provides a focus on, and evidence of, a teacher's developing expertise. In England in 2013 the AST role was abolished and schools were given much more scope to determine teachers' performance-related pay; how this will affect the way schools reward expert teachers is yet to be determined. Some small-scale, qualitative research suggests schools will want to create expert teacher roles perhaps using terms such as 'leading teacher' (Goodwyn, 2015, 2014).

The relatively recent introduction of 'standards' (another global phenomenon) for all teachers is a rather double-edged sword with real potential for teacher development, not least because of the eventually problematic category of 'Excellent Teacher', discussed below. In England, interestingly, standards for initial teacher training were in place for over ten years before those for newly qualified teachers (NQTs) were created in England in 1999; the importance of standards will be discussed later in relation to the competency paradigm. One potent effect in England of the standards for ITT, predicated as they were on a partnership model between universities and schools, was to make far more teachers directly involved in both teacher training and its gatekeeping function (Goodwyn, 1997). Teachers' much greater involvement in ITT has undoubtedly led to far more teacher knowledge about 'learning how to teach'. A great deal of this knowledge is generated through teachers making regular observations of ITT trainees and having to articulate, against explicit standards, how the trainees are accumulating evidence of their teaching expertise and give specific advice on how they need to improve.

The role of the ITT mentor has since risen significantly in status and responsibility since the move to more school-based training. These mentors are usually well trained, typically by a university, and are generally given a certificate that acknowledges their skills. In many such schemes there are opportunities to pursue more demanding training and then to take on a more senior role such as lead mentor. There are often opportunities to undertake master's-level work related to mentoring and teacher development, typically through critically informed investigations of practice. All these developments in school-based ITT build capacity and many more teachers have become skilled in observation, feedback and the interpretation of standards-based evidence gathering. What is most important in this incremental change is the crucial positioning of serving teachers as the gatekeepers for the profession. This has strengthened one of the key elements marking teaching as a potentially top-tier profession. In relation to this change, the introduction of the Graduate Teacher Programme (GTP), often perceived as damaging to the status of teaching (Brookes, 2005), placed more emphasis on schools as training environments. Although a minor route (replaced in 2012/13 by the School Direct training programme, an employment- and hence even more school-based route) into teaching and still questioned by many in the profession, the GTP stabilised into a route of particular suitability for career changers and for teaching assistants upgrading to QTS. However, at the time of writing, England is experiencing such radical change at every conceivable level of the education system that what might emerge in a few years' time is really anybody's guess. Recent research (Goodwyn, 2015, 2014) demonstrated that senior leaders in schools agree that the term 'system' (suggesting a recognisably uniform model of schooling) is increasingly inaccurate and misleading to both the public and applicants to teacher training. We would argue that this increases the need for an independent body to represent the profession (not a union) and also for an external model of teacher recognition that is applicable anywhere; this latter model is a feature of the NBPTS Highly Accomplished Teacher.

The evolution of performative teaching

The apparently consensual term 'teacher' does not come close to capturing what a teacher actually does, *teaching* being only one element within a teacher's actual role. Given that this issue is a global one and could fill a book in itself, the discussion below will limit itself to some relevant initiatives in several developed systems.

It is worth reflecting, very briefly, on the evolution of the concept of 'teacher' as a term (for more detail see Ericsson *et al.*, 2006). This evolution also prefigures some of the conceptualisations of contemporary teaching that will be discussed below. The first accounts of teaching in Western history are associated with Socrates and his pupil Plato. What is significant about this early conceptualisation is that teaching was largely individual and therefore personal, and was also characterised by an open, dialogic approach: it was not didactic. The term 'Socratic dialogue', generally meaning that the teacher mostly asks questions to provoke students to find their own answers, remains in common use. The model of the wise teacher enabling the student has a long and influential history. In the Middle Ages when universities became established and texts (albeit handwritten) became available, the additional dimension developed with the individual student devoting great periods of time to literal study of the authoritative texts. Alongside this development, which was principally associated, as with 'professor' above, with religion, was the emergence of the craft guilds. In the latter model, the craftsman was the expert maker and his apprentice or apprentices, learnt on the job and through observation and imitation. This model has an immediate resonance with much contemporary vocational training, including teaching.

The major change came with industrialisation and the development of schools with a very large number of pupils needing a basic level of competence in order to function in an industrial society. This was when the teacher emerged as the professional, even as teaching itself became a commonplace activity. The important point to reflect on here is that most schools across the world are still dominated by a factory concept and that highly skilled teaching is mostly associated with large groups of students; this *performative teaching* is the dominant paradigm and strongly influences initial teacher training. Concepts of personalised learning currently exist in tension with the performative model, but a distinguishing feature of expert teachers (see below) is their capacity to address individual needs. It seems probable that one role in the longer term for expert teachers is to enable other teachers to develop this facet of personalised attention. One of the rationales for developing the Advanced Skills Teacher in England was exactly the notion that ASTs could directly influence the quality of their colleagues' teaching.

Conceptualising teaching: what is the point of teaching?

As noted above, the concept of teaching went through a massive paradigm shift as a result of industrialisation and it is useful to examine ways of thinking about it. Squires' 1999 analysis is a very helpful starting point. He describes teaching (Squires, 1999, ch. 2) as an activity typically conceptualised in one of six dominant ways as: 'a common sense activity', 'an art', 'a craft', 'an applied science', 'a system', 'a reflective practice' and 'a competence'. All of these conceptualisations have a very definite real world presence and influence and are useful not only for helping us think critically about teaching but also for understanding how others view it. For example, the 'common sense' view may well be that of many parents, whereas the 'system' view may be more favoured by politicians and is evidenced in the McKinsey report's preference for high and low-performing descriptions of teaching. Turner-Bissett offers a clear analysis and application of Squires to effective teaching (Turner-Bissett, 2001, ch. 1).

For our purpose it is worth recognising that these paradigms are present in most discussions about teaching quality and may well influence judgements about what expert teaching is. Considering the paradigms from that perspective, the commonsense view is a pragmatically grounded approach to doing 'what works' and 'getting on with things' without too much reflection. It is antipathetic to any recognition of real expertise. Whereas the 'teaching as art' model immediately offers a richer perspective as it treats teaching as not only complex and highly skilled but also an aesthetic and emotional activity. For example, Eisner in 1985 characterised good teaching as

> sometimes performed with such skill and grace that it can be described as an aesthetic experience; it involves qualitative judgements based on an unfolding course of action; it is contingent and unpredictable rather than routine; and that its outcomes are often created in the process.
>
> *(Eisner, 1985, pp. 175–176)*

An interesting dimension of this paradigm is that it positions the performance of good teachers in a comparative relationship to musicians and other such 'performers'. This is valuable because it suggests that these performances can truly be outstanding, not least because they are *affective* as well as *effective*. Perhaps most importantly, this paradigm suggests that, as with music, the individual artist is the interpreter and in a very creative relationship with the notes/script, etc. Undoubtedly a weakness of this paradigm is that it implies that, as with great performers, there will only be a few such individuals. Teaching may well be an art form but it will always need to position the audience very differently to the (arguably) passive listeners at a concert.

In opposition to the artistic mode, much work has been done to establish teaching as based more on scientific principles: the 'applied science' model. This would imply that the 'rules' of teaching can be discovered and then applied rationalistically. There is plenty of evidence that teaching requires rationalist and systematic approaches, especially at the planning level; however, psychology has demonstrated that professions like teaching are highly concrete and situational (see Hattie, 2003) – strict adherence to rules is a problem and not a solution. Indeed, the Dreyfus model (see Chapter 1) is very clear about the way novices are constrained and inhibited by trying to adhere to 'rules'.

The craft model continues to feature strongly in many education systems as it does in many vocational training models. The essential notion that teaching is learnt partly by 'doing it' and partly by copying others who can already 'do it' is very close to the common sense approach. However, it is fundamentally faulted by the fact that merely reproducing practice is not a way forward and also by the absolute reliance on who the 'demonstrator' might be. It would accurately describe the current 'School Direct' model of training, which essentially offers future teachers the model of 'what works in this school' (rather than many schools).

The 'system' model has had a strong influence on teaching through its focus on processes and how they might be improved. It rightly treats teaching as a complex activity but tends to simplify teaching overall as part of 'school' and 'education' systems. It is possible to see why a government would create a top-down reform such as the National Literacy Strategy (see Goodwyn and Fuller, 2011), believing that 'informed prescription' would force all teachers to teach in a certain way (i.e. what was considered best practice); this led to huge training manuals and highly scripted lessons. The research evidence about teachers' views demonstrates how absurd they found these prescriptions and how they both undermined their performance and eroded their self-esteem (see Goodwyn, 2004a).

The most influential paradigm for many educators has been that of the reflective practitioner, the most powerful among government agencies and politicians has been that of competence; these two models also provide the deepest insights into expert teaching. They consequently have sections of their own.

Reflective practice

It can be argued the notion of reflective practice (RP) has been one of the most powerful influences on thinking about teacher development, especially the idea that teachers (and other professionals) can *continuously develop*. The great exponent of this notion is Donald Schon, and his book *The Reflective Practitioner*, published in 1983, is still the model's bible. His thinking has been widely influential in many professions but it has dominated teaching at all levels, especially teacher education where, for example, the practice of insisting that student teachers keep reflective diaries or journals is widespread on a global scale. There is little solid empirical evidence of a direct link between individual reflection and improved practice. However, the combination of self-evaluation and evaluation by others, e.g. through observation and feedback, has plenty of evidence of direct impact on practice.

It is thus important to examine Schon's original ideas and then to consider their relationship to current concepts of expertise. Schon drew heavily on the traditions of John Dewey and this summary will not do justice to the complexity of his thinking, which would involve looking at his major books in detail. However, it is clear that his original formulation has remained the most significant influence. To Schon, RP was necessary to counteract simplistic and reductive notions of teaching; it both helped teachers move beyond such approaches and revealed how remarkable is the thinking of such professionals. He critiques the simplistic approach:

> If the model of Technical Rationality is incomplete, in that it fails to account for practical competence in divergent situations, so much the worse for the model. Let us search instead for an epistemology of practice implicit in the artistic, intuitive processes which some practitioners do bring to situations of uncertainty, instability, uniqueness and value conflict.
>
> *(Schon, 1983, p. 49)*

He then outlines some key components of RP. Reflection is both continuous (Reflection in Action) and retrospective (Reflection on Action). At all times it is defined by the professional's 'dialogue with the situation' – that is, generating questions related to the situation that need an answer and a solution. It is important to state that Schon was very interested in a range of professions and can often generalise very broadly across several; this can be very stimulating and generative of ideas, but it certainly elides some obvious differences between being an architect and a teacher.

The attraction for teachers is that this model very much puts them in control of their development. The key issues are how to consciously engage in reflection (i.e. 'reflection on the action') and, crucially, how to do this in a way that is time efficient. The relentless business of classroom teaching and the typically frenetic atmosphere of school life would appear to militate very strongly against opportunities for reflection – even to be, by their nature, 'anti-reflective'. Other professions do have both formally and informally what might be described as a more reflective professional paradigm (Schon, 1987). However, Schon's formulation of a 'dialogue with the situation' means that much reflective thinking is done 'in action'.

There are some simple points to add that take us beyond Schon's model without diminishing its value per se. One is that his fascination with highly effective practitioners often led him to focus on the individual to the exclusion of the group and the wider community. It seems likely, if hard to prove, that we can 'do reflection' socially as well as privately. It might be argued that Schon's individualistic model has done teaching as a profession something of a disservice by suggesting that it is simply all about reflection – something that individuals do, as it were, in their own time. It might be one reason why initial teacher education has been so overloaded, because its formulation may imply that, as long as student teachers can *learn how to reflect* they can carry on developing regardless of the 'situation' they find themselves in. This may be a somewhat parodic version of ITT, but teaching as a profession is woefully short of formally provided development time, a part of which should surely be reflective.

It may be useful here to consider the rather broader notions of reflectiveness and their relationship to expertise which can be formulated reductively as merely 'skill'. Underlying all these models is the importance of working memory and cognitive capacity. Teaching has, in the best sense, much that is routine and regular about it; equally, it is full of variety and surprise. Effective teachers develop many strategies for becoming able to distinguish between what does and does not need attention in a classroom. As this capacity increases, it releases mental space (Hattie calls this being more automatic) for focusing on what is significant in the moment of interaction with students. Returning to the musical analogy, one feature of this development involves improvisation. As Schon discusses uncertainty and Eisner artistry, so the notion that the very best teachers improvise in the moment of performance seems absolutely convincing (see Sorensen, 2014). This distinguishing feature has the challenge of being almost invisible, as it tends to be only experts who can detect and appreciate it (as with jazz musicians). Finally, it might be asked how can the idea of 'standards' ever work with the idea of improvisation? This is a question to consider again later.

Competence and standards

It is worth framing this discussion first through the following conceptualisation of conscious competence. It is argued that in acquiring a skill there are, typically, four broad stages:

1 Unconscious incompetence
2 Conscious incompetence
3 Conscious competence
4 Unconscious competence (attributed to Maslow; see Goodwyn, 2010).

It is especially interesting to consider stage 1 because this relates to the earlier discussion of the perception by so many adults that teaching is 'easy'. This was characterised as the 'passenger model', i.e. teaching looks easy when just observing or receiving it but, when you try to actually do it, stage 2 immediately comes into play. After some time, perhaps two or three years, teaching begins to feel like stage 3. Very experienced and competent teachers reach stage 4.

Two points emerge here. Highly effective teachers may well lack some awareness of 'how they do it', especially as the difficulties of learning how to do it recede with time, making them, potentially, unsympathetic to both the novice and the incompetent (see Goodwyn, 1997 and 2010). This is why mentorship training is so important for experienced teachers who need to re-examine how teaching is learnt so they can help novices move on from stage 1. The second point is that, as well as a desirable and necessary stage, 'unconscious competence' may also be a plateau: competent is not expert. Semantically, competent can imply merely 'adequate' and may even be somewhat negative: 'that was a competent performance' can suggest that much was missing.

One outcome of the effort to treat teaching as a set of competences has been the rapid rise globally of 'standards' – that is, descriptive statements of what effective teaching should be like. In this section the focus will be on the pros and cons rather than the detail of this approach. There will be many references to standards throughout the book, especially in relation to how they try to capture expert/excellent levels. The strength of the competence approach is that it offers definitions of aspects of teaching that can be used by a range of professionals to discuss actual teaching. So a novice teacher can be helped to understand what an experienced teacher is achieving by a joint discussion of a particular 'standard'. Such descriptions allow reasonable judgements to be made against evidence accumulated by a teacher. However, the objectivity of standards is fundamentally an illusion. They are very much 'of their time' and are always open to interpretation; indeed, the best teachers use them as a starting point not a finishing point. At worst, competence descriptors produce long checklists that are administered mechanistically and without reasonable judgement. They may become especially limited when applied to expert and innovative performance.

Overall, standards have probably brought more benefits than disadvantages to teachers and researchers because they have helped articulate our knowledge base about teaching and begun to open up a dialogue about how best to capture and describe 'good practice'. The creation in several systems of either a continuum of standards – e.g. England (1998–2012, DoE website) – or standards aimed at the *more than competent* teacher – e.g. NBPTS in the US (later chapters; NBPTS website) and Chartered Teacher in Scotland (GTCS website) – mark a decidedly new departure and offer a very new set of opportunities for the highly effective teacher. For example, Australia is currently employing a relatively new and, we would suggest, quite hierarchical model with Highly Accomplished and Leading Teacher standards. These higher-level standards are not in themselves necessarily any more reliable than other standards; however, they potentially bring into the dialogue the very best teachers and they have certainly begun to establish the concept that such teachers not only exist but can be both helpful to other teachers and themselves continue to improve.

Finally it might be argued that what may matter a great deal is who writes the standards in the first place and then, particularly, who 'owns' them. If teachers themselves felt that the standards, perhaps especially those describing expert teaching, were written by real experts – including practising teachers – they might have more belief in their authenticity and integrity. A provenance of this kind might also lead to them being part of a model of reflective practice in which the standards acted as prompts to reflection rather than mechanistic measures of competence.

Effective teaching?

In most developed systems the most usual term to describe successful teaching is 'effective'; for the purpose of this book this must be seen as the stage before expert teaching, and the stage that a great many teachers will achieve. There are some valuable sources for considering the nature of effective teaching; this section is a selective summary. A useful starting point is the Hay McBer Report (DfEE, 2000), a research study undertaken by consultants rather than educational researchers, which divides teachers into competent, effective and outstanding. This report was especially important in England for a number of reasons, the most striking being that it formed the basis for the introduction of performance management into English schools; 'performance' will be considered below. A second important factor was that the research was conducted by a management consultancy, not educational researchers. This was an interesting tactic as it meant that the authors could ignore all existing research evidence and 'start afresh'. Such an approach is not entirely without merit and the report does have some valuable ideas. It revealed some of its political inflections by using the term 'outstanding' – a categorising term used by Ofsted throughout the 1990s. However, by ignoring previous work the report has a superficiality that undermines its very conclusive rhetoric; it will be further discussed below.

A number of substantial studies have tried to define quality in teaching, using a variety of terms. These include 'good teaching' (Brown and McIntyre, 1993), 'effective teaching' (Perrot, 1982; Cullingford, 1999; Cooper and McIntyre, 1996; Kyriacou, 1997), 'creative teaching' (Woods and Jeffrey, 1996), 'veteran teachers' (Shulman, 1986, 1987), 'quality teaching' (Stones, 1992), 'expert teaching' (Goodwyn, 2010), 'champion teachers' (Lemov, 2010), and teacher 'virtuosity' (Biesta, 2013). A major, relatively recent, examination of teacher effectiveness, the VITAE project (Variations in Teachers' Work, Lives and their Effects on Pupils), published in book form as *Teachers Matter* (Sammons, Day, Stobart and Gu, 2007) also uses the term 'teachers who break the mould' and places particular emphasis on 'resilience'. The 2007 *McKinsey Report* (Barber and Mourshed, 2007), which boldly states that 'the quality of an education system is only as good as the quality of its teachers', adopts the terms 'low performing' and 'high performing'; performance will be considered below.

The term 'effective' has been consistently used over this period and its general applicability makes it particularly useful here. There are a number of texts that cover 'effective teaching' in some detail, Kyriacou's *Effective Teaching* (1997) being a good example. He points out that research began quite early in the twentieth century, mainly focused on teacher attributes. For example, a 1930s study gathered the views of a number of what might now be termed 'stakeholders' (including teachers and pupils), who considered the most important attributes to be 'personality and will', 'intelligence', 'sympathy and tact', 'open-mindedness' and 'a sense of humour'. It seems unlikely that this list has changed much since, as it covers what makes teachers likeable as well as effective. A lot of the early research tended to be of the 'black box' variety (Kyriaocou, 1997, p. 5) – that is, trying to measure the existing attributes of teachers and pupils and then the examination results produced by a particular combination. It was 'black box' because it ignored entirely what actually happened in classrooms. Since the 1960s a much more valid model has emerged, generating much more robust and realistic evidence. Indeed, it laid some foundation for the more recent recognition, as in the McKinsey report, that the absolutely key variable is teacher quality.

The evidence produced suggests that the key focus is always the learning task and activities undertaken by students as generated by the actual teacher. The most productive way to investigate this focal point is through examining the variables associated with context, process and product. The *context* is everything that characterises the situation, such as the teacher's knowledge and training, experience, age, gender, social class and personality, the nature of the class being taught and the occasion (end or beginning of the day, early or late in the school year), the subject or subject matter, the school as an environment and culture, and the immediate community. Even this list is clearly a simplification, especially in a period of government policy prescription that has had a very marked effect on teaching in

England and other countries. Expert teachers have a great deal in common but secondary teachers also have strong subject identities.

Process refers to such elements as the teacher's enthusiasm, organisation, clarity of explanations, questioning technique, use of praise and comment, management strategies, approach to discipline, classroom climate, design of learning tasks and use of resources. Equally, students contribute to process because of the level of their engagement with the lesson, their own interaction with the teacher and each other and their own strategies for learning. Much emphasis is now being placed on the capacity of students to reflect and to 'learn how to learn'.

Product, put simply, is the result of all this interaction between context and process and, in the early twenty-first century, the preferred term is 'outcomes'. Examples of product would be increases in student skill and knowledge, interest in the subject or topic, better intellectual motivation, improved confidence and self-esteem, greater autonomy and independence, or increased social development. A collective term for all this might be 'self-efficacy' – i.e. all these products increasing together in a positive way. However, there can obviously be marked increases in one area and even decreases in another simultaneously. For example, an increase in academic knowledge may be combined with a loss of confidence.

A final point is that *product* suggests something measurable and objectively verifiable. The conclusion of the review of the Highly Accomplished Teacher model in the USA (see Chapter 6 of this book) was that it was simply the wrong approach and probably led to the most salient features of the best teaching being ignored. However, if we were to use the 'common sense' paradigm here, payment by results would make sense – i.e. test students before the teacher starts whatever episode is determined significant (one lesson? one year?) and then repeat the test; if the students do better in the second test, effective teaching must have occurred. In an era of 'high stakes testing' this will lead to incessant testing, a great deal of 'teaching to the test' and huge emphasis on highly visible results per teacher, per school, per school district and per system. This might produce what could be called efficient teaching – i.e. a very narrow focus producing some very particular outcomes – but the evidence is clear that this is not effective education and is also highly damaging to teaching quality (see Sammons *et al.*, 2007; Goodwyn, 2010). One of the underpinning principles in this book is that such a regime is counterproductive to the development of really expert teachers in any phase, subject or country.

The measurement of educational outcomes clearly has its place and the continued application of research and experiment may lead to genuine increases in the accuracy and validity of such measurement. However, the obsession with measurement and what might be termed the 'medical' model of research is unquestionably highly problematic. The medical model adopts a random trial of a large population to see what works – i.e. does drug x work with all ages and types of people? If not, which does it work with and who should therefore avoid it. Over time these findings can be progressively refined. The model is usually predicated on trials on animals first. It is not surprising that governments find this type of approach (does intervention x produce good outcomes for all students) appealing: in England it lies behind the design of the National Literacy Strategy and the obsessive attempts to measure its 'benefits' (Goodwyn and Fuller, 2011). However, teachers and students are not rats – not that rats should be treated inhumanely either.

The key point in considering both effective teaching and expert teaching is that the interrelationship of context, process and product variables is complex and very difficult to measure in a simple and reliable way. This does not lessen its importance nor the value of constantly seeking better ways to achieve it. The point is that teachers are part of the development, not merely subjects in a highly controlled experiment. And something that should be treated as experimental, rather than permanent, is the use of 'standards' in teaching, the ultimate use of the competence paradigm.

Standards and accountability

The introduction of standards into teaching is a global phenomenon (Goodwyn, 2010). In one respect it can be welcomed as further evidence of a determined trend to define what good teaching looks like in practice and several expert models make use of standards to describe that top level. At the same time, it is hugely problematic if it merely prescribes practice and is really driven by managerialist attempts to both measure (in simplistic ways) and control effective teaching. Very good teachers have specific issues with a 'standards' model, not least because their special qualities may be beyond or above what such a model can capture. However, it seems inevitable that standards are likely to be used for the foreseeable future in the service of both developing teachers and controlling them; there will be real tension and expert teachers have a key role in exerting influence towards development.

The very term 'standards' is applied to so many things for so many reasons that it is in danger of becoming a linguistic morass. In an effort to gain some clarity it is worth stating that the next section will endeavour to avoid the 'standards in schools are rising/are falling' debate. Later in the book there will be some discussion of the impact of the standards agenda on experienced and successful teachers, but more in relation to their resilience and their determination to develop. The focus here is on the competence paradigm as it is enacted through the development and use of standards to describe teaching, especially very good teaching.

It is worth noting that the development of national-style standards stemmed initially from the emergence of the teacher appraisal model in England in the 1980s at a time when schools and teachers were the subject of particularly fierce criticism. A recommendation in Better Schools (DES, 1985) became a scheme in 1991 (DES, 1991) and this was mirrored in many countries (Hickcox and Musella, 1992; Goodwyn, 2010). The unions were extremely suspicious of these schemes and tend still to be so, being concerned that such schemes are not only principally managerialist but also driven by a desire to prove incompetence rather than celebrate expertise.

The three main purposes of appraisal, which have not changed over time, can be summed up quite simply (see Kyriacou, 1997, ch. 9). There is a managerial function, which is essentially about understanding teacher quality in a school so that the management (head teacher, head of department, etc.) can understand a teacher's performance and make the best use of it or diagnose any school issues. Equally it is a tool for professional development, and here there are two key aspects: one is feedback on actual performance, especially observed teaching, and the other is feedback on longer-term and career development. When appraisal is undertaken successfully these two major purposes can be complementary, especially for increasingly effective teachers who may be able to undertake much wider roles in the school if their quality is understood – for example, becoming an Advanced Skills or Excellent Teacher. Such teachers may themselves become valuable as appraisers, especially as they may be perceived as not solely managerial and developmental.

It is the third purpose, that of public accountability, that connects most directly with this particular standards agenda. In other words, by assessing the quality of teaching in a school, some kind of measure can be awarded to the school and therefore cumulatively to the school area and then the whole system. If such evidence were reliable and robust it would be possible to state year on year whether standards of teaching were improving. The entire model of inspection in England was based on such an assumption for a considerable period, leading to massive statements in the chief inspector's report about the quality of teaching across the whole of the system. This approach also led to the draconian 'failing school' concept and the notion of 'special measures'. As a conceptualisation of schools and teaching it is deeply flawed and highly controversial. It also makes accountability seem principally predicated on the need to fail teachers and schools. There is abundant evidence (for example, see Sammons *et al.*) that the effect of this model of inspection has been corrosive and destructive. Very good teachers who receive an Ofsted 1 as confirmation of their quality are typically pleased but mostly relieved; a rather paradoxical outcome. The self-evaluative model of inspection that is under development in England may shift paradigms and become a much more reflective model.

One simple initiative to emerge from this complex period of high prescription of both the curriculum (National Curriculum introduced in 1988) and teachers ('Appraisal' introduced in 1991) was the introduction of standards for initial teacher training (ITT) in 1999. It is worth reflecting on the fact that standards were first introduced for student teachers (novices), then later for ASTs (experts) and that the middle part of the continuum (competent) came last! It is also of note that the creation of standards for ITT was bound up with the reformulation from initial teacher *education* to initial teacher *training* and the significant shift from *student* teacher to *trainee* teacher. Much of this stemmed from another government accountability agency, the Teacher Training Agency (TTA). It emerged in 1993 and was very much conceptualised as part of the competence/incompetence paradigm. It can certainly be argued that this was all part of a profoundly negative shift towards downgrading teaching as a profession and imposing very considerable negative control on it at classroom level. It also appears to be a global phenomenon, but with England at the far end of the accountability spectrum. The shift was symbolised by the destruction of the previous Her Majesty's Inspection of Schools model of inspection and the creation of the Office for Standards in Education (Ofsted) in 1992. It is notable that the TTA changed its name in 2005 to the

Training and Development Agency for Schools, signalling an attempt to shift its role towards support for teachers.

Some concluding remarks about the role of the teacher and becoming 'effective'

This chapter has outlined the complicated relationship between the teacher, the teaching profession and some of the key factors that put pressure on that role, some positive and developmental, others more controlling and negative. In all countries with education systems and including the 'private sector', teachers are in the public eye, are seen as highly accountable and are increasingly monitored and regulated. Some of this attention has led to the creation of standards intended to help understand and describe best practice and develop rewards and designations for the best teachers. This drive towards standards is immensely complex as the very term is imbued with all kinds of issues, discussed above, and with the increasingly global challenge of recruiting and then retaining all teachers, including those that are simply competent, not just the very best.

Simultaneously, governments now constantly refer to the need for a 'world class' teaching profession, mostly because they are acutely aware of international educational league tables and their own country's 'performance' and league position. So, as now seems to be the global 'norm', teachers are all highly valued but under the most severe pressure everywhere to 'perform', with most measurement being through the simplistic (and we would argue now outmoded) model of test results. One aspect of all this political pressure and tension has been more emphasis on identifying and retaining the best teachers in the classroom and/or creating some form of career structure that recognises this role – even, in some instances, creating 'leading teachers' whose focus is not managerial but developmental. There have been other, much more educationally sound, reforms such as the development of the Highly Accomplished Teacher in the US (see Chapter 6 of this book) and the Advanced Skills Teacher in Australia (see Chapter 5 of this book), where the major emphasis is on celebrating and rewarding the best teachers, whatever title they might be awarded. Chapter 3 investigates in depth how the recognition and description of the best teachers has become a truly global phenomenon.

References

Barber, M. and Mourshed, M. (2007) *The McKinsey Report: How the World's Best-performing Education Systems Come Out On Top*. New York: McKinsey & Co.

Biesta, G.J.J. (2013) *The Beautiful Risk of Education*. Boulder: Paradigm.

Brookes, W. (2005) The Graduate Teacher Programme in England: mentor training, quality assurance and the findings of inspection, *Journal of In-service Education*, 31(1): 43–61.

Brown, S. and McIntyre, D. (1993) *Making Sense of Teaching*. Buckingham: Open University Press.

Cooper, P. and McIntyre, D. (1996) *Effective Teaching and Learning: Teachers' and Students' Perspectives*. London: McGraw Hill.

Cullingford, C. (1999) *An Inspector Calls: Ofsted and its Effect on School Standards*. London: Kogan Page.

DES (Department of Education and Science) (1985) *Better Schools*. London: HMSO.

DES (Department of Education and Science) (1991) 'School teacher appraisal', Circular 12/91. DES, London.

DfE (Department of Education) (2015) *A World Class Teaching Profession: Government Response to Consultation*. London: HMSO.

Dreyfus, S. L. and Dreyfus, H. L. (1986) *Mind over Machine: The Power of Human Intuition and Expertise in the Era of the Computer*. New York: Simon & Schuster.

Eisner. E. W. (1985) *The Educational Imagination: On the Design and Evaluation of School Programmes*. New York: Macmillan.

Eraut, M. (1994) *Developing Professional Knowledge and Competence*. Brighton: The Falmer Press.

Eraut, M. (1995) 'Developing professional knowledge within a client-centred orientation', in T. R. Guskey and M. Huberman (eds) *Professional Development in Action: New Paradigms and Practices*. New York: Teachers College Press.

Ericsson, K., Charness, N., Feltovitch, P. and Hoffman, R. (2006) (eds) *The Cambridge Handbook of Expertise and Expert Performance*. Cambridge: Cambridge University Press.

Furlong, J. (2013) *Education: An Anatomy of a Discipline*. London: Routledge.

Goodwyn, A. (1997) *Developing English Teachers: The Role of Mentorship in a Reflective Profession*. Milton Keynes: Open University Press.

Goodwyn, A. (2001) 'Second-tier professionals: English teachers in England', *L1-Educational Studies in Language and Literature*, 1(2): 149–161.

Goodwyn, A. and Fidler, B. (2002) 'Advanced Skills Teachers: The emergence of the role'. Paper given at the BERA annual conference, Exeter.

Goodwyn, A. (2004a) 'What's in a frame: The English framework three years on', *English, Drama, Media*, 2, January: 122–131.

Goodwyn, A. (2004b) 'The professional identity of English teachers in England', *English in Australia*, 139, February: 122–131.

Goodwyn, A. (2010) *The Expert Teacher of English*. London: Routledge.

Goodwyn, A. (2014) 'Head teachers' view of expert teachers: Do they see the Advanced Skills Teacher as an innovation benefitting the profession?' Paper presented at the British Educational Research Association, University of London.

Goodwyn, A. (2015) 'Has the Advanced Skills Teacher role been an advance for the profession? The views of principals and other senior leaders'. Paper presented at the American Educational Research Association Conference, Chicago.

Goodwyn, A. and Fuller, C. (eds) (2011) *The Great Literacy Debate*. London: Routledge.

GTCE website: www.gtce.org.uk

Hattie, J. (2003) *Teachers Make a Difference: What is the Research Evidence?* Auckland: University of Auckland.

Hickcox, E. S. and Musella, D. F. (1992) 'Teacher performance, appraisal and staff development', in Fullan, M. and Hargreaves, A. (eds) *Teacher Development and Educational Change* (pp. 156–169). Milton Keynes: Open University Press.

Kyriacou, C. (1997) *Effective Teaching in Schools: Theory and Practice. London*: Nelson Thornes.

Lemov, D. (2010) *Teach Like a Champion: 49 Techniques that Put Students on the Path to College*. San Francisco: Jossey Bass.

Mathieson, M. (1975) *The Preachers of Culture*. London: Allen Unwin.

McBer, H. (2000) *Research into Teacher Effectiveness: A Model of Teacher Effectiveness*. London: HMSO.

Mourshed, M., Chijioke, C. and Barber, M. (2010) *How the World's Most Improved School Systems Keep Getting Better*. New York; McKinsey & Co.

Perrot, E. (1982) *Effective Teaching: A Practical Guide to Improving your Teaching.* London: Longman.

Sammons, P., Day, C., Stobart, G. and Gu, Q. (2007) *Teachers Matter: Connecting Lives, Work and Effectiveness.* Maidenhead: Open University Press.

Schon, D. (1983) *The Reflective Practitioner: How Professionals Think in Action.* London: Temple Smith.

Schon, D. (1987) *Educating the Reflective Practitioner.* San Francisco: Jossey Bass.

Shulman, L. (1986) 'Those who understand: Knowledge growth in teaching', *Educational Researcher,* 15(2), 4–31.

Shulman, L. (1987) 'Knowledge and teaching: Foundations of the new reform', *Harvard Educational Review,* 57(1): 1–22.

Sorensen, N. T. (2014) 'Improvisation and teacher expertise: A comparative case study'. PhD thesis, Bath Spa University. Available via http://researchspace.bathspa.ac.uk/5128/ (accessed 25 October 2015).

Squires, G. (1999) *Teaching as a Professional Discipline.* Falmer: Falmer Press.

Stones, E. (1992) *Quality Teaching: A Sample of Cases.* London: Routledge.

Turner-Bissett, R. (2001) *Expert Teaching: Knowledge and Pedagogy to Lead the Profession.* London, David Fulton.

Woods, P. and Jeffrey, B. (1996) *Teachable Moments: The Art of Teaching in Primary Schools.* Buckingham: Open University Press.

3

THE GLOBAL RISE OF THE EXPERT TEACHER

From effective to expert

Andrew Goodwyn

This chapter explores the idea of the professional teacher, starting with a meta-analysis of expert teaching and then examining a very influential model of stages of expert development. That 'expert teaching' is a global phenomenon is without question and is discussed at some length in Chapters 7 and 8. The emphasis there is very much on evaluating what we now know as a result of the emergence of this phenomenon, seeing it as the beginning of a new era in which nation states can adapt each other's models and share best practice – not merely copying it or, through political imperatives, imposing it on teachers in a different and inappropriate national or even regional context.

We believe this concept of adaptation rather than replication is one of the lessons to be learnt from a plethora of national-level developments (see Chapters 4–6). However, we also argue that there is a useful and generative dimension to this emerging phenomenon, which is about the 'universal' in a Darwinian sense. We continue to evolve as a species and part of that evolution is an increasingly 'adapted mind' (see Chapter 1). So, first, we are increasingly able to learn from each other, especially in a world with rapid and sophisticated communications, much of it visual and not solely dependent on verbal language. Second, we are at a stage in the development of teachers where we are increasingly able to capture some of what we mean by expert teaching: this allows for comparison and contrast, identifying difference and similarity. Third, this knowledge of teacher expertise is not 'political' – that is, it is not entirely controlled by the nation state's government of the day. What governments, certainly most of them, and this has nothing to do with democracy, whatever the rhetoric of the day, *what these governments do* is constantly to attempt to impose an ideological version of the best teaching onto 'their' teaching profession. Unfortunately this is not at all the same as sensitivity towards local needs and contexts. So, fourthly, as this global phenomenon of the expert teacher emerges, we are developing knowledge of global significance and value that allows, at this stage, for local adaptation but also, longer term, of universal substance. This might be articulated, albeit simplistically, as a question: 'To what extent is all the best teaching the same?' A more sophisticated question might be: 'Given that good teaching anywhere is complex and situated, to what extent are the characteristics, at least some of them, helpfully universal?'

Another clearly universal concern is what might be the stages of development in becoming an effective teacher, even an expert one. In all skilled domains there is a simple distinction between novice and competent (see Chapter 1), reflected in the craft tradition as apprentice and master. There is a fundamental recognition that a combination of practice and experience should lead to some 'mastery', whether it be as a jewellery maker or a lawyer: what we are clear about is that experience, by itself, does not produce 'mastery'. More contentious is whether the development of expertise is a gradual continuum or a set of stages or phases, and, if the latter, do the stages have predictable characteristics that might inform our expectations of, for example, what a novice can manage and our understanding of how to develop expertise. Another important aspect of such a concept in modern societies has to do with career structure within a profession.

We thus start this chapter with an examination of what we consider the best meta-analysis with an international scope undertaken of the characteristics of teacher expertise, before moving on to review a seminal model of stages of expertise.

Hattie's characteristics of expert teaching

John Hattie's seminal review of the existing international research evidence, based on half a million studies from around the world (Hattie, 2003), provides a framework for considering expert teachers that we refer to throughout the rest of the book. He first synthesises the findings into five dimensions:

Expert teachers

- A: can identify essential representations of their subject,
- B: can guide learning through classroom interactions,
- C: can monitor learning and provide feedback,
- D: can attend to affective attributes, and
- E: can influence student outcomes.

He then outlines the specific characteristics (Hattie, 2003, pp. 6–10):

A1 Expert teachers have deeper representations about teaching and learning.
A2 Expert teachers adopt a problem-solving stance to their work.
A3 Expert teachers can anticipate, plan, and improvise as required by the situation.
A4 Expert teachers are better decision-makers and can identify what decisions are important and which are less important decisions.

B5 Expert teachers are proficient at creating an optimal classroom climate for learning.
B6 Expert teachers have a multidimensionally complex perception of classroom situations.
B7 Expert teachers are more context-dependent and have high situation cognition.
C8 Expert teachers are more adept at monitoring student problems and assessing their level of understanding and progress, and they provide much more relevant, useful feedback.
C9 Expert teachers are more adept at developing and testing hypotheses about learning difficulties or instructional strategies.
C10 Expert teachers are more automatic.
D11 Expert teachers have high respect for students.
D12 Expert teachers are passionate about teaching and learning.
E13 Expert teachers engage students in learning and develop in their students' self-regulation, involvement in mastery learning, enhanced self-efficacy, and self-esteem as learners.
E14 Expert teachers provide appropriate challenging tasks and goals for students.
E15 Expert teachers have positive influences on students' achievement.
E16 Expert teachers enhance surface and deep learning.

Hattie explains that these are not prescriptive or uniform, but facets:

> Our claim, from a review of literature and a synthesis of over 500,000 studies, is that expert teachers can be distinguished by these five dimensions, or 16 attributes. This is not aimed to be a checklist, but a profile. We see these attributes as 16 facets of the gem-stone, we see there is no one necessary facet, nor the equal presence of all, but the overlapping of many facets into the whole.
>
> *(Hattie, 2003, p.10)*

This use of the metaphor of the gemstone, is, we feel, especially valuable, for making international comparisons. For example, do different models contain all 16? If not, why not? Equally, do they highlight new and different facets?

He also points out that there is nothing here about 'content knowledge', but explains:

> Our argument is that content knowledge is necessary for both experienced and expert teachers, and is thus not a key distinguishing feature. We are not underestimating the importance of content knowledge – it must be present – but it is more pedagogical content knowledge that is important: that is, the way knowledge is used in teaching situations.
>
> *(Hattie, 2003, p.10)*

Hattie is also very deliberately focusing on the teacher as the individual variable inside the classroom; this book treats the expert teacher as an expert professional and a major potential influence on other teachers. For the purposes of this book we offer a slightly simplified version of Hattie's characteristics:

- Deep understanding of teaching and learning
- Problem-solving approach
- Ability to anticipate, plan and improvise
- Excellent decision makers – prioritise decisions
- Create optimal classroom climate for learning
- Recognise the multidimensional nature of the classroom
- Recognise that teaching is context dependent and highly situated
- Constantly monitor student progress and provide valuable feedback
- Test 'hypotheses', i.e. is this working?
- More automatic, i.e. keep plenty of 'mental space' available
- High respect for all students
- Passionate about teaching and learning
- Highly motivating – build students' self-regulation, self-efficacy, self-esteem
- Set appropriate but challenging goals and tasks
- Positively impact on achievement
- Enhance surface and deep learning

Hattie's characteristics therefore offer a very useful framework for considering expert teaching, to some extent anywhere in the world, but they do not capture the full picture of the expert teacher as extended professional because such teachers do a great deal outside the actual classroom, especially in relation to other teachers. Indeed, one of the arguments for identifying the best teachers is so that they can be, put simply, influential outside the classroom as well as inside it.

Arguably stemming from Dewey's work in the 1920s and 1930s, refined by Schon (1970s) then refined again by Shulman and others in the 1980s, there has been a steady focus on the importance of teacher expertise in educational theory and policy development. We review theoretical underpinnings of the concept of the expert teacher from several perspectives: cultural (i.e. societal values and public perceptions), political (i.e. policy) and educational (i.e. teacher as professional and 'carer/developer'). Although this book is not a detailed historical account we do need some historical perspective, partly because there is now clear influence of models across nation states but also because models have 'come and gone' – as with the AST in England, the Chartered Teacher in Scotland and (probably) the AST in Australia. There is something to learn from the provenance of each model and, where relevant, the causes of its demise.

The first appearance of a formal role, as far as we know, was the Advanced Skills Teacher in Australia in the 1980s, a significant moment of expertise recognition; this was closely followed by the HAT in the USA and, a decade later, the AST in England. New ways of describing expert teaching emerged at a time when complex issues of teacher retention and status were having an impact on educational systems around the world. These expert teacher models were attempts to keep the best teaching practitioners in the classroom and halt the rapid departure into management or advisory roles, made partly for status and partly for pay. The AST roles in Australia and in England, for example, were proposed as a solution to both issues. All the models place a fundamental emphasis on continuing development for both the individual teacher and the profession, within the classroom context. The models vary in many ways but share an emphasis on such teachers being both role models and leaders of teacher development – that is, fundamentally not *managers* running parts of the organisation. The models also share, to varying degrees, a view of teachers as intellectuals always seeking new ideas, including those in the latest research.

The influence of the concept of the reflective practitioner, however important and valuable it has been, has tended to place almost all the responsibility for development on the individual. Teacher education programmes around the world focus on developing reflective novice teachers through a host of practical means, perhaps the most fundamental being the reflective evaluation of taught lessons. At this point in most systems the novice has lots of support and stimulus to reflect, and the mentor or mentors – often one from the school and one from the university (or equivalent outside perspective) – provide a constant stream of expert advice. And this advice goes well beyond the apprentice model and, indeed, is reciprocal: good mentors state how much they learn from discussions of teaching (Goodwyn, 1997). However, teaching as a profession is relatively weak on long-term development. Novice teachers tend to experience what feels like a crash course in learning to teach and in many systems that is meant to last them for 40 years. What subsequent training comes their way is often linked to a government initiative, sometimes on a massive scale, as was the case with the National Literacy Strategy in England or No Child Left Behind in the USA (Goodwyn and Fuller, 2011). Teachers can also seek development through subject associations or locally provided courses or even by entering a master's programme.

On this point there is a telling footnote from England. It has already been outlined how the AST role has been terminated and a 'master teacher' designation proposed but not accepted. In the final two years (2009–2011) of the life of the Training and Development Agency for Schools, an attempt was made to set up a structure in which every teacher would eventually achieve a master's degree in teaching and learning. The whole scheme was poorly conceptualised and rushed into place and universities were deeply reluctant to award what they felt was a highly functionalist model based in a very limiting way on individual school practice (Brookes, 2016). For our purposes the key point is that the scheme had barely begun before a new elected government swept it aside, at the same time as abolishing the General Teaching Council for England (see Chapter 2).

Whatever its many and glaring faults, this master's scheme went some way towards recognising that initial teacher education is not sufficient for long-term teacher development or for giving the profession more credibility. The Scottish Chartered Teacher scheme was one of the few to conceptualise teacher development as combining pedagogic, ethical and intellectual growth. So for many teachers it is reflective practice or nothing. We return to the main argument of this book, that while expert teacher designations cannot be claimed to solve all these problems, they do at least recognise high levels of teacher expertise and provide ways for teachers to benefit from having 'excellent' colleagues.

All well-established professions encourage advanced specialisation, usually through the provision of recognised further qualifications, ongoing professional development and career structures that reflect such increased expertise. The next section reviews briefly how the introduction of teacher standards in England was part of the process that established the AST. It then explores a range of issues to do with naming and defining expert teachers.

The emergence of 'models' in England

It is beyond the scope of this book to review the entire history of teaching in England from the perspective of expertise. For most of the twentieth century it seems reasonable to suggest that there were notions of 'great teaching', especially in the popular imagination, but little formal recognition in the system. One role that emerged in the 1970s and 1980s was that of the 'advisory teacher'. This was to some extent a forerunner of the AST, involving as it did a practising teacher being seconded from the classroom by their local educational authority for a period of a few years with the expectation that they would then return to the classroom. The role was based on them using their expertise, for example, as a successful English teacher, to advise other English teachers within the LEA on how to improve their teaching. It had an enhanced salary, significant status and was an 'outreach' model. The role still exists in England but has largely disappeared from the LEAs, not least because of the disappearance of the LEAs from the educational system. Indeed, we speculate that one reason for the introduction of the AST was the rapid diminution of the teacher advisor role in the late 1980s and early 1990s due to LEA reforms and severe budget cuts. As the AST role is analysed in some depth in its own chapter, our focus here is on the standards for the AST as they existed in their last definition.

England, after a period of relative stability in terms of teacher standards (1997–2012), experienced yet more massive change. However, although the government replaced the existing system in September 2012 with a 'single standard' and a tentative proposal for a 'Master Teacher' standard (which will be discussed in the final chapter of this book), the previous system was far more interesting and important from the argument in this book's point of view. Strictly speaking, it was not defined as a model of expertise at all, but if examined from that perspective its implied stages were:

- Achieving Qualified Teacher Status i.e. initial training
- Passing 'Induction' and achieving the core standards i.e. 'probation'
- Post Threshold

- Excellent
- Advanced Skills

The 2009 version of the standards for teachers was set out to suggest that there was a kind of continuum, with the AST positioned as the ultimate 'level'; given that it was conceptualised as 'levels', it might more accurately be described as a hierarchy.

However, they are described in the guidance as essentially career and reward stages:

> The framework of professional standards for teachers set out below defines the characteristics of teachers at each career stage. Specifically it provides professional standards for:
>
> - the award of Qualified Teacher Status (QTS) (Q)
> - teachers on the main scale (Core) (C)
> - teachers on the upper pay scale (Post Threshold Teachers) (P)
> - Excellent Teachers (E)
> - Advanced Skills Teachers (ASTs) (A)
>
> *(DCSF website)*

The mode of description immediately highlights the underlying ideology of the use of the standards as opposed to the nature of the standards themselves; their use is both 'performance related' in a managerial sense and hierarchical rather than developmental. The guidance (DCSF, 2009) made this even more explicit:

> The standards provide the framework for a teacher's career and clarify what progression looks like. As now, to access each career stage a teacher will need to demonstrate that he/she has met the relevant standards. The process for this varies depending on the standards concerned. Teachers seeking Excellent Teacher or AST status need to apply and be assessed through an external assessment process. Teachers seeking to cross the threshold are assessed by their head teacher. The standards for Post Threshold Teachers, Excellent Teachers and ASTs are pay standards and teachers who are assessed as meeting them also access the relevant pay scale.

For the aspiring, or existing, expert teachers this was a clear reminder that 'standards' are always of their time and very likely to be ideologically inflected. They have their uses, as discussed above, but they should be treated critically and subject to constant revision and even improvement. Indeed, a characteristic of an expert teacher is to adopt this stance towards standards and to treat them as generative not prescriptive. Before considering the more apposite Excellent Teacher and AST standards in more detail it is worth noting again that this is a global movement and that most developed systems are trying out this mode of teacher characterisation, producing a variety of 'titles' (see below).

The challenge in finding a highly effective title for 'expert teachers'

One of Shakespeare's best-known lines is 'What's in a name?', which continues: 'a rose by any other name would smell as sweet' (*Romeo and Juliet*). However, the world of education has been much exercised by what to call a 'very good' teacher – and certainly, that term, 'very good', however much used popularly and informally, has not been seen as adequate for the status of what is being described. It is worth reflecting that this partly stems from many other factors (professionalism, unionisation, materiality) covered earlier that bear down on this descriptor once it becomes a status with a title. When the term 'Advanced Skills Teacher' was first imported to England from Australia in 1997 and became a formal term, it was highly controversial. The popular press published cartoon images of 'super teachers', dressed in superman costumes, flying through the windows of classrooms (Goodwyn, 2001b). Although this was largely humorous, it nevertheless symbolises the popular view that, since teaching is a rather ordinary activity, any extraordinary claim about it is rather ludicrous. It is thus clear that the title and/or descriptive term matters very much and may well reflect a highly determining view of what the title bearer is to do with their expertise. Why, for example, does England have both the Advanced Skills Teacher and the Excellent Teacher? Ultimately, it is difficult to decide on the best term because what needs to be captured is so complex.

There are currently a number of terms in use around the world and many are considered in detail at appropriate points in this book. Here we briefly list several that seem 'popular' – by that we mean have been used a good deal rather than especially 'liked'. They include the Advanced Skills Teacher, Master Teacher, Leading Teacher, Highly Accomplished Teacher, Excellent Teacher, Outstanding Teacher and Chartered Teacher. We would argue that this range illustrates the difficulty but also the importance of finding a singular term.

We also consider that the terms bring out differences of *semantic emphasis*. For example, Advanced Skills Teacher treats teaching as a skill with the clear idea of the continuum or stages of skill acquisition; when this term operated in England the AST was at the top of the hierarchical structure of skill levels. One limitation of such a title is it has a *technicist* emphasis rather than a holistic one. There is similar attention to skill and level in a term like 'Highly Accomplished', but 'accomplishment 'suggests a broader range of capabilities. Finally, 'Chartered' focuses much more on the notion of status, that of a top and extended professional; it also deliberately compares teaching to other leading professions with codes of conduct and significant societal status.

Ultimately we believe that these names are highly significant but that the variety is generative and productive: not only is it unlikely that there will ever be a singular term in, for example, the English-speaking world, but the names will probably continue to change with changes to the teaching profession's societal standing. No country to our knowledge has chosen what we consider the most neutral term, *expert*, but this keeps it available for academic and other discussion as the most usefully generic term.

The Advanced Skills Teacher

The use of the term AST (as mentioned above, now discontinued) in England was derived from an attempt in several Australian states to identify and reward the best teachers and retain them, this development has had its own controversies (Ingvarson, 1998; Kleinhenz and Ingvarson, 2004; Ingvarson and Kleinhenz, 2006). These definitions appeared first in 1994 and have been revised but they capture what is also now current in South Australia (see Government of South Australia website).

The AST was introduced in 1994, with the AST2 level added in 2006. The characteristics of these ASTs are a very simple model:

> An AST 1 must be able to demonstrate the possession of high-level skills which enable them to show that they can:
>
> (a) apply a range of effective teaching approaches and methods of evaluating and reporting student's / children's progress;
> (b) generate positive relationships with individual students/children, class groups and groups of children;
> (c) develop ideas gained from their own teaching practice and apply ideas gained from professional development activities to enhance students'/ children's learning;
> (d) apply to their teaching the knowledge of current trends and developments in education;
> (e) work collaboratively with other teachers;
> (f) communicate and work effectively with other teachers, parents and the wider site community;
> (g) contribute to the organisation, planning and development of the site's curriculum;
> (h) assist other teachers in their professional development and supervise, instruct and counsel beginning and student teachers;
> (i) provide professional and personal support to less experienced staff and poorly performing staff to facilitate performance improvements.
>
> *(Government of South Australia website)*

These are recognisably related to Hattie's outline or the Chartered Teacher model, but it seems their rather modest expectations led to a revamped AST2 model in 2006:

> An AST 2 will be able to provide evidence of their sustained role as a teacher leader and the impact that their work has had in challenging, changing and

improving the practice of, at least, 4–6 colleagues at a team, site, district or systemic level.

All criteria should be interpreted with these ideas as the underpinning premise.

1 Demonstrated ability to teach students in an exemplary manner using current learning theories and innovative methodologies.
2 Demonstrated ability to model, develop and positively influence the professional reflection and practice of colleagues.
3 Demonstrated positive collaboration with colleagues and contribution to their professional support and growth.
4 Demonstrated involvement in the critical evaluation of professional practice to challenge, change and improve the quality of teaching of colleagues and the learning outcomes for students.
5 Demonstrated contribution, as a leading practitioner, in the development, implementation and evaluation of a learning area, subject area, program, or a new teaching and learning initiative.
6 Demonstrated ability to effectively influence and expand knowledge and practice of colleagues through mentoring or conducting professional learning opportunities.
7 Demonstrated effective contribution to school/site improvement planning, identification of priorities and to formal school/site decision-making processes.

(*Government of South Australia website*)

What is interesting here is the emphasis on the extended professional concept and also on being a leading practitioner who influences and develops others, something implied in the AST model in England and later stated in the Excellent Teacher model. This 'second stage' – how do you keep developing a highly developed teacher? – is missing from the original idea of the AST in both Australia and England.

In England the AST had its own longevity, having been in operation for over a decade. After an early period of uncertainty and considerable opposition, the role became widely accepted and occupied between 1 and 2% of the teaching workforce. There have been two Ofsted reports (Ofsted 2001, 2003), both broadly favourable, and a review sponsored by the Centre for British Teachers (CfBT) (Taylor and Jennings, 2004). However, there had been no substantive review or research to determine evidence upon which to build future policy. The sudden, ill-fated, arrival of the Excellent Teacher role did not clarify policy intentions. The standards for the AST, in use from 1998 to 2013, were essentially subsumed into those for the Excellent Teacher, leaving just three that were specific to the AST. The ET standards can be clustered as follows:

Be willing to take a leading role in developing workplace policies and practice and in promoting collective responsibility for their implementation.

> Research and evaluate innovative curricular practices and draw on research outcomes and other sources of external evidence to inform their own practice and that of colleagues.
>
> Have a critical understanding of the most effective teaching, learning and behaviour management strategies, including how to select and use approaches that personalise learning to provide opportunities for all learners to achieve their potential.
>
> *(DCSF website)*

These standards focused on teaching and learning and gave the ET a leading role and also a degree of criticality, although nothing like as strong or autonomous as that of the Scottish Chartered Teacher. The next group focused on assessment and curriculum:

> Know how to improve the effectiveness of assessment practice in the workplace, including how to analyse statistical information to evaluate the effectiveness of teaching and learning across the school.
>
> Have an extensive and deep knowledge and understanding of their subjects/curriculum areas and related pedagogy gained for example through involvement in wider professional networks associated with their subjects/curriculum areas.
>
> Have an extensive knowledge on matters concerning equality, inclusion and diversity in teaching.
>
> Take a lead in planning collaboratively with colleagues in order to promote effective practice.
>
> Identify and explore links within and between subjects/curriculum areas in their planning.
>
> *(DCSF website)*

It is notable that the Hatti-style word 'deep' only appears once, whereas the vaguer term 'extensive' is much used. The next three are about being exemplary:

> Have teaching skills which lead to excellent results and outcomes.
>
> Demonstrate excellent and innovative pedagogical practice.
>
> Demonstrate excellent ability to assess and evaluate.
>
> *(DCSF website)*

There is something very reductive here about merely repeating the word 'excellent' as if it is self-evident what that means. It is an interesting question how far expert teachers are exemplary in all respects; clearly the extended professional communicates to a range of audiences, hence this standard was highly appropriate:

> Have an excellent ability to provide learners, colleagues, parents and carers with timely, accurate and constructive feedback on learners' attainment, progress and areas for development that promotes pupil progress.
>
> *(DCSF website)*

Equally, and rather like technology, an addition to teachers' knowledge base can now come from data-rich school environments:

> Use local and national statistical data and other information, in order to provide:
>
> - a comparative baseline for evaluating learners' progress and attainment,
> - a means of judging the effectiveness of their teaching,
> - and a basis for improving teaching and learning.
>
> *(DCSF website)*

Finally, there was a section about working outside the classroom and collaborating with and developing others:

> Work closely with leadership teams, taking a leading role in developing, implementing and evaluating policies and practice that contribute to school improvement.
>
> Contribute to the professional development of colleagues using a broad range of techniques and skills appropriate to their needs so that they demonstrate enhanced and effective practice.
>
> Make well-founded appraisals of situations upon which they are asked to advise, applying high-level skills in classroom observation to evaluate and advise colleagues on their work and devising and implementing effective strategies to meet the learning needs of children and young people leading to improvements in pupil outcomes.
>
> *(DCSF website)*

These standards were very much a mixture of discourses. Some are literally pedagogical, e.g. 'Demonstrate excellent and innovative pedagogical practice'. However, compared to, say, Hattie's definition of what characterises excellent teachers, we can only guess at what such pedagogy might look like. The discourse of managerialism was evident throughout: 'Be willing to take a leading role in developing workplace policies and practice and in promoting collective responsibility for their implementation'. This implied that such policies are morally and educationally neutral; in summary, you should do what the management tell you to do as they know best. The word 'critical' appears once, reflection is never mentioned, affective terms such as 'enthusiasm' and 'passion' are entirely missing. Did they appear in the final section in the standards for ASTs?

> Be willing to take on a strategic leadership role in developing workplace policies and practice and in promoting collective responsibility for their implementation in their own and other workplaces.
>
> Be part of or work closely with leadership teams, taking a leadership role in developing, implementing and evaluating policies and practice in their own and other workplaces that contribute to school improvement

> Possess the analytical, interpersonal and organisational skills necessary to work effectively with staff and leadership teams beyond their own school
>
> *(DCSF website)*

These standards were even more explicitly managerial and implementational than those for the Excellent Teacher. The only interesting aspect was that they make explicit the operational distinction between the Excellent Teacher focus on their school (inreach) and the AST focus on other schools (outreach). Outreach was one of the most imaginative and generative aspects of the AST role, essentially requiring teachers to spend a day a week in other schools or settings. Early research (Goodwyn and Fidler, 2002) suggested that this was highly valued and could be very effective. However, there has been little research of any depth to evaluate these early positive findings; the work by Goodwyn and others (see Chapter 4) has had to rely principally on the self-report of ASTs themselves.

It seems reasonable to say, then, that the AST role was significant within the English system; what the Excellent Teacher role would have added is unclear. This is especially the case as the scheme was three years old at the time of the sole review of the role, sponsored by the DCSF, which concluded:

> The Excellent Teacher Scheme (ETS) came into being in September 2006 to provide a new career route for experienced teachers as an alternative to management and leadership posts. It was envisaged that over time, some 20% of eligible teachers would be employed as Excellent Teachers (ETs). However, by December 2008, only 59 teachers in England and Wales had undergone assessment and fully met the ET Standards.
>
> *(Hutchings* et al.*, 2009)*

The review was a thorough one and gathered data widely and principally from head teachers and teachers who had not taken up the role in their schools as well as undertaking case studies of ETs. One of their striking findings was how much the ETs themselves disliked the title:

> The vast majority of ETs strongly disliked the title Excellent Teacher; only one positively liked it. Most of them told of being teased by colleagues. While much of this was 'jokey', the cumulative effect of this had made some of them miserable. They felt the title placed an onus on them to be excellent in all aspects of their work, and this was hard to live up to. They were also aware that there were many other excellent teachers in their schools. In two schools, the title was not used at all, and in others, the ET discouraged its use. All this contributes to the invisibility of the scheme. But they also complained that in some public contexts and research contexts, ET is not included as an option, and this also tends to make the whole scheme invisible.
>
> *(Ibid., p. 12)*

Other teachers were also negative: 'While most interviewees identified at least some positive aspects of the ETS, the majority gave much more emphasis to negative aspects, and in particular to concerns that the scheme, and the title ET, are potentially divisive (ibid., p. 10).

So clearly, while AST did become accepted, 'Excellent' did not. The introduction of the ET role, the report concluded, had been a hugely wasted opportunity. Most teachers knew little about it; those who did were completely confused by its relationship to other roles and especially to the AST role. It might be argued that the role just needed time, as the AST role certainly did (Goodwyn and Fidler, 2002), to become 'normal' and credible. The review team suggested a clearer relationship with the AST role:

> Many of the schools also employed ASTs. While the key difference between the two roles was generally identified as the AST doing outreach work while the ET did not, this was not always the case; a number of the schools employed 'inreach' ASTs. In these circumstances, there was little difference between ET and AST roles. Generally, however, ASTs were perceived as being better paid and having higher status. They were also seen as more likely than ETs to move into management roles, while ET was described by some as a '*dead end*' in terms of career progression.
>
> *(Hutchings* et al., *2009, p. 4)*

In order to achieve this clarity they suggested 'bringing together AST and ET into one route under the AST title (this being more familiar and accepted); this route could then include "AST outreach" and "AST inreach" (ibid., p. 5). This would certainly have been a pragmatic solution, but it ignored the question of the culture in which the term Excellent Teacher was rejected: presumably Expert Teacher would have been even more unpopular. The teaching profession will need to come to terms with its own expertise at some point soon!

With only 57 teachers the ET scheme could not have had any significant impact, but surely the AST role, after ten years, must have an evidence base. In fact, very little evidence was gathered on which to evaluate the importance of the AST role at any level during that time; work by Goodwyn and others came much later. Had it added any status to the profession in the eyes of the public, the media or politicians? Did pupils have any positive awareness of the role? Did great numbers of teachers aspire to the role? Had it produced any identifiable 'gains' to the school system? Had the role itself inspired and/or developed expert teaching? Did we now know more about expert teachers through this particular AST characterisation? Had it been money well spent?

We do not have clear answers, but we do know, if we trust Ofsted, that there are many excellent teachers who, for whatever reason, do not have a designation as such but who have been recognised through inspection.

References

Brookes, W. (2016) The Master Teacher Programme in England: a critical evaluation, unpublished Phd. Reading: University of Reading.

DCSF website: www.gov.uk/government/organisations/department-for-children-schools-and-families

Goodwyn, A. (1997) *Developing English Teachers: The Role of Mentorship in a Reflective Profession*. Milton Keynes: Open University Press.

Goodwyn, A. (2014) 'Head teachers' view of Expert teachers: Do they see the Advanced Skills Teacher as an innovation benefitting the profession?' Paper presented at the British Educational Research Association, University of London.

Goodwyn, A. and Fidler, B. (2002) 'Advanced Skills Teachers: The emergence of the role'. Paper presented at the BERA Annual Conference, Exeter.

Goodwyn, A. and Fuller, C. (eds) (2011) *The Great Literacy Debate*. London: Routledge.

Government of South Australia website: www.sa.gov.au

Hattie, J. (2003) *Teachers Make a Difference: What is the Research Evidence?* Auckland: University of Auckland.

Hutchings, M., Mansaray, A., Minty, S., Moreau, M.P. and Smart, S. (2009) *Excellent Teacher Scheme Review*. London: DCSF.

Ingvarson, L.C. (1998) 'Teaching standards: Foundations for the reform of professional development', in A. Hargreaves, A. Lieberman, M. Fullan and D. Hopkins (eds), *International Handbook of Educational Change*. Dordrecht: Kluwer.

Ingvarson, L.C. and Kleinhenz, E. (2006) 'Advanced teaching standards and certification: A review of national and international developments'. Report for Teaching Australia (Australian Institute for Teaching and School Leadership). Camberwell, VIC: Australian Council for Educational Research. Available at: www.teachingaustralia.edu.au/ta/go/home/projects/standards

Kleinhenz, E. and Ingvarson, L.C. (2004) 'Teacher accountability in Australia: Current policies and practices and their relation to the improvement of teaching and learning', *Research Papers in Education*, 19(1): 31–49.

Ofsted (2001) *Advanced Skills Teachers: Appointment, Deployment and Impact*. London: HMSO.

Ofsted (2003) *Advanced Skills Teachers: A Survey*. London: HMSO.

Taylor, C. and Jennings, S. (2004) *The Work of Advanced Skills Teachers*. Reading: CfBT.

4

THE ADVANCED SKILLS TEACHER IN ENGLAND

Carol Fuller

This chapter details the development of the English expertise model within the policy context and explores the assessment process, funding and initial reactions to the Advanced Skills Teachers (AST) designation. This chapter also reports on a national survey and follow up-interviews with English ASTs in 2010 and 2012 to offer an illustrated picture of how ASTs experienced being expert teachers. The views of these ASTs are used to exemplify the complex interconnections between professional development and practice and the intrinsic and extrinsic value of expert teacher awards in England. This is considered within the broader concern of teacher status and esteem in England and the ways that professional development models that recognise and reward expertise can contribute to their significant elevation.

Development of the Advanced Skills Teacher role in England

In many Western industrialised countries, substantial policy pressure has been directed at the greater accountability of teachers in improving the quality of classroom education and student results. With the teacher also identified as the most important variable in any high-performing educational system (Barber and Mourshed, 2007), a number of international policy initiatives now acknowledge and reward those teachers assessed and thus considered to be expert (SMHC, 2009). From the Highly Accomplished Teacher in the USA to the Chartered Teacher in Scotland and Advanced Skills Teacher in Australia and England, what international policies have in common is an understanding that harnessing the skills of expert teachers within the classroom is essential for educational reform and its development (Hopkins, 1996; Ingvarson, 2009).

Background

In response to a national and international context of sustained educational underachievement, the Excellence in Schools white paper was published in England in 1997 by the then Labour government. Central to the key reforms proposed within the policy was a clear and targeted focus on teaching. The teacher was framed as being at the absolute heart of raising standards in schools and heralded as the 'key to improving performance and remedying underachievement' (DfEE, 1997, p. 45). Key within the discourse of improving outcomes in the classroom was the value placed on the dissemination of the professional knowledge and practice of expert teachers. The white paper also acknowledged that 'experienced teachers were reluctant to stay within a profession which does not offer rewards for the highest quality teaching standards' (p. 48). The Advanced Skills Teacher grade was thus proposed as a new model of teacher designation for expert teachers that would be sufficiently well remunerated to keep teachers in the classroom and would focus very directly on the sharing of best practice. As a result, the AST grade was introduced into maintained schools in England in 1998, with the government's intention that they would, in time, make up 3–5 per cent of the teaching workforce.

Research by Berry (2008) suggests that while expert teachers should be well remunerated, policies that focus on salary incentives alone are not enough to attract and retain good teachers. To be most effective and to remain in the classroom, expert teachers require, among other things, high-quality professional development. This view is also supported by the work of Day (2007). Thus, as well as the growing recognition of the need to attract and retain excellent classroom practitioners, the policy initiative also demonstrated an appreciation that until then, promotion into management had been the typical and often only career route available for many teachers. The AST pathway was therefore also positioned as an attractive professional development opportunity and alternative career route for teachers. It made it possible for 'excellent classroom practitioners to progress as class teachers without having to take on management responsibilities and to be rewarded accordingly' (DfES, 2001, p. 3).

As well as a need to raise standards in schools, the then UK government was also concerned with the professionalism of teachers and ongoing issues with low morale. Despite teaching being the first-choice profession for university graduates and public opinion positioning teachers second only to doctors and nurses in terms of their professional status and prestige (Institute for Public Policy Research, 2001), research in the UK suggested that teachers still believed they had much lower status than other professions. Large-scale research by the General Teaching Council (UK) in 2002 found that 65 per cent of the 70,000 teachers surveyed believed that the public, media and government had little respect for the teaching profession, with later research by Hargreaves *et al.* (2006) finding much the same. With teacher job satisfaction considerably lower today than in 1962 (Klassen and Anderson, 2009) and ongoing issues with teacher recruitment and retention, there was also a clear drive to enhance the status of teachers both within and outside of the profession (Swann *et al.*, 2010). In 2001 the then secretary for education Estelle Morris outlined the importance of addressing teachers' low morale and the need to boost both their confidence and sense of professional status. Central to this agenda was what she considered to be the crucial need for teachers to redefine and renegotiate their professionalism in line with other professions of the modern world. Her main assertion, however, centred on establishing greater trust between government and teachers; with an implied critique in her declaration that the days were long gone when 'teachers could say with a straight face, "trust me, I'm a professional"' (Morris, 2001, p. 19). The purpose of the AST grade was therefore threefold. It was a means to raise standards by sharing best practice, it offered a career and professional development route that kept teachers in the classroom, and it was also a medium by which to recognise and reward teaching expertise and thus – in time – raise the status of the teaching profession more broadly.

Funding[1]

Up to March 2006, most AST posts were funded by the dedicated AST Standards Fund grant, a fund established to help local authorities (LAs) and schools raise standards. Half the costs were met by the DfES and the other half by the LA. The grant was for the additional costs of the post, i.e. salary enhancement and cover for outreach and an amount towards the LA costs of supporting and managing AST outreach (DfES, 2006)

From April 2004 the AST Standards Fund grant was designed to support existing AST posts in each LA. DfES noted that in 2006 this represented just over 1 per cent of the teaching workforce nationally. In 2005/6 the funding allocations were based on an average annual cost for each AST post of £15,500, made up of £6,200 for outreach costs and £9,300 for salary-related costs. In addition, the total allocation to the LA included £300 per AST post (with a minimum of £5,000) towards the cost to the LA of coordinating AST outreach work, supporting ASTs and monitoring the AST programme (DfES, 2006).

In March 2011 the ring-fenced funding for ASTs ceased. In April 2013, the central funding to local authorities for ASTs also ceased and the AST designation was therefore effectively abolished.

Assessment

Prior to being awared the grade of AST, candidates underwent a comprehensive assessment to satisfy a set of standards designed to demonstrate 'an excellent classroom teacher' (CfBT, 2004, p. 4). Once appointed, ASTs moved to a pay scale that was comparable to management and designed to reflect the expertise and challenges of the role, while offering a realistic alternative to the leadership and management route.[2] Alongside a range of additional responsibilities geared towards increasing the quality of teaching and learning in their own schools, there was also a clear expectation that at least 20 per cent of an AST's time would be spent on 'outreach' work in other schools, where the primary focus was on using their expertise to improve the practice of others.

In order to ascertain that potential applicants to an AST post had the requisite skills to carry out the role, all applicants underwent a one-day assessment, carried out by an external assessor. In addition, candidates completed an application form where they evidenced how they met each of the required standards for ASTs. The application process also required that a candidate's head teacher provide supporting evidence under each of these standards, and further evidence, included in a folder and provided to the assessor on the day of the assessment, was also necessary. Once approved, ASTs needed no further re-assessment for five years.

There was no requirement that a teacher be Post Threshold[3] before applying to become an AST; however, a main-scale teacher applicant had to satisfy a set of 26 standards. These standards reflected the Core (C), Post Threshold (P) and Excellent Teacher[4] (E) standards alongside three additional standards specific to ASTs (A).

The standards that a main-scale teacher had to demonstrate are outlined in Box 4.1.

BOX 4.1

Professional attributes

Frameworks

P1 Contribute significantly, where appropriate, to implementing workplace policies and practice and to promoting collective responsibility for their implementation.

E1 Be willing to take a leading role in developing workplace policies and practice and in promoting collective responsibility for their implementation.

A1 Be willing to take on a strategic leadership role in developing workplace policies and practice and in promoting collective responsibility for their implementation in their own and other workplaces.

Personal professional development

E2 Research and evaluate innovative curricular practices and draw on research outcomes and other sources of external evidence to inform their own practice and that of colleagues.

Professional knowledge and understanding

Teaching and learning

P2 Have an extensive knowledge and understanding of how to use and adapt a range of teaching, learning and behaviour management strategies, including how to personalise learning to provide opportunities for all learners to achieve their potential.

E3 Have a critical understanding of the most effective teaching, learning and behaviour management strategies, and including how to select and use approaches that personalise learning to provide opportunities for all learners to achieve their potential.

Assessment and monitoring

P3 Have an extensive knowledge and well-informed understanding of the assessment requirements and arrangements for the subjects/curriculum areas they teach, including those related to public examinations and qualifications.

P4 Have up-to-date knowledge and understanding of the different types of qualifications and specifications and their suitability for meeting learners' needs.

E4 Know how to improve the effectiveness of assessment practice in the workplace, including how to analyse statistical information to evaluate the effectiveness of teaching and learning across the school.

Subject and curriculum

P5 Have a more developed knowledge and understanding of their subject/curriculum area and related pedagogy including how learning progresses within them.

E5 Have an extensive and deep knowledge and understanding of their subjects/curriculum areas and related pedagogy gained for example through involvement in wider professional networks associated with their subjects/curriculum areas.

Achievement and diversity

E6 Have an extensive knowledge on matters concerning equality, inclusion and diversity in teaching.

Health and well-being

P6 Have sufficient depth of knowledge and experience to be able to give advice on the development and well-being of children and young people.

Professional skills

Planning

P7 Be flexible, creative and adept at designing learning sequences within lessons and across lessons that are effective and consistently well-matched to learning objectives and the needs of learners and which integrate recent developments, including those relating to subject/curriculum knowledge.

E7

a. Take a lead in planning collaboratively with colleagues in order to promote effective practice;
b. identify and explore links within and between subjects/curriculum areas in their planning.

Teaching

P8 Have teaching skills which lead to learners achieving well relative to their prior attainment, making progress as good as, or better than, similar learners nationally.

E8 Have teaching skills which lead to excellent results and outcomes.

E9 Demonstrate excellent and innovative pedagogical practice.

Assessing, monitoring and giving feedback

E10 Demonstrate excellent ability to assess and evaluate.

E11 Have an excellent ability to provide learners, colleagues, parents and carers with timely, accurate and constructive feedback on learners' attainment, progress and areas for development that promotes pupil progress.

Reviewing teaching and learning

E12 Use local and national statistical data and other information, in order to provide (a) a comparative baseline for evaluating learners' progress and attainment, (b) a means of judging the effectiveness of their teaching, and (c) a basis for improving teaching and learning.

Team working and collaboration

P9 Promote collaboration and work effectively as a team member.

E13 Work closely with leadership teams, taking a leading role in developing, implementing and evaluating policies and practice that contribute to school improvement.

A2 Be part of or work closely with leadership teams, taking a leadership role in developing, implementing and evaluating policies and practice in their own and other workplaces that contribute to school improvement.

P10 Contribute to the professional development of colleagues through coaching and mentoring, demonstrating effective practice, and providing advice and feedback.

E14 Contribute to the professional development of colleagues using a broad range of techniques and skills appropriate to their needs so that they demonstrate enhanced and effective practice.

E15 Make well-founded appraisals of situations upon which they are asked to advise, applying high-level skills in classroom observation to evaluate and advise colleagues on their work and devising and implementing effective strategies to meet the learning needs of children and young people leading to improvements in pupil outcomes.

A3 Possess the analytical, interpersonal and organisational skills necessary to work effectively with staff and leadership teams beyond their own school.

(TDA, 2007)

The standards that a teacher was expected to demonstrate related to *Professional Attributes*, *Knowledge and Understanding* and *Professional Skills* and reflected the dimensions that Tsui (2009) suggests are the important qualities of 'expert' teachers: an 'ability to integrate aspects of teacher knowledge in relation to the teaching act . . . and their ability to engage in reflection and conscious deliberation' (2009, p. 421).

Three of the 26 standards were specific to the AST and distinguished the expertise of an AST from the Post Threshold or Excellent teacher. These are:

A1 Research and evaluate innovative curricular practices and draw on research outcomes and other sources of external evidence to inform their own practice and that of colleagues.

A2 Be part of or work closely with leadership teams, taking a leadership role in developing, implementing and evaluating policies and practice in their own and other workplaces that contribute to school improvement.

A3 Possess the analytical, interpersonal and organisational skills necessary to work effectively with staff and leadership teams beyond their own school.

(TDA, 2007)

These standards related to critical and analytical skills as well as the inter-personal and organisational skills required in managing others. Distinctive to the AST was the focus on the leadership and managerial characteristics required to support and promote change. When combined with the Excellent Teacher standards, particularly those that were target focused and concerned with student 'outcomes' (E8; E15), the suggestion was that the core skill required of an AST was one of impact: an ability to 'change', 'improve' and 'promote'.

As we saw in Chapter 3, for Hattie (2003) it is the teacher who accounts for 30 per cent of the variance in student achievement; it is what teachers know, do and care about in learning outcomes. For Hattie, the five major dimensions of expertise in teaching relate to what a teacher can do. An expert teacher can:

- identify essential representations of their subject,
- guide learning through classroom interactions,
- monitor learning and provide feedback,
- attend to affective attributes, and
- influence student outcomes.

(Hattie, 2003: 5)

When considered in relation to the 16 prototypic attributes within these, the AST standards appeared to capture them. However, the inherent characteristics of expertise that Hattie also identifies as important, the unique qualities that relate much more to an expert's personal attributes – a teacher's passion, respect for students, autonomy, awareness of context, decision making and ability to anticipate – appear not to have been reflected so well. The traits, which appear to resonate far more strongly with the lexicon of a profession and, in combination, reflect both the cognitive and emotional aspects of an expert – and the ways these play out in practice; i.e. the important inter-connection of teachers' personal and professional selves (Day *et al*., 2005) – appear to be neglected.

Unlike the Dreyfus model, expertise within the English context is recognised as non-linear in that years of experience are not positioned as equating with expertise and so do not determine when a teacher is eligible to apply to become an AST; a teacher did not to have to be Post Threshold. However, the English 'standards' clearly suggested that it was outcomes that were the key indicator of expertise; that is, that successful teaching is achieved with reference to standards and is thus primarily concerned with demonstrating the achievement of end results (Berliner, 2001). The English model can therefore arguably be considered as far more prescribed and strategic than both the Australian and American, which are much more concerned with deep subject knowledge (USA) and pedagogy (Australian). This clearly makes sense within a political environment that strongly articulates an ideological framework of performance and accountability yet fails to make allowance for the fluidity and context specificity of teaching. As we will see later in this chapter, this onus appears to have proved highly detrimental for ASTs in England and has implicitly been the death knell for the funding associated with the role. The English context resounds with the demands of performativity – 'a culture and a mode of regulation that employs judgements, comparisons and displays as means of incentive, control, attrition and change based on rewards and sanctions' (Ball, 2003, p. 216). The AST model of expertise encapsulated these ideas and rewards accordingly.

Initial reaction and the views of ASTs

Despite initial hostility from teaching unions and school principals in England over concerns that the grade would be divisive, Office for Standards in Education (Ofsted) studies in 2001 and 2003 and a more thorough review undertaken by CfBT in 2004 were all largely encouraging about the overall value of the AST role in terms of its impact and value. In interviews with 70 ASTs, head teachers and LA coordinators, Ofsted (2001) found that for half the ASTs interviewed, their impact on teaching and learning in their own school was judged as good, and for just over a further third, judged as very good or excellent. The impact of the outreach work of two-thirds of the ASTs was also 'judged at least good and for two-fifths it was very good or excellent . . . where impact was judged to be less than satisfactory this was principally because of the limited amount of work which had taken place' (2001, p. 6). In looking ahead, their research indicated that head teachers believed that there was an important role for ASTs in school, particularly in the area of performance management. In a follow-up survey of 800 ASTs in 2003, Ofsted found that ASTs had significantly improved the quality of teaching and learning in over three-quarters of the schools inspected in the survey and that head teachers felt that the improvements in teaching and learning attributable to the ASTs meant that they were well worth the extra cost of their employment. While it is not clear from the report how the impact of ASTs was measured aside from self-report, it is interesting to note that Ofsted draw attention to the fact that '*procedures are rarely in place for schools to make clear judgements about the value for money ASTs are providing*' (2003, p. 5). The justification and link between performance and financial investment is clear.

Chapter 2 discussed the competing theoretical definitions of expertise. Given the ideological context in which standards are framed, the often unconscious nature of expert practice as well as the pragmatic issues relating to an ability to demonstrate expertise and thus pass an assessment (Watkins, 1994), the use of standards to capture an expert teacher is highly problematic. Jackson (2006) argues, however, that a teacher's ability to satisfy and meet performance indicators has become much more significant than qualifications and years of teaching experience within the teaching profession and certainly within England, performativity appears to be a key driver of changes within the teaching profession. In an increasingly globally driven market place, demonstrable skills via additional credentials have become particularly important. Competition requires people to advertise their 'individuality . . . uniqueness of their work and of their accomplishments' (Beck and Beck-Gernsheim, 2001, p. 33) and for Bourdieu, credentials provide a key source of status distinctions between groups (in Swartz, 1997). If, as Giddens (1984) contends, identities emerge through standardised markers, such as age and gender, then awards such as the AST grade arguably work in the same way and are therefore an important means by which teachers are able to define their professional identities via a model that recognises their expertise; thus there are intrinsic as well as extrinsic values in achieving the award.

Because of the 'objective' criteria that had to be satisfied prior to the award of AST status, in many ways the AST grade can be observed as having established, at least for a time, both the parameters of teaching expertise in England and also that of a teaching professional. As to what a teaching expert should look like, the AST was in many ways positioned as the embodiment. However, despite the grade existing for more than 12 years, research on ASTs in England was almost non-existent. Given that the emphasis of the role was very much one of 'impact',[5] this remains rather surprising. In the following section I discuss the findings of a large-scale study of 849 ASTs carried out in England in 2010[6] and a follow-up study with 205 ASTs in 2012.[7]

The research

A comprehensive mapping of the literature in England indicated a real dearth of any large-scale, in-depth study of ASTs. What did exist were either small-scale qualitative case studies or larger studies (as reported above) that focused on specific aspects of the role. Research that explored ASTs' motivations for taking on the role, their experiences and views of the value of it, as well as its use as a professional and career development opportunity, was non-existent. The two research projects reported here attempted to address this gap.

Study 1

Data in the 2010 study was collected using a mixed method research design, through online survey and in-depth interviews with ASTs in England. Using a national database of 1,200 ASTs as our sampling frame, ASTs were invited to participate in the study via email. In total, 849 ASTs from across England participated in the online survey, giving an extremely high response rate of 71 per cent. A further 40 follow up in-depth telephone interviews were then carried out.

Of those included in the 2010 survey, 75 per cent were female and 25 per cent male. Forty per cent of ASTs worked in secondary schools; 33 per cent in primary and 7 per cent in special and 'other' schools – for example, sixth form, pupil referral unit, etc. All curriculum subject areas were captured in the survey, with science (12 per cent), English (9.5 per cent) and maths (9 per cent) most frequently represented – this replicated the main subject areas for ASTs in the English secondary sector. Significantly 85 per cent of AST posts were funded by their local authority (LA), with the remaining 15 per cent being funded by their employing school.[8]

Study 2

In the follow-up snapshot survey carried out in 2012, the same sampling frame was used but the response rate was much lower, with 205 responding to the online survey. An interesting sub-feature of the research, however, was the volume of email correspondence received. From the original survey, more than 40 made contact to inform us that they were no longer employed as ASTs, largely due to the cessation of funding for their role, in light of the Second Review of Teaching Standards published in December 2011, which recommended the discontinuation of the three existing Post Threshold, Excellent Teacher and Advanced Skills Teacher standards and the introduction, instead, of a single higher-level standard called the Master Teacher standard. A particular feature of the second survey was therefore a far greater emphasis on more open-ended questions that sought ASTs viewpoints about the then current changes.

Of those included in this survey, 72 per cent of ASTs were female and 28 per cent male. Fascinatingly, all worked in secondary schools (age 12–16/18). All curriculum subject areas were captured in the survey: with English (13 per cent), maths (9 per cent) and science (8 per cent) most frequently represented and replicating the main subject areas for ASTs in the English secondary sector. Significantly, 63 per cent of AST posts were funded by their LA (local authority), with the remaining 27 per cent being funded by their employing school.

English Advanced Skills Teachers

Needing a new challenge was the primary motivating factor in deciding to become an AST for a quarter of the teachers surveyed in 2010. Other factors were also important including: an opportunity to stay in the classroom (21 per cent) and a desire to share skills (19 per cent). Teachers opting to undertake the AST route discussed having reached a point in their career development where they needed greater challenge and responsibility; yet remaining connected to the classroom as well as their subject were also very important to the type of professional lives the teachers wanted. The AST role was thus seen as an important career opportunity offering professional development without the '*sheer administration . . . of the Senior Management Route* (SMT)'. This commitment to the classroom was clearly evident in AST future career plans. Although 27 per cent of ASTs planned to move into management in the future, 66 per cent of ASTs intended to remain in an AST role for the foreseeable future.

Eighty-five per cent of respondents enjoyed being an AST 'most of the time', with more than two-fifths stating that the role is what they expected it to be. However, almost all ASTs found the role demanding, primarily because of large workloads (24 per cent) and the amount of time it required (33 per cent). Levels and perceptions of support varied but primarily centred on practical issues that related to the facilitation of outreach work and appropriate preparation time. A key focus for the work of an AST was the 20 per cent of teaching time spent on outreach. However, issues around timetabling, lesson cover, as well as attitudes of the head and the SLT to the role, had an important impact on how well this requirement was facilitated.

It is difficult to definitively outline an AST's role as much of their work was dependent on local authority and school priorities. Focus ranged from 1:1 mentoring support for a struggling teacher, INSET training provision to departmental or whole-school intervention strategies. Interestingly, only just over half of ASTs believed their schools were allowing them to make the best use of their skills. In addition, a shift in emphasis over recent years saw a far greater focus on schools in special measures:

> 'the job isn't what it was when I first started as an AST, it's a lot harder now. I used to go into any school that asked for my support but now it's just the schools on special measures . . . and it's about dealing with either poor teaching or poor leadership . . . it makes it harder because often they don't want you there, well not at first. It's just a really challenging environment and I guess it's that which makes the role harder than it was.'

Based on feedback, teachers were clear they were having an impact, with support of teachers (38 per cent) and the training provision (31 per cent) being their biggest contribution as an AST:

> 'my greatest impact is with NQTs, because they've been successful . . . from the feedback . . . they stay in the school.'
>
> *(Female, secondary)*

> 'well, results have gone up, department-wise, and [when I work with individuals] teaching quality has gone up . . . from the informal feedback [I get] from teachers.'
>
> *(Female, secondary)*

> 'when you get asked to do things more than once, that feels like they value what I do and get a lot out of it. Some of my work comes as a request from people who have spoken to other people so, it's sort of "word of mouth". That feels like a way of measuring impact. The things I organise outside of school time; that are voluntary in terms of attendance, they are repeatedly well attended and people are keen to take part. This is informal evidence to show my role as an AST is effective'
>
> *(Male, secondary)*

Quantifying this 'impact', however, was clearly problematic given the diverse ways that ASTs are deployed and utilised:

> 'I can't generalise on my impact because the role is so varied . . . and it would depend on how you measure these things.'
>
> *(Female, secondary)*

In terms of the government's policy initiative and the key aims behind the introduction of the grade of AST, almost all teachers agreed that the role was achieving what the government intended it to in terms of raising standards:

'all I can say is that I do really think that ASTs are shaping educational policy in the classroom.'

All teachers require support and instruction from expert teachers over extended periods of time (Elmore, 2002, pp. 18–19) for new practices to be incorporated into teaching styles and adapted to subject requirements. Equally, a group of ASTs held strong views on the need for more structured and frequent CPD for expert teachers themselves. Training that focused on building their AST networks and collegiality while also regularly sharing their best practices and innovative pedagogical approaches were seen as essential to maintaining their professional excellence and the impact and credibility of the role.

Several core features of training were desired by ASTs. These were: 1) a *focus on content* that deepens and improves the content knowledge of ASTs rather than focusing on generic methods of teaching. Some thought AST conferences were useful only in terms of its generic information and networking but not for specific curriculum and subject matters; 2) *deliberate active learning opportunities* for ASTs to engage with other ASTs, creating new understandings of their role and an AST professional culture by leading discussions, practice delivery sessions, being observed or observing others (Hawley and Valli, 1999); 3) *coherent training* aligned with system-based curriculum standards and assessments (Ingvarson, 1998) and teachers' own classroom and/or leadership goals (Porter *et al.*, 2004, p. 133).

Just over 20 per cent of ASTs surveyed did not receive any training either between assessment and starting the role or after. Over a fifth of ASTs (22 per cent) had not attended any additional training since becoming an AST, primarily because it was not offered or available (49 per cent). Others viewed the training scheduled as inappropriate to their needs (24 per cent) or too difficult to find the time to attend (21 per cent). Of these ASTs, the vast majority (76 per cent) imagined it would be useful for their role.

The Training and Development Agency for Schools (TDA) Professional Standards for ASTs in England (2007) clearly stated the important contribution ASTs make to other teachers training and CPD:

> ASTs provide models of excellence and innovative teaching and use their skills to enhance teaching and learning by undertaking school improvement activities and CPD for other teachers. They carry out developmental work across a range of workplaces and draw on the experiences they gain elsewhere to improve practice in their own and other schools.
>
> *(TDA, 2007, p. 3)*

While the survey and interview respondents largely agreed with the TDA premise and believed they fulfilled these responsibilities, the professional standards and contractual entitlement to 'effective, relevant and professional development throughout their careers' (TDA, 2007, p. 3) was seen as much less structured and rigorously adhered to. This meant many ASTs enjoyed supporting other teachers but felt their own training and professional development was limited unless they created opportunities for themselves.

Although ASTs had successfully completed the external assessment process, not all felt suitably 'prepared' or 'trained' to mentor adult colleagues. Different skill sets are required for different learning relationships. Being a role model for one teacher at a special measures[9] school differs from facilitating a curriculum workshop for newly qualified teachers (NQTs) organised by a local authority. Some ASTs talked of a 'taken-for-grantedness' by head teachers and local authorities, that being an expert teacher implied training was not as necessary and that expertise already featured in all aspects of their teaching life:

> 'I thought there might be some training and there hasn't been. It makes me laugh because I am supposed to know everything and I've had no official training . . . nothing for me – only helping others.'

> 'I do all the delivering (of training). I would love some input and be delivered to. I would love to watch more experienced colleagues and the range of skills they have . . . most of it comes from gut feeling at this point. There should be standardised training that allows you to do a layer of development before you start. I haven't had that as an AST.'

We were interested to explore how the title of AST was experienced in terms of the ways it was seen to encapsulate levels of expertise or not. Alternatives to the title of Advanced Skills Teacher – for example, 'highly accomplished teacher', 'experienced teacher' or 'expert teacher' – were preferable for almost 75 per cent of ASTs. However, over half the teachers agreed that the title sums up well their level of expertise. From interviews it is apparent that the award of Advanced Skills Teacher status conferred a sense of professional recognition that was important to teachers, contributing significantly to their sense of professional self-esteem and well-being:

> 'I got through the assessment process so, I do feel recognised.'
>
> *(Male, primary)*

> 'you feel you have status, you've got it on paper and they can't take that away from you. There is some pressure that comes with it but, in the end, you've earned it.'
>
> *(Female, secondary)*

> 'I feel more respected, because of my role.'
>
> *(Female, secondary)*

> 'you are not in the same position as a deputy or assistant head but you have a range of knowledge and expertise so, yeah, your colleagues hold you with a certain amount of esteem.'
>
> *(Male, secondary)*

> 'I feel recognised and rewarded. Outside of my school I get quite a bit of kudos before I meet anyone. It gives you a head start, which is good. I don't feel I have to prove myself and people trust my word a little bit more.'
>
> *(Female, secondary)*

> 'my status has grown and I feel good for it.'
>
> *(Female, secondary)*

> 'I know that the parents of my kids like the fact I am an AST, they feel that their children are being taught by an expert and they seem to respect me for it.'
>
> *(Male, primary)*

The AST route was clearly observed to be achieving one of the government's key aims in that these highly skilled teachers remained in the classroom. The ASTs who were surveyed and those spoken to directly were adamant about their need for career challenges and for professional development. It is highly probable, therefore, that without this viable alternative to leadership and management these accomplished teachers might well have been lost from the classroom. In terms of the policy initiatives, teachers were clear they were having an impact. Establishing this in quantifiable terms is exceedingly difficult, however.

ASTs firmly articulated that their AST role also contributed in meaningful ways to their sense of professional efficacy, satisfaction and enjoyment. The ASTs expressed a sense of enhanced professional status yet there was some tension with this feeling in relation to anxiety around possible misconceptions as to levels of expertise. Thus, while the AST award appeared to impact in positive ways, the benefit of this outcome appeared to be more in terms of its intrinsic value, especially in raised self-esteem. Paradoxically, ASTs liked feeling that the grade was recognising and rewarding their expertise, but they were also reticent about being perceived as having all the answers; thereby exemplifying 'expertise':

> 'I am quite embarrassed by it to be honest with you, which is not necessarily a good thing. It shouldn't be embarrassing.'

> 'Because of the term "advanced teachers", people think you are going to be goody, goody. You're successful every time.'

> 'everybody expects you to be perfect all the time.'

This reticence may well have reflected ASTs' understanding of the broader political issues within teaching, defined by standards, accountability and outcomes. It may also have reflected a deeper concern with what defines 'an expert'. Yet, with a need to justify funding by proving 'impact', ASTs' reluctance can also be interpreted as reflecting concerns that they were supposed have 'all the answers' to the many challenges and issues experienced in the context specific classroom. An element of reserve allows for a circumnavigation around ideas of 'magic wands' and thus avoids the risk of 'failing'.

As Beck (1992) notes, we live in an increasingly credentialised society, and as the teachers in this research reiterated, feeling increased status and being more appreciated can result from being formally recognised. Hence, as ASTs felt their status as a professional was enhanced by objectivising their skills it remains evident that credentials and therefore designations such as AST do matter, as Beck suggests. Exploring the ways that the objective shapes the subjective, in terms of teachers' professional identities, it could appear then, to be in part understood as a process of social reflection. The enhanced sense of professional identity, the status and esteem of the ASTs included in this research, reflects and resonates very strongly with external/'objective' recognition of their skills and expertise. Thus, if policy is used to recruit and retain excellent teachers in the classroom, awards such as the AST 'work'.

In our follow-up study in 2012, nearly all ASTs surveyed still enjoyed their role despite it being very different to that of two years previously, as reported by 85 per cent of particpants. In terms of impact, ASTs were still clear that the role retained value and made a significant contribution to teaching and learning, primarily through 1:1 mentoring of struggling teachers (74 per cent); subject-specific support (71 per cent) and the coaching and mentoring of new teachers (68 per cent).

In light of the changes to funding highlighted earlier in this chapter, only a quarter of ASTs were confident of continued funding for their role post-2012 and as a result, 70 per cent were unsure whether they would remain in their current post or even in the classroom. In terms of future career plans, 11 per cent of ASTs stated that if their AST role ended they would seek a consultancy role; 13 per cent would leave teaching and 42 per cent would pursue a management and leadership role. Primarily, this is because the removal of allocated funding left little alternative in terms of choice:

> 'I love being an AST and think it is a great shame that my role is being ended. I always thought that in the future I would seek a leadership role but instead feel that my hand is being forced as the alternative is to be a classroom teacher with no other responsibilities which given the skills I have is a waste.
>
> The only way to increase your pay now is to move into management and out of the classroom – a very, very tragic fact for our children.'

In terms of the proposed 'Master Teacher' standard (see Chapter 8), nearly all ASTs were familiar with the proposal yet only 10 per cent felt this to be a potentially positive development for the teaching profession; most expressed ambivalence. However, with respect to impact on the AST role specifically, almost 60 per cent felt it to be overwhelmingly negative:

> 'AST status brings responsibility and financial rewards – which is what 'expert' teachers deserve. The Master Teacher role doesn't appear to offer those things.'

Interestingly, ASTs felt that the distinctiveness of the AST role, in terms of the rigour of assessment and pay rewards, meant it was an aspirational, exclusive route, not open to all. The notion of a Master Teacher standard, potentially more easily accessible and attainable and most likely without financial recognition, reduced both its value and desirability. However, and more importantly, implicit in some teachers' comments was a sense that such a standard was patronising and left little in the way of career alternatives inside the classroom:

> 'Why do the government think that good staff will be motivated to go for this? For the kudos? Out of the good of their hearts? Unrewarded gives the clear message – unvalued!! This proposal has left me feeling highly demoralised in a profession and post that I used to love. This government seems to be doing everything it can to demotivate and demoralise young and ambitious members of the teaching profession. I do not see why I should take such a backwards step in my career, having achieved, and I believe contributed, a lot in my first ten years of teaching. I do not wish to leave the classroom to go into management, but these proposals may leave me no alternative.'

The key aim of the introduction of the AST designation was to keep excellent practitioners in the classroom yet by removing the allocated funding, and potentially, and by default, the AST role, many ASTs were left feeling demoralised and disenfranchised. It was inevitable then that the only career progression route left open appeared to be leadership, management or consultancy. As one AST noted, 'pay is not the only reason to become an AST but, in the current climate, it is a way of justifying your decision to stay in the classroom'. However, rather more worrying was the planned exit from teaching altogether. No official research has been conducted into what 'happened' to the AST workforce. Research by Goodwyn (2014, 2015) will be reviewed in Chapter 8.

The future of expertise

In considering the model of teacher expertise advocated in England between 1998 and 2012, the standards that had to be achieved before one could be recognised as an Advanced Skills Teacher suggest that expertise in the English context was understood as a demonstration of a specific set of skills that produced particular outcomes. Expertise and consequently teaching was framed as a skilled craft with characteristics that produce high-quality results in the classroom – for both students and teachers. While it is beyond the scope of this chapter to engage in a theoretical debate as to how 'expertise' in teaching should be conceptualised (see Chapters 2 and 3), it is worth exploring nonetheless what a particular definition might mean, in terms of its potential consequences for the teaching profession, using the AST example from England.

In a report outlining the evidence presented to the School Teachers Review Board in May 2012, the Department for Education drew attention to the recommendations made in the Second Review of Teaching Standards published in December 2012. This review suggested that the existing standards for Post Threshold, Excellent Teachers (ETs) and Advanced Skills Teachers be discontinued and that a new Master Teacher standard should replace them. The review recommended that the proposed Master Teacher standard should not be linked to pay but could be used for schools to form a professional judgement and determine how they should reward their top performing teachers: the DfE made clear it endorsed this recommendation.

There is clearly a case for linking expertise with outcomes. It is undeniable that student attainment is, and will remain, a core concern for every school and educational system around the world and invariably schools and governments will want to reward teachers that do this particularly well. However, models of expertise that focus solely on, and reward accordingly, these performance indicators miss the other important ways that expertise is evident. Models of expertise need to capture the juxtaposition of teaching qualities and skills and recognise that the intrinsic and extrinsic skills of expert teachers – and how these manifest – are not always so easily captured with measures of performativity. How does one capture the increased confidence of a previously struggling teacher who has been supported by an AST, for example? Teaching expertise clearly involves a nexus of skills and a policy focus which is solely concerned with performance indicators – invariably student attainment – offers a clear message that within the profession, more inherent skills matter little. This policy message has important consequences in relation to the prestige and status of the teaching profession in England as well as the recruitment, retention and career development of teachers. The AST model in England went from being an unpopular and problematic innovation to a well-respected and profoundly credible alternative career route for some of the best teachers. In that sense it was a bold and successful experiment and its demise has never been justified by any substantive evidence. It offers a valuable lesson to other countries with the importance of 'outreach' an especially significant part of its legacy. It is also salutary that its demise was political and not evidence based, as so often happens with changes to education systems and especially to the role of teachers, even those clearly identified as some of the best in the profession.

Notes

1 Information included here is taken from DfES 2006 document.
2 Salary range for 2010 is £37,461 to £59,950 for ASTs outside of London (TES Connect, July 2010).
3 Qualified teachers who reach the top of the main pay scale can apply to be assessed against eight national standards and if they meet the standards, can cross the 'threshold' to the upper pay scale. The threshold provides an opportunity for good classroom teachers to progress from M6 to a higher salary range. Progression on the upper pay scale is performance based and governing bodies make the decisions on progression, based on recommendations from heads. Teachers don't normally move through the upper pay scale more frequently than every two years (www.tes.co.uk/article.aspx?storycode=6000193).
4 The Excellent Teacher scheme is similar to the AST although there are two key differences: a sole focus on in-reach and less remuneration. An Excellent Teacher applicant must be Post Threshold in order to apply. Take-up of this route, however, was very poor. ASTs in our 2010 survey cynically saw this as a cheaper option to the AST role.
5 Compared to the Highly Accomplished Teacher, for example, that has a much broader focus on teaching and learning.
6 This research was carried out with Goodwyn, A. and Francis-Brophy, E.
7 This research was carried out with Goodwyn, A.
8 Prior to commencing both studies ethical clearance was sought from the University of Reading Ethics Committee and all ethical procedures and guidelines were complied with in carrying out the research.
9 'Special measures' is an Ofsted designation applied to schools in England and Wales that are considered to be failing and lack the leadership capacity necessary to secure improvements. A school in special measures will have regular short-notice Ofsted inspections to monitor improvement. A school usually has two years to improve and if poor performance continues the school may be closed.

References

Ball, S. (2003) 'The teacher's soul and the terrors of performativity', *Journal of Education Policy*, 18(2): 215–228.

Barber, M. and Mourshed, M. (2007) *How the Worlds' Best-performing School Systems Come Out On Top*. New York: McKinsey & Co.

Beck, U. (1992) *Risk Society: Towards a New Modernity*. London: Sage & Sons.

Beck, U. and Beck-Gernsheim, E. (2001) *Individualization*. London: Thousand Oaks; New Delhi: Sage Publications.

Berliner, D. (2001) 'Learning about and learning from expert teachers', *International Journal of Educational Research*, 35(5): 463–482.

Berry, K. (2008) Staffing high-needs schools: Insights from the nation's best teachers' *Phi Delta Kappan*, 89(10): 766–771.

CfBT (Centre for British Teachers) (2004) *The Work of Advanced Skills Teachers*, report. Reading: CfBT.

Day, C. (2007) *Teachers Matter: Connecting Work, Lives and Effectiveness*. Maidenhead: Open University Press.

Day, C., Kingston, A., Stobart, G. and Sammons, P. (2005) 'The personal and professional selves of teachers: Stable and unstable identities', *British Educational Research Journal*, 32(4): 601–616.

DfEE (Department for Education and Employment) (1997) *Excellence in Schools*, white paper. London: HMSO.

DfES (Department for Education and Skills) (2001) *Advanced Skills Teachers, Promoting Excellence*. London: HMSO.

DfES (Department for Education and Skills) (2006) *Advanced Skills Teachers: Promoting Excellence*. London: HMSO.

DfES (2012) *Evidence to STRB: The Case for Change*. London: HMSO.

Elmore, R. F. (2002) *Bridging the gap between standards and achievement*. Washington, DC: Albert Shanker Institute.

Fuller, C., Goodwyn, A. and Francis-Brophy, E., (in press) 'Advanced Skills Teachers: Professional status and identity, *Teachers and Teaching: Theory and Practice*.

General Teaching Council (2002) *Teachers on Teaching: A Survey of the Teaching Profession* (MORI). London: GTC.

Giddens, A. (1984) *The Constitution of Society*. Cambridge: Polity Press.

Hargreaves, L., Cunningham, M., Everton, T., Hansen, A., Hopper, B., McIntyre, D., Maddock, M., Mukherjee, J., Pell, T., Rouse, M., Turner, P. and Wilson, L. (2006) 'The status of teachers and the teaching profession: Views from inside and outside the profession', Research Report RR755. DfES, London.

Hattie, J. (2003) 'Teachers make a difference: What is the research evidence?' Australian Council for Educational Research Annual Conference on Building Teacher Quality, October.

Hawley, W. and Valli, L. (1999) 'The essentials of effective professional development: A new consensus', in L. Darling-Hammond and G. Sykes (eds) *Teaching as the Learning Profession: Handbook of Policy and Practice* (pp. 127–150). San Francisco: Jossey-Bass.

Hopkins, D. (1996) 'Quality teachers, quality schools: International perspectives and policy implications', *Teaching and Teacher Education*, 12(5): 501–517.

Ingvarson, L. (1998) Professional development as the pursuit of professional standards: The standards-based professional development system, *Teaching and Teacher Education*, 14(1): 127–140.

Ingvarson, L. (2009) 'Developing and rewarding excellent teachers: The Scottish Chartered Teacher Scheme', *Professional Development in Education*, 35(3): 451–468.

Institute for Public Policy Research (2001) *Transforming Teacher Status: The Future of the Teaching Profession*. GTC conference: London.

Jackson, A. (2006) 'Teachers, the reluctant professionals? A call for an individual response'. BERA Conference, Warwick.

Klassen, R. M. and Anderson, C. J. K. (2009) 'How times change: Teachers' job satisfaction and dissatisfaction in England in 1962 and 2007'. *British Educational Research Journal*, 35(5): 745–759.

Morris, E. (2001) *Professionalism and Trust: The Future of Teachers and Teaching*. London: Department for Education and Skills.

Ofsted (2001) '*Advanced Skills Teachers: Appointment, Deployment and Impact*, HMI Report.

Ofsted (2003) *Advanced Skills Teachers: A Survey*, HMI Report.

Porter, A. C., Birman, B. F., Garet, M. S., Desimone, L. M. and Yoon, K. S. (2004) *Effective Professional Development in Mathematics and Science: Lessons from Evaluation of the Eisenhower Program*. Washington, DC: American Institute for Research.

SMHC (2009) *Taking Human Capital Seriously: Talented Teachers in Every Classroom, Talented Principals in Every School*. Madison: Consortium for Policy Research in Education.

Swann, M., McIntyre, D., Pell, T., Hargreaves, L. and Cunningham, M. (2010) 'Teachers' conceptions of teacher professionalism in England in 2003 and 2006', *British Educational Research Journal*, 36(4): 549–571.

Swartz, D. (1997) *Culture and Power: The Sociology of Pierre Bourdieu*. Chicago: Chicago University Press.

TDA (Training and Development Agency for Schools) (2007) *Professional Standards for Teachers: Advanced Skills Teachers*. London.

Times Educational Supplement (2010) 'Advanced Skills Teachers pay scales for 2010', TES Connect, July.

Tsui, A.M.B. (2009) 'Distinctive qualities of expert teachers', *Teachers and Teaching: Theory and Practice*, 15(4): 421–439.

Watkins, P. (1994) 'Advanced Skills Teachers: Progress and problems in their establishment in Australia', *International Journal of Educational Management*, 8(4): 5–10.

5

AN AUSTRALIAN VIEW

From Advanced Skills Teacher to national standards

Ellie Francis-Brophy

> The greatest resource in Australian schools is our teachers. They account for the vast majority of expenditure in school education and have the greatest impact on student learning, far outweighing the impact of any other education program or policy.
>
> *What Teachers Want: Better Teacher Management* (Jensen, 2010, p. 5)

Introduction

This chapter examines a fascinating period of development when one of the earliest models of expert teaching was created. What is especially valuable about this case study is it demonstrates the complex matrix of forces that shaped the Advanced Skills Teacher and especially the role of teacher unions and state and federal governments in a very long-drawn-out process of struggle and contestation to define the concept of expert teacher best suited to the Australian context. Unlike the USA's National Board, this story is full of political intervention and rhetoric which leads, perhaps ironically, to a national consensus 30 years later and to dropping the AST designation (although not entirely) and to the adoption of the US-originated term Highly Accomplished Teacher (see Chapter 8). As discussed elsewhere, a perfect illustration of the global context of expert teaching with national systems adopting and adapting both key terms and also the infrastructural contexts of other countries.

For over three decades Australian governments grappled with ways to bring back the best and brightest into schools, retain excellent teachers in the classroom and develop a viable long-term career structure that is well paid and rewarding. There is a shared acknowledgement that 'teachers matter' and those who can matter most for students' learning outcomes, and by extension the productivity of a country, are the expert teachers (see OECD, 2005), referred to and championed in many Australian policy documents. But, like all policy instruments and cycles, the Australian experience of implementing and adapting the Advanced Skills Teacher (AST) status follows a course marked by disputes, rejections and 'rethink'. Considerations about the combination and focus on reforming pay systems, performance measures and improving the status and professionalism of teaching impact on policy discourses and eventual uptake by unions, teachers and the wider community.

The chapter provides a brief history of the AST status and its variations across the states in the Australian federal system. It describes its evolution, contentious features and more recent refocus on teacher quality, recognition and deployment factors. In Chapter 8 there is a more detailed examination of the recent development of the new Highly Accomplished Teacher model and the other professional designations that are briefly commented on in the final section of this chapter. Expert teachers work and respond as leaders in various communities of practice, from their own classroom, school and local educational area. Australia has experienced challenges in finding ways to integrate leadership and career (reward or incentive-driven) perspectives to keep talented teachers in the classroom rather than losing them to management and principalship.

The first part of the chapter provides a contextual overview of the Advanced Skills Teacher (AST) policies in the early 1990s. The AST model is a knowledge and skills-based system that bases pay increases on demonstrated improvements in teacher practice – in particular, improvements to enhanced learning outcomes for students. The role of an AST was to support student teachers, undertake staff development and take a lead in key aspects of teaching and learning policy.

A formal AST classification served to open up a much wider debate on the need to develop career pathways within the classroom for expert teachers. This approach, compared to a merit pay scheme, has broadly tended to receive more support from teachers overall, especially if teachers play an active role in developing standards and the assessment procedures and process. This has been more the case in recent years of the policy's morphing into Highly Accomplished Teacher (HAT) status.

Two examples are considered: the Western Australian Level 3 classroom teacher model and the South Australian AST2 model.

The second part reviews more recent and significant changes to a number of schooling policies in Australia. Policymakers and teachers alike are faced with multiple, competing agendas related to career progression for teachers who want to remain in classroom teaching and also be involved in school effectiveness. While the AST classification was strongly linked to performance pay, it served to open up a much wider debate on the need to develop career pathways within the classroom for expert teachers. In order to halt the classroom exodus of highly experienced and quality teachers and demonstrate to ambitious graduates the scope within a teaching career, a growing group of stakeholders are considering ways to implement the most effective performance pay system that integrates professionalism (standards and development) and teaching quality.

Educational governance in Australia

Constitutionally, schooling in Australia is a state responsibility and state and territory governments are the major employers of teachers. The Commonwealth of Australia is a federation with six individual states comprising New South Wales, Victoria, Queensland, South Australia, Western Australia and Tasmania, together with the Australian Capital Territory and Northern Territory. As in America, Australia's federal system means the allocation of responsibilities for attracting, developing and retaining effective teachers is widely distributed, with many aspects of education (e.g. teacher employment, school curriculum) being the prerogative of the state. However, the federal government is the major funder of teacher education programmes in universities – the principal source of new teachers and upgraded teacher qualifications – and is becoming increasingly involved in school funding and policy. Australia has a substantial and growing non-government school sector (mostly independent or Catholic) that enrolls one-third of all primary and secondary students. The federal government sees its role as providing 'educational leadership' and working with state and territory governments and other school education stakeholders to ensure 'teaching and learning for all Australian school-age children is the highest quality' (DEEWR, 2011).

Within the teaching profession in Australia there remains a number of qualified teacher workforces characterised by their state and territory location, government and non-government school sector, primary and secondary level of schooling, and subject area specialisation. Teaching career paths and salaries are regulated by collective industrial agreements between state and territory governments, unions in the public sector (branches or associated bodies of the Australian Education Union), non-government school authorities and the Independent Education Union.

Collectively, public and private education sector union membership is at an estimated 250,000 people. Funding for the non-government school sector varies considerably – though this will change under the *Better Schools Plan* (see below) – with the least wealthy schools receiving up to 90 per cent of their budget from the state. For other elite schools their significant resources mean they can pay higher salaries than the relevant award in order to retain exceptional teachers.

Leading the way? The Australian Advanced Skills Teacher initiative

By combining their strengths, Australian teachers and their unions in the late 1960s disassembled the teaching inspection system. Inspection was discredited as being unfair, discriminatory, paternalistic and contrary to the growing professionalism of teachers. What resulted, however, is teachers being formally evaluated only if they sought promotion or were seen as incompetent and under threat of dismissal.

With a relatively loose structure to scrutinise the strengths and weaknesses in teachers' professional practice, the Advanced Skills Teacher (AST) programme emerged in the late 1980s and early 1990s as a concerted attempt by unions and the government to establish a career path for classroom teachers and to differentiate skills within the profession. It also signalled the Commonwealth governments' endorsement of 'globalisation' and their significant movement towards neo-liberal political practices. Hence, policies are not thought up or practised in a value-free discourse that is apolitical. The way teachers' work is conceptualised and regarded has changed over time, influenced by various social and political pressures, for example:

> with respect to both its formal characteristics and the nature of the content discussed. . . . The concept of teacher as intellectual carries with it the political and ethical imperative to judge, critique and reject those approaches to authority that reinforce a technical and social division labor that silences and disempowers both teachers and students.
>
> *(Giroux and McLaren, 1986, pp. 225–226)*

The AST policy emerged out of several factors. First, in the late 1980s the federal Hawke Labour government and the Australian Council of Trade Unions (ACTU) initiated a campaign to reform the industrial awards. By August 1988 the Australian Industrial Relations Commission (AIRC) introduced a restructuring process, known as the structural efficiency principle. It implemented awarded unions an initial 3 per cent wage rise and a further commitment of 3 per cent if they restructured their members' industrial awards. The Labour government's comprehensive market restructuring process pushed policies that would increase the productivity of the nation (Bluer and Carmichael, 1991) and international competitiveness, hence pay rises were made conditional on trading of rights and conditions. Prior to 1988, teachers' employment conditions were determined by state industrial relations commissions and distributed as 'an award'. The award was binding on all employers and legally enforceable.

Declining international economic competitiveness and low productivity performance was linked in part back to the Australian education system and the quality of school teachers. Building the nation had to involve building the expertise of teachers so future citizens could participate fully in the economy and society. Despite Australia's strong union heritage, trade unions largely accepted the initiative, with many actively advocating the changed emphasis on workplace industrial relations. Angus (1991, p. 82) argues that the inclusion of the ACTU was deliberately planned by the government, mindful that 'the wider involvement of unions in educational reform is a recognition that educational reform has frequently fallen short of the mark because of the opposition of unions'.

High on the restructuring agenda were issues such as establishing skill-related career paths, broadening the range of work tasks within a position, building in greater flexibility in work patterns and arrangements, and interconnecting and relativising categories of workers with the industrial award and at the enterprise level. Any advantages of enterprise bargaining – e.g. short lead time to implementation, tailored to a school's individual needs and potentially the working conditions of teachers relevant to a school – should be balanced against the numerous differences between schools enterprise bargaining agreements, resulting in significant variations in employment conditions and salaries for teachers. Across the board, significant restructuring of industries and sectors such as education was occurring. Furthermore, Milligan, Ashenden and Quin (1994, p. 10) write of the

> discussions in the industrial arena (. . .) extending their scope from a focus largely on improving conditions of work for teachers to more encompassing issues such as how to generate improvements in learning, thus reflecting the concerns for productivity framing industrial agreements in other industries.

Unions were involved in discussions about pay incentives and rewards to keep excellent teachers in the classroom at the same time as the educational research sector prioritised investigations into the nature of teachers' work and the quality of school education. Key impacts of the award restructuring on teachers, aside from the category of the AST, included strengthening of merit-based access to careers; the introduction of the notion of 'productivity' into schools; pay relativities for teachers; redefining many aspects of teachers' career development in terms of skills or competencies; and professional development and some form of appraisal to become a more integral and ongoing part of teachers' careers (Milligan *et al.,* 1994: 10).

Second, with increased public scrutiny of teachers following a spate of poor student results, efforts to establish greater teacher accountability and keep effective teachers in the classroom was fertile ground for the advancement of the AST career path classification. In a 1990 paper prepared by the Schools Council for the National Board of Employment, Education and Training entitled 'Australia's teachers: An agenda for the next decade', the Australian classification of AST was recommended. The paper argued for the need to recognise, through definable career roles and structures, the fundamental importance of classroom teaching and the sense of fulfilment for many classroom teachers in student teaching rather than moving into education management or administration careers. The Commonwealth government strongly supported the restructuring of the teaching workforce in state and independent education systems via the AST category. It was framed by the Commonwealth government as a way to foster a consistent, national basis for salaries and conditions of employment irrespective of location.

Third, the AST classification coincided in the late 1980s and early 1990s with the production of various position papers on teacher quality – for instance, the Schools Council of the National Board of Employment, Education and Training (NBEET) issued papers in 1989 and the work of the National Project on the Quality of Teaching and Learning (NPQTL) in 1996 involved federal and state governments, unions and employers. Earlier, in June 1986, federal and state ministers, through the Australian Education Council, came together to focus on an agreed agenda for Australia's schools.

At the same time, state education systems were undergoing change. For example, the Queensland review, *Focus on Schools* (Department of Education, 1990) addressed topics such as leadership and management and professional development. In these state-based policies, leadership was at the heart of a teacher's role and practice within the profession. Effective teaching relies on creating the social conditions for learning, establishing learning and outcomes expectations and directing the pathway of learning. With a new weighting, the AST policy was concerned with the teacher's ability to influence their colleagues, take the initiative in institutional development and contribute to the building of professional knowledge.

Defining Advanced Skills Teachers

Although variation exists in eligibility, salary and professional status across different states and education systems, the basic notion of an AST is similar i.e. a classroom teacher with superior teaching skills supporting and influencing the professional development of other teachers. The introduction of the classification demonstrates how policy is formulated to shape the working lives of teachers through patterns of performance and reward, standardised criteria and quality (judged in terms of results and often with international comparisons).

The overall classification 'AST' was segmented into three levels:

1. AST1 working mostly at classroom, subject/faculty or school level
2. AST2 at faculty, school or school district level and
3. AST3 at a macro-school district or system level.

Each state government endorsed the AST policy – for example, in June 1990 the Industrial Relations Commission of Victoria ratified the three levels of AST, describing the classification as a significant initiative within the Victorian Teaching Service aimed at supporting expert teachers to stay in school classrooms. In 1992, the New South Wales Department of School Education accepted the classification of AST with their localised definition that 'An Advanced Skills Teacher is a classroom teacher who provides educational leadership and guidance to classroom teachers' (Weppler and Bourke, 1994).

The governments of South Australia and Western Australia are the two that have continued with the AST model, expanding it into AST 2 and Level 3 Classroom Teacher classifications respectively. In applying for AST status teachers needed to demonstrate high levels of competency in classroom teaching and student learning – often by outlining their involvement and contribution to: professional development of other teachers including beginning teachers; curriculum development; student progress and involvement in improving the educational outcomes of students (Jasman and Barrera, 1998). A few unique conditions set out by the NSW Department of School Education also applied including applicants must have fulfilled minimum service requirements (i.e. reached the final step of their salary scale).

Supporting the initiative, Bluer and Carmichael (1991) write of the nationwide classification of AST as a positive attempt to provide classroom teachers with greater rewards for demonstrating superior classroom teaching skills. In their view, this was a major boost for the development of a career restructure and was seen as providing greater motivation and incentive for experienced teachers, fostering new and supportive relationships between ASTs and other teachers, building systematic on-the-job skills acquisition programs for teachers and rearranging the methods for organising teachers' work.

In each state and territory the application process entailed both a written and interview component. In NSW there were three possible outcomes:

- Awarded an AST appointment
- Considered suitable without gaining appointment (most common due to a lack of available AST positions) or
- Given a ranking of unsuitable.

Continuing with the NSW example, their ASTs were appointed for an initial 12 months, which was then followed by a review and continuation or termination. Teachers who were three-year trained gained permanent four-year-trained salary status through AST appointment, even if the appointment was for one year only. Four-year-trained teachers were given a set allowance for the 12-month AST contract. But in NSW the AST classification was introduced and *then*, within a couple of years, as a condition in a salary agreement, it was phased out in the early 1990s.

Many teachers in NSW opposed the categorisation on grounds of causing division within the teacher community of practice and failing to meet its purported objective of keeping highly experienced teachers in the classrooms, as many ASTs still moved into school administration positions. Weppler and Bourke (1994) found in their research, involving survey responses from over 400 ASTs and classroom teachers in the Hunter Valley region of NSW, that these conditions had important implications on teacher attitudes towards the AST classification and the selection process. They concluded that results indicated mixed feelings among teachers on the effects (both positive and negative) of ASTs in schools in regards to teacher efficiency, student outcomes and overall school effectiveness. They identified five major reasons for applying to be an AST: recognition, personal satisfaction, financial gain, career/promotional opportunities and encouragement from others. Of those who decided not to apply for AST classification, the main reasons combined professional and moral philosophies: where teachers distrusted the system, lacked confidence, felt a lack of support from school executive and had an unwillingness to compete with colleagues (Weppler and Bourke, 1994).

Thematic analyses of qualitative data on ASTs in Australia (e.g. Weppler and Bourke, 1994) and interpretative explanations help us to better understand how these policies unfold in real time for teachers, schools and states. In recognising certain skills as advanced (and thereby nominating others as of less value), Smyth, Shacklock and Hattam (1997) argue the AST process has discursively encouraged a specific type of development by the many experienced teachers who seek advanced status. Gaining AST status means experienced and very able teachers are expected to fulfil leadership roles in their own school and in neighbourhood schools. Their impact is to be felt by graduate and proficient teachers within a number of classrooms, across schools and into the profession.

Perceived problems concerning AST eligibility overshadowed the view that ASTs were teachers with superior teaching skills. Research such as Scott's (1998) based on surveying ASTs found most were more likely to be dissatisfied with teaching than their colleagues, were more stressed and experienced significant role conflict. Adding insult to injury, these ASTs felt that their promotion had caused them to slip backwards in their classroom effectiveness, compared to their output prior to taking up the role. They were also suspicious that principals (head teachers) used them as 'waste-paper baskets' to store and handle the most difficult or intractable problems. Finally, the process of allocating AST posts was felt to be *ad hoc*, and they were frequently cynical about the AST role, seeing it as tokenistic or a good idea badly implemented (Scott, 1998).

Within a few years the definition of superior teaching skills became a contested issue for revision and debate. By the late 1990s, with teachers and unions unimpressed by the shape of their AST policies, few state governments continued with overt AST application awarding processes. With a few notable exceptions, such as the Level 3 classroom position in WA, the Advanced Skills Teacher concept of a career path in teaching, based on evidence of professional development and teacher leadership, was reluctantly absorbed back into the traditional notion of career ladders based on movement out of professional practice into management hierarchies. Policymakers and teachers were, once again, faced with competing agendas and expectations on how to balance career progression 'in the classroom' for effective teachers with student outcomes and greater workplace productivity.

Shadlock and Smyth (1998, p. 92) write, in their substantial critique of the Australian AST experience, that different constructed discourses of ASTs prevailed. These ranged from:

> the official or policy aspiration; the lived realities of how the official aspirations were lived out at the level of process of selecting the teachers; and, the accommodation, contestation and resistance displayed by teachers as they acted to give voice to their own local or indigenous definitions of skilful teaching. It was clear that these various constructions were not always heading in the same direction, nor were they one and the same thing.

The Western Australian Level 3 Classroom Teacher

Ingvarson and Kleinhenz (2006) selected the Western Australian Level 3 Classroom Teacher in their analysis of four international advance teachers systems because 'arguably (it is) the most rigorous and the most interesting' of the Australian examples. Level 3 classroom teachers are defined by the WA government as exemplary teachers recognised and rewarded for their exceptional teaching practices. The aim is for these teachers to play an important part in the provision of quality teaching and leadership in schools. The Level 3 (Highly Accomplished Teacher) category follows on from a beginning teacher (Level 1) and competent teacher (Level 2). The initiative was a major outcome of the 1996 Enterprise Bargaining Agreement (National Award Restructuring reforms outlined earlier in this chapter) negotiated between the State School Teachers Union of Western Australia (SSTUWA) and the Education Department of Western Australia (EDWA). It featured in a larger Teacher Career Path project whose key goals centred on:

- Retention of quality teachers
- Giving greater status and recognition to teachers' commitment to their colleagues, school communities and their professional development
- Expanding career paths within the classroom and
- Using teachers' expertise to maximise student learning and results.

Through a competitive tendering process with funding by the Department of Education (DOE) of Western Australia and overseen by a reference group comprising representatives of the employer and the union, Murdoch University was tasked with developing processes for selection of Level 3 teachers, establishing a competency framework and the use of portfolios and performance-based assessment exercises to assess these competencies. Practising teachers played a significant working role in the competency development. This, along with assessment transparency, generated support from within the education profession and did not lead to union concerns. The subsequent competency framework contained five competencies:

1. Use innovative and/or exemplary teaching strategies and techniques in order to more effectively meet the learning needs of individual students, groups and/or classes of students.
2. Employ consistent exemplary practice in developing and implementing student assessment and reporting processes.
3. Engage in a variety of self-development activities, including a consistently high level of critical reflection on one's own teaching practice and teacher leadership, to sustain a high level of ongoing professional growth.
4. Enhance teachers' professional knowledge and skills through employing effective development strategies.
5. Provide high-level leadership in the school community through assuming a key role in school development processes, including curriculum planning and management and school policy formulation.

Level 3 teachers are expected to be leaders and mentors of other teachers and time is allocated away from their own teaching to fulfill this. Their work is seen as improving teaching and learning across a whole school, as well as within a classroom context. Any teacher can apply, not just those at the top of the scale.

For those at the top of the scale the pay rise is about 10 per cent. While there is no limit or quota on the number of teachers who can become a Level 3 classroom teacher, the assessment process is seen as very rigorous and not all applicants each year are successful. A total of 141 teachers from schools across WA achieved Level 3 Classroom Teacher status in 2010. A record 304 teachers applied in 2011 – an increase of 13 per cent on 2010 applications. In early 2011 there were 796 Level 3 teachers working in public schools throughout WA.

The Level 3 competencies are aligned with Phase 3 of the WA Teacher Competency Framework. Two trained assessors review each candidate's application. These assessors engage in consensus moderation and could be employed as Level 3 classroom teachers, head of learning areas, principals or deputies. Assessments occur in two parts:

1 A portfolio with supporting evidence and referees' verifications
2 Participation and facilitation in a collaborative group 'reflective review' sessions.

Concepts such as reflective inquiry featured as part of the AST application and assessment process as a more formal way to reinforce how 'reviewing, reconstructing, re-enacting and critically analysing one's own and the class's performance' (Shulman, 1987: 15) offers value for professional development. The key benefits of becoming a Level 3 Classroom Teacher include:

- Formal recognition of your expertise and dedication
- Career advancement that enables you to stay in the classroom
- Sharing your experience and professional learning with colleagues
- Taking on a leadership role
- Permanent employment (if you are on a fixed term contract) and a salary increase.

But initiatives such as the Level 3 status seem to have varying effects. Retention issues persist; for instance, the Edith Cowan University report, *Wellbeing of Regional Professions: Policing, Nursing and Teaching in Western Australia* (2006) involved almost 3,600 responses from teachers and a response rate of 40 per cent. Over 80 per cent of the 2,000 teacher respondents who were based in rural and remote areas indicated an intention to remain in the profession for the foreseeable future.

Riding revolutionary waves of reforms: professionalism changes and funding controversies

Since the 2008 signing of the Melbourne Declaration (effective for 2009–2014) by the Commonwealth, state and territory governments on the national goals of schooling, a number of wide-reaching reforms have been endorsed such as the *National*

Plan for School Improvement (NPSI) policy programme, which aims to secure Australia in the top five countries in the world in reading, writing and maths by 2025.

To be phased in over six years from 2014, it includes the funding plan for schools and training and professional development for teachers and principals throughout their careers. The Australian Education Bill protects both the NPSI core directions (Quality teaching; Quality learning; Empowered school leadership; Meeting student need; and Greater transparency and accountability) and the new school funding model. Connected policies and initiatives include:

- The National Education Agreement
- National testing and reporting
- *MySchool* website
- A national curriculum
- The Australian Early Development Index
- National Professional Standards for Teachers
- A Charter for the Professional Learning of Teachers and School Leaders
- National Teacher Performance and Development Framework.

Additionally, many education initiatives across the federal and state systems attempted to improve outcomes for Aboriginal and Torres Strait Islander children, such as the Australian government-funded programmes *Dare to Lead, What Works, Stronger Smarter,* and *Teach Remote*. State and territory governments implemented numerous programs to attempt to 'close the gaps' in educational achievement between Aboriginal and Torres Strait Islander and non-Indigenous students under their jurisdictions (Ma Rhea and Anderson, 2011). Increasingly, there has been movement towards a more coordinated provision of government services nationally, through the Council Of Australian Governments (COAG), in key areas of focus under the 'Closing the Gap' strategy.

Improving the effectiveness and capability of the teaching profession in Australia was a key priority among this wave of reforms. In 2010, the Australian Institute for Teaching and School Leadership (AITSL) was established by the Australian government to provide national leadership for the Commonwealth, state and territory governments in promoting excellence in the profession of teaching and school leadership. Reporting to all state and territory ministers responsible for education, the AITSL has relatively quickly, given the complex governance structure, created new levels of teacher professionalism. In consultation with the teaching profession, National Professional Standards for Teachers were introduced in 2012 to define the requisite skills, knowledge and capacities across the four stages of a teacher's career – the graduate, proficient, highly accomplished and lead teacher stages. Future teachers will have achieved the Graduate Standards in their teacher training courses and be 'classroom ready'. The rapid emergence of this new model is discussed at more length in the final chapter of the book; here we recount how this national model of expert teaching came into being.

The Proficient Standards underpin a nationally consistent approach to teacher registration, whereas the Highly Accomplished and Lead Teacher Standards are voluntary career stages for teachers to aspire to and progress towards as their career continues; other new guidelines such as the National Professional Standards for Principals place greater emphasis on the principal as an educational leader and mentor of teaching staff. As outlined earlier in this chapter, attempts to construct professional competencies for expert teachers (whether described as ASTs or otherwise) have played an important, re-occurring role in Australia's vision of education and its multifarious benefits.

An acceptance of shared responsibility for ongoing individual and organisational learning has resurfaced in the *Charter for the Professional Learning of Teachers and School Leaders (*AITSL 2012b). It names three main characteristics of professional learning: relevant, collaboration and future focused. Collaboration describes how sharing professional learning magnifies the effect of an individual teacher and a school. The role of other teachers as mentors in a 'disciplined and purposeful' way is part of this professional learning that:

- promotes teacher and leader ownership of their learning through active involvement in the design, content, practice and evaluation of their learning
- provides opportunities to receive feedback on practice, and observe the practice of others
- offers support to change practice through coaching, mentoring and reflection
- provides opportunities to access and learn from experts
- develops professional learning communities within and between schools
- uses technology to enrich collaboration and learning (AITSL, 2012b).

Connected to teacher expertise and the capacity to achieve expected teaching standards is the problematic issue of allocating equitable funding to government, independent and Catholic schools – an issue governments in Australia struggled with in the 1970s and during subsequent periods of neo-liberal policies. The most recent response to funding issues was former Labour prime minister Julia Gillard's review of school funding, chaired by David Gonski (chancellor of the University of New South Wales and chairman of various not-for-profit and for-profit organisations). *The Review of Funding for Schooling*, known as the Gonski review (DEEWR, 2011), criticised the unnecessarily complex current school funding arrangements and their overall lack of coherence and transparency.

Government schools were assessed as the ones most in need, due to the significant student numbers and greater concentration of disadvantaged students. It was proposed that there should be additional funding to take into account disadvantage factors such as school size and location, low socio-economic status, indigeneity and limited English language proficiency. On the basis of extensive modelling, the review specified indicative ranges within which these loadings should be determined by negotiation between the states and the Commonwealth.

In June 2013, Kevin Rudd won the leadership vote against Julia Gillard becoming (once again) prime minister. He renamed the Gonski reforms the *Better Schools Plan* and ensured the reforms passed federal parliament within a month of taking up office. In a joint statement with the education minister, Bill Shorten, Kevin Rudd wrote: 'This is not just an investment in schools. This is a down payment on the long-term strength of the Australian economy, and will underwrite higher productivity for decades to come' (press release).

Some states and territories were reluctant to sign up to the Gonski reforms; citing concerns that it signalled a significant shift in responsibility for education towards the Commonwealth, reducing the capacity for schools to apply their autonomy and flexibility to manage themselves and innovatively address the characteristics and needs of their communities. The university and student support system were to take heavy budget cuts to help pay for the government's school funding plan and lobbied the Gillard government to scrap the cuts (Rudd's government agreed to 're-examine' the cuts). Others criticised the style of secrecy in negotiating with states and the resultant 'different agreements with different sectors, states and territories' (Donnelly, 2013). Various tactics across political sides such as deadlines, public denouncements and private talks with hold-out states were needed before New South Wales, Tasmania, South Australia, the Australian Capital Territory, independent schools and Catholic schools signed up to the reforms. At the time of writing, Victoria, WA, Queensland and the Northern Territory were still negotiating the terms.

National consistency on what makes an expert teacher: a focus on quality and standards

Having professional standards for teachers, leaders and school principals can impact not only on aiding reflection and self-development and attracting and selecting suitable candidates for teaching positions and promotions to greater levels of responsibility, they also express the current values, knowledge and practices of teachers in Australia. Ma Rhea and Anderson (2011) argued that standards-based education in Australia has established benchmark expectations for academic achievement nationally which allows measurement of the efficiency and effectiveness of education services provision to specific groups such as Aboriginal and Torres Strait Islander children.

Over the past few decades, each state and territory, often involving professional associations, jurisdictions, employers and educational systems, designed varied teaching standards and frameworks including employing and appraising. These were not always transferable when a teacher moved from one state to another. Hence a shared recognition emerged for national professional standards for teachers (at four career stages) (Ingvarson and Rowe, 2007; Kleinhenz and Ingvarson, 2007; Ingvarson and Hattie, 2008). A comprehensive national consultation process agreed to four levels and their titles, before AITSL finalised the process and ensured the standards were endorsed nationally. The four levels for teachers became designated as:

1 Graduate
2 Proficient
3 Highly Accomplished
4 Lead.

High Accomplished Teachers are expected to increase, through mentoring less experienced or proficient, their peers' teaching quality so they can develop 'successful learners, confident and creative individuals and active and informed citizens' ('Melbourne declaration on educational goals for young Australians', MCEETYA, 2008). In early 2012, the education ministers at the Standing Council on School Education and Early Childhood (SCSEEC) endorsed the *Certification of Highly Accomplished and Lead Teachers in Australia* (AITSL, 2012a) document.

Quality teachers are differentiated according to expertise – excellent practitioners, like the Highly Accomplished and Lead teachers, can demonstrate through a staged assessment process how they meet the seven national standards. These are grouped in three domains of teaching: Professional Knowledge, Professional Practice and Professional Engagement. Reflecting on their own practice, throughout their assessment process, is also considered beneficial for their professional development. Combined, these big-picture policy mechanisms, along with the new Australian curriculum, potentially provide an ideal catalyst to engage and support teachers to develop their skills and knowledge.

SUMMARY CHARACTERISTICS OF HIGHLY ACCOMPLISHED TEACHERS AND LEAD TEACHERS

Highly Accomplished teachers

Highly Accomplished teachers are recognised as highly effective, skilled classroom practitioners and routinely work independently and collaboratively to improve their own practice and the practice of colleagues. They are knowledgeable and active members of the school.

Highly Accomplished teachers contribute to their colleagues' learning. They may also take on roles that guide, advise or lead others. They regularly initiate and engage in discussions about effective teaching to improve the educational outcomes for their students.

They maximise learning opportunities for their students by understanding their backgrounds and individual characteristics and the impact of those factors on their learning. They provide colleagues, including pre-service teachers, with support and strategies to create positive and productive learning environments.

Highly Accomplished teachers have in-depth knowledge of subjects and curriculum content within their sphere of responsibility. They model sound teaching practices in their teaching areas. They work with colleagues to plan, evaluate and modify teaching programs to improve student learning. They keep abreast of the latest developments in their specialist content area or across a range of content areas for generalist teachers.

Highly Accomplished teachers are skilled in analysis student assessment data and use it to improve teaching and learning. They are active in establishing an environment which maximises professional learning and practice opportunities for colleagues. They monitor their own professional learning needs and align them to the learning needs of students.

They behave ethically at all times. Their interpersonal and presentation skills are highly developed. They communicate effectively and respectfully with students, colleagues, parents/carers and community members.

Lead teachers

Lead teachers are recognised and respected by colleagues, parents/carers and the community as exemplary teachers. They have demonstrated consistent and innovative teaching practice over time. Inside and outside the school they initiate and lead activities that focus on improving educational opportunities for all students.

They establish inclusive learning environments that meet the needs of students from different linguistic, cultural, religious and socio-economic backgrounds. They seek to improve their own practice and to share their experience with colleagues.

They are skilled in mentoring teachers and pre-service teachers, using activities that develop knowledge, practice and professional engagement in others. They promote creative, innovative thinking among colleagues.

Lead teachers apply skills and in-depth knowledge and understanding to deliver effective lessons and learning opportunities and share this information with colleagues and pre-service teachers. They describe the relationship between highly effective teaching and learning in ways that inspire colleagues to improve their own professional practice.

They lead processes to improve performance by evaluating and revising programs, analysing student assessment data and taking account of feedback from parents/carers. This is combined with a synthesis of current research on effective teaching and learning.

Lead teachers represent the school and the teaching profession in the community. They are professional, ethical and respected individuals inside and outside the school.

Source: *Certification of Highly Accomplished and Lead Teachers in Australia* (AITSL, 2012a)

Conclusion

Teacher and school leadership is recognised internationally as a vital factor in improving teacher quality, student achievement and school effectiveness (Schleicher, 2012; Barber, Whelan and Clark, 2010; Harris, 2009; Day *et al.,* 2009; Dinham, 2007, 2012;). Policy attention towards formulating professional standards and frameworks for school leaders (both principals and highly accomplished teachers) to define the full diversity of roles and to inform professional learning, selection, appraisal and accountability processes (Leithwood, Jantzi and Steinbach, 2002, pp. 863–875).

For the first time Australia has an Australian Professional Standard for Teachers, for Principals and a national curriculum. These changes will impact on the recognition of ASTs and their nationally renamed Highly Accomplished Teachers' work in the classroom and beyond and its potential to transform how teaching is viewed in contemporary society. Given the years of difficult collaborative work to co-produce agreed standards by teaching professional associations, researchers, policymakers and parents, it will remain important to monitor and assess the long-term impact on expert teachers' career paths in and out of the classroom and the reshaping of a professional from a combined policy perspective.

This short history of the AST reveals much about how, in some ways, expert teacher models can emerge almost haphazardly and yet create an increasing momentum for a national-level model of substantive and systemic importance. Australia was one of the first countries to experiment with the expert teacher concept and is reaching a new level of maturity (see Chapter 8) in establishing its fully national model, drawing strongly on international developments and ensuring that other models are locally inflected and nuanced for the benefit of teachers and students.

References

AITSL (Australian Institute for Teaching and School Leadership) (2012a) *Certification of Highly Accomplished and Lead Teachers in Australia.* Carlton South, VIC: Education Services Australia.

AITSL (Australian Institute for Teaching and School Leadership) (2012b) *Charter for the Professional Learning of Teachers and School Leaders.* Carlton South, VIC: Education Services Australia.

Angus, M. (1991) 'Award restructuring: The new paradigm for school reform', *Unicorn,* (17)2: 77–84.

Australian Commonwealth Government (1991) '*Commonwealth Submission to AIRC in Relation to Review of AST1 Classification in ACT Schools*', Government Sector, 17 December.

Australian Government Press release and statement: www.pm.gov.au/press-office/tasmania-signs-national-education-reforms (accessed 30 July 2013).

Barber, M., Whelan, F. and Clark, M. (2010) *Capturing the Leadership Premium: How the World's Top School Systems Are Building Leadership Capacity for the Future.* New York: McKinsey & Co.

Bluer, R. and Carmichael, L. (1991) 'Award restructuring in teaching', *Unicorn,* 17(1): 24–29.

Day, C., Sammons, P., Hopkins, D., Harris, A., Leithwood, K., Gu, Q., Brown, E., Ahtaridou, E. and Kington, A. (2009) *The Impact of School Leadership on Pupil Outcomes, Final Report.* Nottingham: University of Nottingham.

DEEWR (Department of Education, Employment and Work Relations) (2011) *Review of Funding for Schooling: Final Report.* Canberrra: DEEWR.

Department of Education (1990) *Focus on Schools: The Future Organisation of Educational Services for Students.* Queensland: Department of Education.

Dinham, S. (2007) *Leadership for Exceptional Educational Outcomes.* Teneriffe, Queensland: Post Pressed.

Dinham, S. (2012) 'Walking the walk: The need for school leaders to embrace teaching as a clinical practice profession'. Available at: http://research.acer.edu.au/cgi/viewcontent.cgi?article=1137&context=research_conference

Donnelly, K. (2013) 'A dog's breakfast stifling innovation and creativity', *The Australian*, 30 July. [Kevin Donnelly was director of conservative think tank, Education Standards Institute.] Accessed at: www.theaustralian.com.au/national-affairs/opinion/a-dogs-breakfast-stifling-innovation-and-creativity/story-e6frgd0x-1226687773736

Edith Cowan University Report (2006) *Wellbeing of Regional Professions: Policing, Nursing and Teaching in Western Australia.* Joondalup, WA: Edith Cowan University.

Giroux, H.A. and McLaren, P. (1986) 'Teacher education and the politics of engagement: The case for democratic schooling'. *Harvard Educational Review,* 56(3): 213–229.

Harris, A. (ed.) (2009) *Distributed Leadership.* Dordrecht, The Netherlands: Springer.

Ingvarson, L. and Kleinhenz, E. (2006) Advanced Teaching Standards and certification: A Review of National and International Developments. Canberra: Teaching Australia: Australian Institute for Teaching and School Leadership.

Ingvarson, L. and Rowe, K. (2007) 'Conceptualising and evaluating teacher quality: Substantive and methodological issues'. Report for the Teaching and Learning and Leadership at ACEReSearch, Australian Council for Educational Research. Available at: http://research.acer.edu.au/learning_processes/8

Ingvarson, L. and Hattie, J. (eds) (2008) *Assessing Teachers for Professional Certification: The First Decade of the National Board for Professional Teaching Standards,* Advances in Program Evaluation, vol. 11. Amsterdam: Elsevier Press.

Jasman, A. and Barrera, S. (1998) *Teacher Career Structure: Level 3 Classroom Teacher: Final report.* Perth: Murdoch University and Nexus Strategic Solutions.

Jensen, B. (2010) *What Teachers Want: Better Teacher Management.* Melbourne: Grattan Institute.

Kleinhenz, E. and Ingvarson, L. (2007) 'Standards for teaching: Theoretical underpinnings and applications'. Report for the Teaching and Learning and Leadership at ACEReSearch, Australian Council for Educational Research. Available at: http://research.acer.edu.au/cgi/viewcontent.cgi?article=1000&context=teaching_standards

Leithwood, K., Jantzi, D., and Steinbach, R. (2002) 'School leadership and the new right', in K. Leithwood and P. Hallinger (eds), *Second International Handbook on Educational Leadership and Administration.* Dordrecht, The Netherlands: Kluwer.

Ma Rhea, Z. and Anderson, P.J. (2011) 'Economic justice and indigenous education: Assessing the potential of standards based and progressive education under IL0169', *Social Alternatives*, 30(4): 25–31.

MCEETYA (Ministerial Council on Education Employment Training and Youth Affairs (2008) 'The Melbourne declaration on educational goals for young Australians'. Available at: www.curriculum.edu.au/verve/_resources/National_Declaration_on_the_Educational_Goals_for_Young_Australians.pdf

Milligan, S., Ashenden, D. and Quin, R. (1994) 'Women in the teaching profession'. Commissioned Report no. 32. NBEET, Canberra.

National Board of Employment, Education and Training (1990) *Australia's Teachers: An Agenda for the Next Decade*. Canberra: AGPS.

National Project on the Quality of Teaching and Learning (1996) *National Competency Standards for Beginning Teaching*. Sydney: Australian Teaching Council.

OECD (Organisation for Economic Co-operation and Development) (2005) *Teachers Matter: Attracting, Developing and Retaining Effective Teachers*, 6th edn. Paris: OECD Publishing.

Schleicher, A. (ed.) (2012) *Preparing Teachers and Developing Social Leaders for the 21st Century: Lessons from Around the World*. OECD Publishing. http://dx.doi.org/10.1787/978 9264xxxxxx-en

Scott, C. (1998) 'Australia's superteachers', *Times Educational Supplement*, 20 March.

Shacklock, G. and Smyth, J. (eds) (1998) *Being Reflexive in Critical Educational and Social Research*. London: Falmer.

Shulman, L. (1987) 'Knowledge and teaching: Foundations of the new reform', Harvard Educational Review, 57(1): 1–22.

Smyth, J., Shacklock, G. and Hattam, R. (1997) 'Teacher development in difficult times: Lessons from a policy initiative in Australia', *Teacher Development*, 1(1): 11–20.

Weppler, M. and Bourke, S. (1994) 'Advanced Skills Teachers: Dilemmas and demands'. Paper delivered at the annual conference of the Australian Association for Research in Education, Newcastle, NSW.

6

THE HIGHLY ACCOMPLISHED TEACHER IN THE USA

Andrew Goodwyn

As this book offers a perspective on the global phenomenon of expert teaching, it is especially important that it includes a view of the US model, the Highly Accomplished Teacher (HAT). This is because it is now, to our knowledge, the longest surviving model of its kind in the world and also because its influence has spread to the new Australian model discussed in Chapters 5 and 8. We would argue that the adoption of the HAT descriptor at national level in Australia to (possibly) replace the Advanced Skills Teacher designation (which was only available in some states) is an example of the positive adaptation of a success from one major education system to another, not least because it is a real adaptation, not a mere cloning or copying.

Another important element in the story of the HAT model is that it is a national model in a very federal education system. The US has arguably the most fiercely and defensively federal system in the world; however, Australia is not so very different and may well have seen the HAT model, which can be described as 'supra-federal', as especially relevant to learn from. One undoubted success of the HAT concept was making it 'portable' – that is, making it a national certification not limited by any particular state's conditions of teacher qualification or service. Indeed, it was designed to allow a teacher from one state to move easily to another without having to requalify as a teacher. However, there is no real research evidence about whether this has actually happened to any significant degree. The challenge of reconciling state-level teacher licensure with a national certification is further discussed below.

The HAT model is offered by the National Board for Professional Teaching Standards (NBPTS), a robustly independent and secure organisation completely distinct from government at either state or federal level. The establishment of the NBPTS and its longevity (so far) offers a valuable example of how a model of expert teaching may reach maturity over time. At the same time, the model has had nothing like the national impact of identifying effective teachers envisioned by the policymakers who called for its instigation, and it has had relatively little impact on the profession of teaching in the US and the raising of its status compared to other professions that is a theme of this book. The history of the NBPTS is thus especially valuable for our account, providing examples of successes and limitations that contribute much to our understanding of the concept of expert teaching from an international perspective. It was also the subject of an extremely thorough evaluation by the National Research Council (NRC) of the National Academy of Sciences, which produced a book-length report (NRC, 2008) and other supporting documents in 2008, following three years of evidence gathering by the Committee on Evaluation of Teacher Certification for the National Board for Professional Teaching Standards, which was fully endorsed and supported by the Department for Education.

Policy context

The NBPTS was created in 1987 in response to the direct recommendations made by the Carnegie Task Force on Teaching as a Profession. Their report, 'A nation prepared: Teachers for the 21st century' (Carnegie Corporation, 1986), called for systemic reforms in the training and long-term development of the teacher workforce. This initiative in turn owed much to 'A nation at risk', a 1983 report by the National Commission on Excellence in Education, a commission set up in 1981 by the secretary of education, T. H. Bell (see NRC, 2008, pp. 16–25); its genesis was national concern about poor student performance and the report adjudged that the US would lose its economic viability unless there was serious reform. Its main recommendations were that there needed to be far more robust ways of measuring and improving student performance, a longer school day, and the introduction of new ways to attract good graduates into teaching and then retain them in a better respected profession (NRC, 2008, p. 39).

What this chain of linked policy documents clearly reveals is an almost hysterical anxiety about the school system and a perception that the teaching profession was deeply problematic. It might be argued that this was a rather predictable conclusion and that other governments (including the US national and state-level legislatures to this day) continue to pursue this theme.

What was different about the above period is that it led to real action to support the long-term development of the teaching profession. Whatever the limitations of the NBPTS, it has survived and thrived and escaped the whims of short-term political policy change. One reason for this was the character of the Carnegie commission's task force, which included policymakers, educators, leaders of the teaching unions and business leaders whose minds were concentrated by the national anxiety to develop some kind of workable consensus (NRC, 2008, p. 39). The origins of the Chartered Teacher in Scotland started out in a similarly consensual way (Goodwyn, 2010) and the emerging Australian adaptation of the HAT model had an equally broad-based and inclusive set of partners and stakeholders backing the initiative (see the website of the Australian Institute for Teaching and School

Leadership). The Carnegie report's main theme was that student performance generally needed to reach levels that had previously been considered only possible for a minority and that this could only be achieved through a higher-quality teaching profession. They were also mindful that there was a need to find a way to have more of the best teachers working in the most disadvantaged schools. They then focused on how this might be achieved over time and provided a blueprint for the NBPTS as they recommended better initial preparation for teachers and, much more significantly, that the goal be highly accomplished teachers with a higher level of certification than the 'basic'. They emphasised that such teachers would need to be able to demonstrate a:

- deeper understanding of subject content;
- better understanding of how knowledge developed in the disciplines could be made relevant to students;
- much deeper appreciation of how students learn and develop including in diverse and differing contexts;
- much wider repertoire of teaching techniques especially in relation to diverse student populations;
- a higher level of skill in assessing student needs and outcomes.

(NRC, 2008, ch. 3)

Their most important recommendation was that this higher level of certification should be used to identify and reward these accomplished teachers, who could then be mobilised to improve teaching and learning wherever they were working but especially in low-achieving school districts. Their summary recommendations are quoted in full below (NRC, 2008, p. 41) to illustrate the commendable ambition of the project for the NBPTS, which partly explains why its achievements are still quite limited.

1 Create a National Board for Professional Teaching Standards, organised with a regional and state membership structure, to establish high standards for what teachers need to know and be able to do, and to certify teachers who meet that standard.

This aim has been largely achieved, although there is still huge variation in different states' support for the Board and there is not yet a recognisable regional structure.

2 Restructure schools to provide a professional environment for teaching, freeing them to decide how best to meet state and local goals for children while holding them accountable for student progress.

3 Restructure the teaching force, and introduce a new category of 'Lead Teachers' with the proven ability to provide active leadership in the redesign of schools and in helping their colleagues to uphold high standards of teaching and learning.

Goal 2 is a long way from being achieved – with the exception of accountability, as the US has become dominated by high-stakes testing. Again, individual states have very different approaches to recognising their best teachers. Goal 3 has not been achieved in any national sense. The term 'Lead Teacher' has been taken up more fully in the new Australian model and has increasing presence in England (Goodwyn, 2014, 2015). Perhaps more importantly there has been little national utilisation of the Highly Accomplished Teacher. It is both a strength and limitation of HAT teachers that certification is a recognition but not a designation.

4 Require a bachelor's degree in the arts and sciences as a prerequisite for the professional study of teaching.
5 Develop a new professional curriculum in graduate schools of education leading to a Master's in Teaching degree, based on systematic knowledge of teaching and including internships and residencies in the schools.

The majority of US teachers have an undergraduate degree but it is not a uniform requirement. Similarly, some states require teachers to reach master's level but most do not (Angus, 2001). Schools of education have not received any federal funding aimed at creating a system that would give all teachers access to a higher degree. It is worth noting in passing the brief experiment in England of the MTL (Master's in Teaching and Learning) that was launched by the Teaching and Development Agency (TDA) in 2008 with the intention of making every teacher reach master's level; it was scrapped by the new government in 2010, as was the TDA. It is also notable that Finland, almost always close to the top of the international league tables for educational attainment (see Chapter 7), does have a master's degree-level teaching profession.

6 Mobilise the nation's resources to prepare minority youngsters for teaching careers.

There has been no systematic or strategic approach to this goal.

7 Relate incentives for teachers to school-wide student performance, and provide schools with the technology, services and staff essential to teacher productivity.
8 Make teachers' salaries and career opportunities competitive with those in other professions.

Goal 7 remains at the discretion of individual states and certainly most schools and districts only relate teachers' pay (if they do at all) to the performance of their particular students. Goal 8 remains a state-level responsibility, but there is certainly no comparison, least of all in pay, with the 'top' professions of medicine and law. This remains a global phenomenon, with occasional exceptions. As discussed in Chapter 4, the AST role in England was a genuine career route and relatively well paid for the small number (1 to 2 per cent) of teachers who achieved the status. The NBPTS can quite rightly claim that many states do reward HAT status and that it is now a well-established and credible aspect of the profession of teaching, but the goal of making teaching comparable to other 'top' professions remains an aspiration.

The nature of the NBPTS and its model of certification

As mentioned above, one of the aims of the HAT model was to create an expert teacher model recognised across the extremely diverse USA state-led system. It is relevant, therefore, to summarise the extent of the diversity in question to help illustrate how great the task was to design a coherent 'supra' system. It also helps to explain the exceptional level of details in the HAT descriptors, which had to be robustly applicable across a problematically broad range of state systems. At the time of the research review of the NBPTS in 2008 (NRC, 2008, ch. 3), the following statistics were accurate concerning the initial licensure of teachers across the USA. Of the 50 states and the District of Columbia, eight developed their own examinations for teacher licensure; 26 used some combination of the three components of the PRAXIS series offered by the Educational Testing Service (ETS); and nine required some other combination of assessments (Baber, 2007). Of the states that did have a testing requirement, three also used a testing requirement to certify advanced teachers. Arkansas and Ohio used PRAXIS III for this purpose, and New York had its own assessment. In general, entering teachers, who have met the entry-level requirements, received a probationary certificate and then had a three-year period in which to complete additional requirements. Teachers who had satisfied these requirements received a standard certificate, qualified for tenure and were referred to as 'advanced' teachers (some states identified as advanced only teachers who had earned a master's degree). This picture of state-level diversity appears not to have changed significantly. There are some policy shifts in the US that are significantly affecting teacher education and schools and may produce more commonality, but only by reducing the quality of teacher preparation (see Christenbury, 2014).

Goal 5, quoted again:

> Develop a new professional curriculum in graduate schools of education leading to a Master's in Teaching degree, based on systematic knowledge of teaching and including internships and residencies in the schools.

This goal has not only been mostly ignored but recent policy changes suggest a weakening of the influence of universities in teacher education. In 2008, the majority of public school teachers were educated at a school of education. Fewer than 40 per cent of these programmes were nationally accredited and as a group they were regarded as having comparatively low standards for admission and modest success in preparing excellent teachers (Levine, 2006; Murray, 2001). It is important to note that these programmes varied in many respects, and that prospective teachers were not evenly distributed among them – as many as 50 per cent of graduates came from teacher education programmes in five states (California, Illinois, New York, Pennsylvania and Texas) and more than one quarter were in just two states: New York and California (NRC, 2008, p. 53).

In 2008, the NBPTS was approaching its twentieth year and, despite the limitations noted above, was firmly established. One considerable strength was that its five core propositions had successfully stood the test of 20 years, and these will now be examined briefly (for all NBPTS documents, see their website, NBPTS.org).

The five core propositions

1 Teachers are committed to students and their learning:

- Teachers recognise individual differences in their students and adjust their practice accordingly;
- Teachers have an understanding of how students develop and learn;
- Teachers treat students equitably; and
- Teachers' mission extends beyond developing the cognitive capacity of their students.

These characteristics conform closely with the literature on effective teaching and the standards for teachers in several countries (Goodwyn, 2010). The final point is especially interesting as the research report commented on the importance of aspects of teacher efficacy that go beyond the cognitive but acknowledged that they are hard to describe and even harder to measure (NRC, 2008, ch. 12). In a sense, this finding from the review *and* the retention of the final bullet point above help us see how future research must be focused. As students around the world spend more time in school and the world school population grows, it becomes ever more imperative that we understand how expert teachers engage with and communicate with students beyond the 'cognitive'.

2 Teachers know the subjects they teach and how to teach those subjects to students:

- Teachers appreciate how knowledge in their subjects is created, organised and linked to other disciplines;
- Teachers command specialised knowledge of how to convey a subject to students; and
- Teachers generate multiple paths to knowledge.

This section fits especially well with the findings from Shulman's work on, amongst other things, Subject Pedagogical Knowledge, as in 'how to teach those subjects' (Shulman, 1986, 1987). The Board has also the most developed set of descriptors (see below) that have ever been produced and, again, they have robustly stood the test of time. This strength of the NBPTS also offers a research challenge for other developed systems to undertake subject descriptor development work.

3 Teachers are responsible for managing and monitoring student learning:

- Teachers call on multiple methods to meet their goals;
- Teachers orchestrate learning in group settings;
- Teachers place a premium on student engagement;
- Teachers regularly assess student progress; and
- Teachers are mindful of their principal objectives.

This is a very straightforward and incontrovertible section, again soundly based on the literature and very close to the actual words of Hattie's research (Hattie, 2003). It might be criticised for sounding rather unsophisticated and simplistic but, again, the 25 years of successful operation contradicts any such concern.

4 Teachers think systematically about their practice and learn from experience:

- Teachers are continually making difficult choices that test their judgement; and
- Teachers seek the advice of others and draw on education research and scholarship to improve their practice.

This section, especially the first two points, appears to draw principally on Schon (1983, 1987) and subsequent work on the reflective practitioner model. The third point is a feature of a number of other expert teacher models, most notably the Chartered Teacher model in Scotland, and of policy emphases in some jurisdictions about teachers achieving a master's-level qualification, as again in Scotland or in the ill-fated and poorly conceptualised MTL in England (see Chapter 3). Another strong feature of the assessment process to become a HAT, is the 'testing' (see below) of the academic knowledge of the candidates. The assessment requires candidates to demonstrate their ability to understand educational research and to use their critical judgement, drawing on their practical experience, to make evidenced judgements about the value and potential of the research. An unusual strength of this approach is that it challenges the much-mentioned tension between practical wisdom and theoretical knowledge. This is something we believe should be a feature of expert teacher development and assessment, not least because it places teaching on a par with other 'learned' professions and, we would argue, therefore enhances the status of the whole profession.

5 Teachers are members of learning communities:

- Teachers contribute to school effectiveness by collaborating with other professionals;
- Teachers work collaboratively with parents; and
- Teachers take advantage of community resources.

The first point in this section strongly echoes the work of Lave and Wenger (1991) and their emphasis on 'communities of practice'. It also depicts HATs as extended professionals whose impact and influence reach out to the community; this is an interesting emphasis in the new Australian version (see Chapter 8). It is also another example of an important aspect of the work of the best teachers that is especially hard to measure. With the AST model in England, the assessment process involved the assessor meeting with a group of parents, which at least recognised this dimension of excellent teaching (Goodwyn, 2010). The emphasis on community has been very influential on the emerging Australia HAT model (see the website) and offers more opportunity for approaches to research into expert teaching that try to evaluate the less tangible but fundamentally important impact that such teachers have on both the parents of students and also the whole community, of which they are a key part.

In summary, these core propositions have admirably stood the test of time (NRC, 2008) and the independence of the NBPTS has kept them safe from short-term political interference, helping to build the reputation of the Board and provide incremental credibility to the propositions and standards that were developed to form the basis for the certification process.

The process of certification

A consistent theme in this book is the vital importance of fair and credible assessments used to identify excellent teachers. These assessments also need to be part of any system that employs some degree of external input: the AST in England, for example, involved a two-day visit from an accredited assessor (Goodwyn, 2010). The new HAT model in Australia also employs external input, while it has some interesting differences of emphasis (see Chapter 8) from the US model outlined below.

The NBPTS spent a great deal of money and time (NRC, 2008) in developing the certificates and it currently offers 25, all inflected by teacher knowledge (in, for example, languages, arts, maths, etc.) and also, typically by age range (such as elementary, middle or high school). This distinguishes the model from the majority of systems that opt for generic and/or hierarchical descriptors. In some systems, subject-orientated style associations have developed more subject-based models (e.g. STELLA in Australia, or various chartered models in England such as science, geography, English; for an overview, see Goodwyn, 2010). However, the Australian-adapted model emphasises teacher subject knowledge but is not developing subject or age-specific certification. Another major difference is the emphasis, in fact reliance, on psychometric testing (see below). The process of gaining certification has remained essentially the same since 1993:

- To begin the process of earning board certification, a candidate must first establish that he or she is qualified to apply.
- The candidate must have completed a bachelor's degree, have completed at least three full years of teaching or counselling before beginning the

application process, and have had a valid teaching or counselling license throughout that period.
- After submitting documentation of eligibility, the candidate receives more detailed instructions about the procedures for completing the entire assessment.
- The candidate must also submit payment of the test fee, which is currently $2,500.

This is the simple starting point and is notable for being entirely self-nominated. This is partly because, whatever the NBPTS suggests, this is not fundamentally a career change. Certified teachers do not have a new job to do once successful, unlike the AST in England. There are also very significant variations in state-level support and encouragement, as outlined on the NBPTS website. The most prevalent incentive across the states is that the candidate's fees will be reimbursed and there may be a pay rise. It can be argued, therefore, that the motivation for undertaking certification must be largely intrinsic. It is noteworthy that research by Fuller, Goodwyn and Francis-Brophy (2012) found that the AST workforce in England was adamant that the main drive in taking on the role was not the salary (welcome though it was) but rather the status and the challenge that the role offered.

It is certainly clear that undertaking NBPTS certification is demanding on a number of levels and is a complex process compared, for example, to the AST model as it was in Australia or England.

- The assessment consists of 10 exercises administered in two parts: a computer-based assessment of content knowledge that includes 6 constructed-response exercises, and a portfolio that consists of 4 exercises.
- Responses to the computer-based exercises and the portfolios are scored at designated times during the year, so the time that elapses between submitting an application and receiving certification depends on the time of year the candidate initiates the process, as well as on how long he or she takes to complete the portfolios and schedule the computer-based assessment.

The detail of these assessments will be analysed below but the other significant point is how much time a teacher must give to the process.

- National board staff estimate that the typical candidate spends up to 400 hours on the 10 exercises.
- Given the deadlines throughout the year and the volume of work to be included in the portfolios, most candidates complete the process in approximately 12 to 18 months.
- The national board will allow candidates to take as long as 3 years to complete all of the requirements before voiding early scores and asking the candidate to start again.

Of the various models around the world this is certainly one of the most individually onerous. There is no guaranteed local support and the applicant's school is not necessarily involved. This approach is therefore very much the lonely mode of reflective practice which, it has been argued (Goodwyn, 2010), places a great burden on the individual teacher and ignores the need for a more social model of support. It is also a neat way, in neo-liberal times, of suggesting that teacher development does not need a properly funded model of professional development but rather that exceptional teachers will individually prove themselves. There is evidence that this is the case (Goodwyn, 2010), but it ignores the key issue about the potential of many more teachers being able to move to the expert, or extended professional, level if they had appropriate challenge and support. However seminal Schon's work (1983, 1987) remains and should remain, its emphasis on the dialogue between the lone reflective professional and the practice situation can be misinterpreted to suggest that it is always the individual teacher who can improve if only they try hard enough.

The master's-level teacher proposal in England clearly implied this when it stated:

> Master Teachers are reflective and self-critical regarding their own teaching and make critical appraisals of new developments and techniques, which they use judiciously. A thorough understanding of the developmental and social backgrounds of pupils further supports and informs their practice.
>
> Master Teachers command the classroom, skilfully leading, encouraging and extending pupils. They have the respect of both pupils and parents. They are at ease in their role, and discipline and dialogue are unselfconscious and effective.
>
> *(DfE, 2011, p. 9)*

The first two sentences suggest that such teachers, having somehow become 'reflective and self-critical', are now so judicious that they should (third sentence) 'command' their classrooms. Later, the recommendations state firmly that Master Teacher status should have no link to pay or reward. There are also statements about their potential collegiality:

> Master Teachers are highly regarded by colleagues, who want to learn from them. They willingly play a role in the development of school policies and in the professional life of the school. They work in collaboration with colleagues on pastoral and wider pupil-related matters, giving advice as appropriate. They engage with and contribute to professional networks beyond the school.
>
> They are analytical in evaluating and developing their own craft and knowledge, making full use of continuing professional development and appropriate research. They recognise the vital importance of out-of-school and extra-curricular activities, both academically and personally, and play a leading role here and in the wider life of the school.

> Master Teachers are open in the giving and receiving of professional advice, which may include coaching or mentoring colleagues and less-experienced teachers. They work to significant effect with other adults in ensuring high quality education for the pupils they serve.
>
> *(Ibid.)*

There is a very real tension here between the assumptions being made about these remarkably generous and exemplary teachers and the intensely demanding nature of daily life in schools where no time is provided for such sharing of expertise. However, there is some truth in the assumptions as there are many teachers who, our experience shows, do give in this generous way. Ultimately, the underlying weakness in these assumptions is that they are of little value to a system that is trying to identify and optimise the importance of the best teachers: it is simply good luck should a teacher happen to benefit from working alongside a remarkable teacher.

It might be argued that, even if remarkable teachers can prove their capability, the profession as a whole will only ever identify a tiny proportion of such teachers. For example, ASTs in England formed at best 1–2 per cent of the workforce; in the US, HATs were even less, as the NBPTS data only reveals how many have passed over 25 years (1,000,000), not how many are currently employed. The NBPTS mission is about advancing the profession. The certification process has much to recommend it in terms of rigour, but a weakness may be its focus on identifying teachers who can, in a sense, rise above local circumstances rather than looking at how the Board might work with school districts to enable far more teachers to develop the confidence to undertake the certification process. It might be suggested, as with the Master Teacher above, that the reward of certification is not about pay but a combination of status enhancement and opportunity to work with and influence other teachers.

The certification process

A strength of the certification process has been its consistency, something commended by the NRC review (NRC, 2008, ch. 4), which considered that one of the Board's major successes was that its selection of Highly Accomplished Teachers had been consistently accurate and credible within the profession. In summary:

> the certification process for National Board Certification is designed to collect standards-based evidence of accomplished practice. In all certificate areas, candidates for National Board Certification are requested to complete four components: three portfolio entries, which you submit online, and a computer-based assessment, which is administered to you at a testing center.
>
> *(NBPTS website)*

The computer-based, essentially psychometric element of the certification process is currently, to our knowledge, unique in the world of assessing expert teaching.

It may well be that this element is something that other systems might wish to adopt as it gives some objectivity to the process of selection. There are concerns that these tests are pseudo-rationalistic judgements that elide the much more important and more holistic significance of site visits and expert evaluations of actual teaching seen in the AST model in England and the emergent HAT model in Australia. Equally, most inspection systems or school-based performance management systems are highly dependent on carefully managed and focused observations by local colleagues, completed in real time. Put simply, expert observers are observing (potentially) expert teachers in almost (given that all observations affect the teacher and students) authentic circumstances. The NBPTS can certainly argue that the thoroughness of its development stage and the consistency of its application of its original model demonstrate the reliability of the computer-based assessment, which covers 'Component 1: Content Knowledge'. Portfolio entries comprise:

- Component 2: Differentiation in Instruction
- Component 3: Teaching Practice and Learning Environment
- Component 4: Effective and Reflective Practitioner.

(Ibid.)

The components

A general description of each component follows. The specific instructions vary by certificate area, as do the standards assessed by each component. It can be argued that this computer-based approach gives an objective validity to the entire assessment process. Almost all other models rely on more human judgements through observation and interview, so are therefore reliant on the application of human expertise to human expertise. In its own way this is a 'tried and tested' method and a dominant mode of assessment in the domain of teacher training in many countries. It is important to stress that this computer-based task is only one part of the holistic judgement.

Content Knowledge

> In this computer-based assessment, you demonstrate knowledge of and pedagogical practices for teaching your content area.
>
> - You must demonstrate knowledge of developmentally appropriate content, which is necessary for teaching across the full age range and ability level of your chosen certificate area.
> - This is assessed through the completion of three constructed response exercises and approximately 45 selected response items (SRIs).
> - You will have up to 30 minutes to complete each of the three constructed response exercises and up to 60 minutes to complete the selected response section.

The next component is more typical of models of expert teaching in that it emphasises the selection of relevant material by the candidate, so allowing autonomy of judgement; it also stresses student development over time, giving weight to a more nuanced view of student progress than test scores alone. It also focuses on differentiation rather than the raw outcomes of, for example, very successful students, so allowing candidates to include students whose work is not outstanding but shows significant progress.

Differentiation in Instruction

- This classroom-based portfolio entry is primarily comprised of samples of student work and an accompanying written commentary.
- You will submit selected work samples that demonstrate the students' growth over time and a written commentary that analyzes your instructional choices.

Currently, this remains the only model, as far as we know, that puts video evidence and commentary at the heart of the assessment process. The approach has been robustly tested over the life of the NBPTS. There are a number of projects employing the latest video technology, perhaps the most spectacular being the Measure of Effective Teaching Project, sponsored by the Gates Foundation (see below; metproject.org/). The NBPTS portfolio seems to combine the tradition of reflective practice with, again, teacher autonomy in the selection of classroom episodes. The use of video in teacher development, and especially expert teaching, is likely to be one of the features of the future of research and practice in an evidence-based approach to defining and refining the best teachers.

Teaching Practice and Learning Environment

- This is a classroom-based portfolio entry that requires video recording(s) of interactions between you and your students.
- A written commentary in which you describe, analyze and reflect on your teaching and interactions will also be submitted.
- Both the video and the written commentary should demonstrate how you engage students and impact their learning.

The final portfolio is soundly based in the concept of the extended professional, particularly featured in models such as the Chartered Teacher and the emergent Australian Highly Accomplished Teacher. This element of teacher effectiveness remains one of the hardest to evidence but is almost certainly, in terms of underpinning why we might identify and accredit expert teachers, the most fundamentally important. The search to demonstrate how expert teachers support and develop less expert teachers must be one of the key aims of future research in the field.

Effective and Reflective Practitioner

- This is a portfolio entry that requires evidence of your impact across your professional responsibilities as an educator including your students, peers, and community.

It is worth returning to the other robust feature of the NBPTS, which is its recognition of the nuances of teacher expertise as inflected by both subject and phase-specific knowledge. The Board currently offers certification in 16 content areas of specialisation covering seven age groupings, for a total of 25 individual certificates. This is combined with the recognition that neither kind of knowledge is static – indeed, they are conceptualised as importantly and developmentally dynamic; the certificate is effective for ten years and then must be renewed. Such a view is closer to other professional models such as medicine and law where practitioners are required, not just encouraged, to constantly refresh their professional knowledge so as to be up to date with changes in the field (Eraut, 1995). Far too much teacher 'development' is actually merely pragmatic and functional instruction in how to implement some politically driven policy imperative, often conceptualised as technicist and 'teacher proof'; an excellent example would be the National Literacy Strategy in England, which used a model of 'informed prescription' (see Goodwyn and Fuller, 2011, for a full account).

Conclusions

We argue that the NBPTS is a remarkable model of expert teaching, not just because of its longevity and independence from political interference, vital as those elements are, but also because of its richness and evolving complexity. The study of *Assessing Accomplished Teaching*, much referred to above, was clear that NBPTS had achieved a huge amount but had some significant goals for the future. When the report was completed its recommendations were:

- The NBPTS should conduct its work according to the highest standards for credentialing programs, make its operations accessible to external scrutiny and conduct regular evaluations of its assessments to ensure continuous improvement.
- The NBPTS should pursue an ongoing research agenda to evaluate progress toward its goals.
- The NBPTS should periodically review its assessment model, both to evaluate how it has worked in practice and to adapt to changes in the policy environment and advances in research. As part of such ongoing evaluation efforts, the board should consider whether adjustments are needed in the types of information used as the basis for certification,

which might include classroom observations, objective tests of content knowledge or measures of student performance.

- The NBPTS should continue to invest in its larger mission of influencing the teaching field in broad, comprehensive ways.

(NRC, 2008, pp. 261–262)

In Chapter 8, which reviews some of the future potentialities of the various extant models, the NBPTS is further discussed because it has demonstrated its response to some of these recommendations, especially at the level of influencing the teaching field in broad and comprehensive ways. However, it is less clear what the HAT workforce has done to raise the status of the profession. The National Board (see Chapter 8) works hard at state and federal level to lobby for the profession as a whole but there appears to be no research on what the HAT workforce contributes to teacher status or esteem. There is also little evidence of how the different states deploy these accomplished teachers; it might well be that local models could be reviewed for their national and even international potential.

Whatever else, the NBPTS seems to have a secure future and thus now has the capacity to take the long view. It has the vital ability to commission much needed research into expert teaching and its relationship not just to student achievement but to the less tangible influences that expert teachers have on other aspects of student development, on their colleagues and, indeed, on their local communities. Some other schemes are being dismantled for no evidential reason as a result of political interference; an example is the ending of the AST scheme in England and the vague notion of its replacement by the Master Teacher, a recommendation that has received no attention in four years. The Chartered Teacher scheme in Scotland, underpinned at its beginning by a great consensus, has faltered and was closed in 2012 (Kidner, 2012). On a more positive note, the Australian government has adopted aspects of the US HAT model to replace the state-level versions of the AST and introduced a nationwide and systemic approach to developing teacher expertise.

Singapore continues to expand its cadre of expert teachers by offering an increasing range of titles and specialisms; rather than closing one model and replacing it with another, its approach is a steady expansion but also refinement of the model. This approach is an example of a genuine strategy within a politically stable context and in September 2014 the government announced that its policy will:

> widen the reach and impact of highly skilled teachers in lifting up the practice of the entire teaching fraternity, MOE will continue to develop and appoint more Principal Master Teachers, Master Teachers, Lead Teachers, and Senior Teachers in recognition of their key roles in leading professional learning and in deepening the culture of teachers growing teachers. In this regard, MOE will work with schools and clusters to actively encourage more teachers to deepen their skills and take up these appointments.

This expansion is supported not by a reliance on reflective practitioners or self-challenging teachers who might choose a scheme like the NBPTS model but instead offers a system of support and reward:

> Appointed Senior Teachers and Lead Teachers have the opportunity to attend Teacher Leaders Programme which is designed to further deepen their professional knowledge and skills. MOE will look to raising the apex grade for the teaching track to recognise the national role of Master Teachers in developing and raising the competencies of the entire teaching service.
>
> MOE will continue to strengthen professional development opportunities and support our teachers to be lifelong learners, so that they too can be role models of lifelong learning for our students. With more skilful, caring and effective teachers in every school, we will be able to bring out the best in every child.
>
> *(Singapore MoE, 2014)*

Conclusion

So the NBPTS model must be admired for its longevity, independence and resilience, but at the same time it should be wary of complacency: it may need to look at international models such as Singapore's, which offers fresh ideas and an expansionist approach, or Australia's, where the HAT concept is being redefined. However, both these schemes, however well intentioned, are government led; there is no suggestion that the NBPTS should surrender any of its precious independence. That many of the systemic aspirations for the original remit of the NBPTS considered above have remained unfulfilled is certainly disappointing but equally unsurprising. A universal feature of all the models discussed in this book is that they are voluntary, and the HAT model may be considered especially voluntary in that it has very ill-defined career benefits for the individual teacher. The strength of this volunteer model is well proven by the history of the NBPTS. However, looked at specifically from the needs of students, especially those in disadvantaged communities, it remains clear that most HAT teachers work in 'good' schools and have no incentive to move to more challenging environments. It is also clear that the NBPTS cannot show any evidence of its work having attracted more ethnic minority students into the teaching profession. These final points demonstrate very simply that although identifying expert teachers and certifying them is a very valuable step, it cannot, by itself, address deep systemic problems such as social and economic disadvantage.

References

Angus, D. L. (2001) *Professionalism and the Public Good: A Brief History of Teacher Certification.* Washinton, DC: Thomas B. Fordham Foundation.

Australian Institute for Teaching and School Leadership, www.aitsl.edu.au (accessed 1 Jan 2015).

Baber, A. (2007) 'State-level testing requirements for teacher certification', Education Commission of the States. Available at www.ecs.org.clearinghouse/72/92/7292.pdf (accessed 20 Nov 2007).

Carnegie Corporation (1986) *A Nation Prepared: Teachers for the 21st century. The Report of the Task Force on Teaching as a Profession*. Minnesota: University of Minnesota.

Christenbury, L. (2014) 'Is it the endgame for teacher preparation in US universities?', in A. Goodwyn, L. Reid and C. Durrant (eds), *International Perspectives on Teaching English in a Globalised World*. London: Routledge.

DfE (Department for Education) (2011) *Second Report of the Independent Review of Teacher's Standards*. London: HMSO.

Eraut, M. (1995) *Developing Professional Knowledge and Competence*. London: Falmer Press.

Fuller, C., Goodwyn, A. and Francis-Brophy, E. (2012) 'Being an advanced skills teacher: Professional identity and status', *Teachers and Teaching: Theory and Practice* 19(4): 463–474.

Goodwyn, A. (2010) *The Expert Teacher of English*. London: Routledge.

Goodwyn, A. (2014) 'Head teachers view of Expert teachers: Do they see the Advanced Skills Teacher as an innovation benefitting the profession?' Paper presented to the British Educational Research Association, University of London (September).

Goodwyn, A. (2015) 'Has the Advanced Skills Teacher role been an advance for the profession? The views of principals and other senior leaders'. Paper presented at the American Educational Research Association Conference, Chicago (April).

Goodwyn, A. and Fuller, C. (2011) *The Great Literacy Debate*. London: Routledge Falmer.

Hattie, J. (2003) *Teachers Make a Difference: What is the Research Evidence?* Auckland: University of Auckland.

Kidner, C. (2012) *Teacher Training and Employment*. Edinburgh: The Scottish Parliament.

Lave, J. and Wenger, E. (1991) *Situated Learning: Legitimate Peripheral Participation*. Cambridge: Cambridge University Press.

Levine, A. (2006) *Education School Teachers*. Washington, DC: Education Schools Project.

MoE (Ministry of Education) Singapore (2014) *Growing Our Teachers, Building Our Nation*, MoE press release, September. Available at: www.moe.gov.sg/media/press/2014/09/growing-our-teachers-building-our-nation.php

National Board for Professional Teaching Standards, nbpts.org (accessed 20 May 2016).

NRC (National Research Council) (2008) *Assessing Accomplished Teaching: Advanced-Level Certification Programs*. Washington, DC: The National Academies Press.

Schon, D. (1983) *The Reflective Practitioner: How Professionals Think in Action*. London: Temple Smith.

Schon, D. (1987) *Educating the Reflective Practitioner*. San Francisco: Jossey Bass.

Shulman, L. (1986) 'Those who understand: Knowledge growth in teaching', *Educational Researcher*, 15(2): 4–31.

Shulman, L. (1987) 'Knowledge and teaching: Foundations of the new reform', *Harvard Educational Review*, 57(1): 1–22.

7

EMERGING MODELS OF EXPERT TEACHING

Andrew Goodwyn

Current national models of expert teacher recognition share an understanding that harnessing the skills of these teachers is essential for countries wishing to achieve national educational priorities and, if they are motivated by international comparisons, secure any prominence further afield. Some emerging paradigms of expert teacher programmes, such as the Chartered Teacher (Scotland), offered a broader conceptualisation of expert teaching, with a stronger emphasis on the teacher as a fully extended professional and role model for other teachers, than more narrowly focused models such as the AST in Australia and England. Ensuring international coverage, this chapter includes examples of European and Asian models, such as the high-performing Finnish model that prompted other countries to think about teaching as a master's level profession. There will also be a comparison with Chartered Teacher models in England, which come from non-governmental institutions such as subject associations.

The problematic rise of global measures

It has been stressed in our argument that the rise of the expert teacher is a global phenomenon. There is no truly explicit evidence about teacher quality in international comparison models such as the PISA (Programme for International Student Assessment) system but it is very clear that the making of international comparisons now has huge political importance. An interesting, if rather populist, example has emerged recently with the Varkey Foundation's Global Teacher Status Index. The website (Varkey Foundation, 2016) boldly asserts:

> The Global Teacher Status index is the world's first comprehensive attempt to compare the status of teachers across the world. It is based on in-depth opinion by Populus in 21 countries that explores the attitudes on issues

> ranging from what is a fair salary for teachers to whether they think pupils respect teachers to how highly people rank their own education system. There have been many international comparisons in education, but this is the first time that the role of teacher status has been studied in-depth.

As if this were not 'exciting' enough, the Foundation then launched a 'Nobel prize' for teaching:

> The Varkey Foundation launched the Global Teacher Prize in 2014 to raise the stature of the teaching profession. We seek to celebrate the best teachers – those who inspire their students and community around them. The Foundation believes that vibrant education awakens and supports the full potential of young people. The status of teachers in our cultures is key to our global future. The award – the 'Nobel Prize' of teaching – operates under the patronage of His Highness Sheikh Mohammed bin Rashid Al Maktoum, UAE Vice President, Prime Minister, and Ruler of Dubai.
>
> *(Varkey Foundation, 2016)*

Are these moves merely media gimmicks or are they part of a shift towards a global recognition of the stature of the profession and a deepening understanding of the nature of the status of teachers? We certainly consider that much of this particular move is about promoting the Varkey Foundation at a time when corporations of all kinds are moving into the provision of educational services of all types. However, it does seem to be part of the more fundamental globalisation of education as a series of competing systems, all measurable by a set of outcomes. The Varkey work on teacher status claims to be research based but has not been subject to much independent scrutiny; nevertheless, the work of PISA and equivalents, while much contested methodologically, has a great deal of influence and credibility amongst governments.

The effect of such widely publicised and globally influential league tables leads to implied findings about teacher quality. Political parties around the world now make part of their education policy about moving up the PISA table, to be 'world leading' and so on. Just how genuinely robust such international comparisons are is much contested. Developed systems can be compared but they should also be contrasted and it is astonishingly hard to adjust for variables that might include the philosophy and culture of a system. How comparable are China and the USA, or Finland and England? What is an expert teacher in China or Africa compared to an expert teacher in the Middle East or Australia? We argue that examining the emergent models has real value and can help each of the different systems reflect on what their own model is predicated upon and how other systems may offer new ideas and innovations. It is perhaps striking that Finland, which has so often come top in international comparisons, can only be described as a most unusual and atypical country: this is examined below.

A good example, in our view, of the unintended and damaging consequences of a system like PISA has occurred in the UK, where the government reacted

(DfE press release, February 2014) to what it considered poor performance in maths (UK was 50th out of 148 systems in the World Economic Forum's (WEF) competitiveness ranking in Maths and Science Education) by deciding that teachers in the UK should adopt the approach of teachers in Shanghai (which came top in the WEF table). In February 2013 a large group of teachers from 46 UK schools visited Shanghai and the UK minister for education visited in early 2014. There is, of course, every reason for looking at excellent practice in another system, learning from it and adapting it to the local culture. However, we would argue that this is another example of an attempted quick fix, the intention being to simply copy the pedagogy of Shanghai maths teachers and import it to the UK. There is not space here for detailing the crucial differences between teaching maths in the Shanghai and UK jurisdictions; sufficient to say that they are very considerable. This initiative to copy Shanghai has continued in the UK up to the time of writing, mostly reported in the press with very little citing of evidence other than the Shanghai league table position. A later posting (TLTP Education, 2014) quoted Charlie Stripp, director of the National Centre for Excellence in the Teaching of Mathematics, as saying:

> Shanghai teachers employ a mastery approach to maths teaching that fits in well with the structure of our new national curriculum – and I firmly believe it can, and should, be embedded deeply and widely throughout our schools.

In this book we are less concerned with reductive comparisons, as in 'what is the best expert teacher model', and more with the global phenomenon and what it means.

Influencing policy: the McKinsey reports

There have been other, arguably more valuable, influences on political thinking – for example, the two reports produced by McKinsey & Co. The first report, *How the World's Best-performing Schools Come Out On Top* (Barber and Mourshed, 2007), concluded that the main issues were, first, recruiting and retaining the best people to be teachers, second, developing them into effective instructors, and third, ensuring that the system enables this high-quality teaching to reach every child. The chapter headings of the report spell out the fundamental necessity of having excellent teachers:

1 The quality of an education system cannot exceed the quality of its teachers.
2 The only way to improve outcomes is to improve instruction.
3 High performance requires every child to succeed.

This report was highly influential, so much so that in England (not the UK) it led to the rapid creation of the Masters in Teaching and Learning as an ill-conceived attempt to achieve higher PISA rankings (see Chapter 2). This has been discussed elsewhere as yet another politically motivated ideological reform rather than evidence-based change. That a master's degree for all teachers might raise outcomes is still to be tested in England, but the evidence from Finland does suggest what might be achieved in at least one developed system (see below).

Their second report, also very influential, was a follow-up to 2007 entitled *How the World's Most Improved School Systems Keep Getting Better*. Published in 2010, it argued that successful school reforms are replicable and that poor performance can be turned around to become excellent in all developed systems. The evidence comes from:

> 200 interviews with system stakeholders, and analysis of 600 interventions carried out by these systems – together comprising what we believe is the most comprehensive database of school reform ever assembled.
>
> *(Mourshed, Chijioke and Barber, 2010, Introduction)*

This study and others are now claiming that the contact between a student and very good teachers is not just a crucial learning variable but also makes a massive difference to the economic well-being of students in adult life. To us this is both a large and contentious claim.

However, the simple point is that if a student spends the majority of classroom time being taught by the best teachers, possibly in the optimal learning climate of a school full of such teachers, it is probable that their learning experience will be excellent and their chances of being a highly effective adult much enhanced. It can be argued that systems that endorse private education (England, the USA) are allowing parents to pay for such a model. It is beyond the scope of this book to examine the claims for private versus public education and their different merits. We are primarily concerned with the great majority of teachers around the world who work in the public sector – usually in learning environments that are not 'optimal', though they may be close to optimal – and who are part of large-scale systems designed to educate children and young people regardless of social background and parental income.

As previously discussed (Chapter 1), governmental rhetoric everywhere extols the importance of teachers and their contribution to society. The actual experience of teachers can feel very different from such rhetoric. Indeed, a more striking global phenomenon than the rise of the expert teacher is persistent political pressure on performance management of teachers coupled with inexorable rise of high-stakes testing: there is sufficient controversy around these linked areas for a whole other book. However, the key point is that in 'data rich' schools, the claim is made that each teacher's year-on-year performance can be measured and calibrated to the level of each student's 'achievement'. This brings back into fashion the Victorian phrase from England, 'payment by results'. At its worst, performance management is a means of forcing teachers and their students only to cover in the classroom what can be easily measured by a test and then judging every element of achievement in a narrow, mechanistic and formulaic way, the exact opposite of the approach in, for example, much-lauded Finland. In such a bleak scenario, why would a teacher spend any time helping another? Their salary depends on them 'out-performing' that colleague and, very likely, losing their job entirely should they have a bad year.

Mixed up in this draconian and punitive model there is also some focus on removing 'bad teachers', very often claimed as a central tenant of performance management and cheerily suggesting that all that is happening is proper reward for the best teachers and exposure and dismissal of the incompetent. There is clear evidence that teachers do demonstrate very different levels of competence. Some of this range simply relates to development, with the Dreyfus model providing a helpful framework to help adjust expectations by enabling judgements to relate to recognised phases.

In any profession there are colleagues who are less effective than others; it is a difficult matter to decide, we would argue, whether identifying such colleagues should lead to their removal from the profession or be a trigger for additional help and support. In England, one of the strengths of the *outreach* function of the AST was to enable these excellent teachers to support teachers identified as needing support. It was an additional benefit that the AST came from a different school and so their judgement was not clouded by local issues or managerial prejudice. Our research (Fuller, Goodwyn and Francis-Brophy, 2010) demonstrated that ASTs felt this was an important aspect of their work. We recognise that teachers who are not effective or who are, for whatever reason, no longer effective and who do not respond to support and advice should be helped to make a dignified exit from the profession. Again, in order to maintain the professional credibility of teachers with the public, and especially parents, it is important that this is a rare outcome. A figure like an AST is in a good position to offer expert judgement on such matters and to advise a school accordingly.

Returning to the theme of performance management for most teachers, expert teacher designations provide some support and benefit to the profession. In most countries discussed in this book, such designations are based on rigorous assessment of each candidate with a strong external element, giving them significant credibility inside and outside the profession. In an age of performance management it is thus another argument for continuing to develop such models, so that teachers have a champion whose focus is to be an excellent teacher and to help others to develop – a measure of counterbalance to narrow managerialist and, in a sense, anti-teacher approaches.

Models and environments that foster expert, ethical and extended professional modes of teaching

One development worthy of mention, partly as a different kind of concept, was the General Teaching Council for Scotland (GTCS) 2002/3 'Chartered Teacher' initiative (GTCS, 2009). This scheme turned out to be a short-lived experiment, coming to an end after only a few years, effectively in 2010 (see Donaldson, 2010).

However, there remains a strong view within the Scottish system that it was a valuable project and offers valuable insights for the future (see below). The project was underpinned by a similar wish to retain the best teachers in the classroom and at first glance looks very comparable to England's AST. For example, the Scottish scheme identifies these components:

- Professional values and personal commitments;
- Professional knowledge and understanding;
- Professional and personal attributes;
- Professional action (GTCS website).

In England, the components until 2013 were:

a professional attributes;
b professional knowledge and understanding;
c professional skills (DCSF, 2009).

However, the Chartered model was intended for all experienced teachers who wished to achieve 'the standard'; this could be done either via a master's-style programme or by 'stating a claim' to the GTCS, which then had to be validated. The Chartered model was developed consensually in Scotland and gave the Scottish GTC an important role in improving the status of the profession, something completely missing in England. The use of the term also implied a strong equivalence with other professions that identify and celebrate their own Chartered professionals. The term 'chartered' exists (see further discussion below) across a very wide range of professions (chartered architect) and professional domains (chartered chemist); it is a recognition of high competence and bestows status. It is an award by an independent professional body, not affected by political change or control or conditions of employment. In the UK (and the Commonwealth) it has a somewhat archaic dimension since historically the awarding body had to have a Royal Charter, something only the monarch could grant. Although this still pertains to an extent, professional bodies have begun to use the term without such royal imprimatur, the Chartered Teacher in Scotland being such an example. The key question for teaching is whether this focus on professional capability is comparable to that of other prestigious and well-established professions where the term 'chartered' conveys a sense of gravitas and high-status credibility.

This term has also been adopted for teachers in Wales, and some subject associations in England – notably science and geography, more recently English – have developed their own chartered teacher models. Before considering the Scottish model in detail, there is an unusual scheme to consider, the Chartered London Teacher (CLT), available exclusively to teachers in London. This model is of interest less because it uses the term 'chartered' – although that is significant – and more because it focuses on teachers in a huge city with a remarkably diverse society and all the demands of a challenging and wildly unequal economic context.

As so many teachers are working, and will increasingly work, in just such complex, intensely urban settings, it seems likely to be generative of global comparison and insight. The standards for this model are very simple; that may be a limitation in some ways, but it might also provide a starting point for evidence-based comparisons.

The award in London could be achieved by both beginning teachers after five years and highly experienced teachers after two years (see the Chartered London Teacher website, www.clt.ac.uk). This is yet another scheme that will be discontinued from September 2016, although certified teachers will retain their status.

To give an idea of the London-centric focus, the standards are quoted below (from the website). They are worth quoting in full because of their emphasis on community and diverse populations. Given that this chapter opens with how global league tables like PISA lead to governments trying to copycat success (an example being the UK government's focus on learning from maths teaching in Shanghai), a valuable question might be whether expert teachers from different systems can learn from more directly comparable contexts – for example the mega cities of the twenty-first century? So, despite caveats indicated by reservations about, for example, the Shanghai-influenced project in England, it seems worth reviewing a chartered teacher model which focuses on being a highly competent teacher in the particular urban context of a major twenty-first-century city.

Chartered London Teacher standards

The four areas of standards, (1) Pedagogy and pupil learning, (2) Subject specialism and/or phase knowledge, (3) Whole-school issues and (4) Diversity, communities and cultures are a much simpler and more manageable model than the very much more sophisticated models we have reviewed so far. For example, the standards in area 1:

Pedagogy and pupil learning

1 Create and manage a classroom environment to ensure a secure and supportive achievement culture and behaviour strategy to meet the needs of London's diverse and mobile pupil population.
2 Apply a wide range of teaching and learning strategies to reduce individual barriers to learning and to meet the variety of pupil needs in London.
3 Develop and implement inclusive practices in a range of learning settings appropriate to the diversity of pupils in London and the complexity of their personal learning, including support for Special Education Needs, to raise pupils' achievements.
4 Progress partnerships within and beyond the classroom with support staff, teachers, other professionals, agencies and community resources, to promote pupils' achievements, learning, development and well-being.

5 Analyse and use relevant data to inform and promote the highest possible aspirations for pupils and to target expectations and actions to raise pupil achievements.

These standards are almost purely descriptive and avoid both rhetoric and any suggestion of levels of skill; they are focused on the London context and desirable teacher activities, defined by the simple verbs 'create', 'apply', 'develop', 'progress' and 'analyse'.

Subject, specialism and/or phase knowledge

6 Demonstrate ongoing development and application of subject, specialism and/or phase knowledge and expertise, drawing on opportunities and resources in London to enrich the learning experience.
7 Identify and use the knowledge and experiences that pupils, their families and other communities bring from outside the school to enrich curriculum development and teaching practices.

Whole-school issues

8 Contribute to the development and application of whole school policies and activities, to extend opportunities for pupil and school achievements in London.
9 Promote and apply shared professional learning and other forms of support and development for teachers to learn and work together, taking account of teacher mobility, to strengthen collective knowledge and expertise across teachers in London.

Diversity, communities and cultures

10 Build on, extend and apply knowledge of the range of communities, cultures and sub-cultures in London, to inform and promote individual pupils' learning.
11 Promote and implement policies and practices that encourage mutual tolerance and respect for diversity, challenge discrimination and widen pupils' understanding of their contribution to society.
12 Demonstrate a capacity to deal constructively and sensitively with conflicting community and cultural values in classrooms and schools.

There is certainly nothing contentious in these standards for most educators (politicians might not be so agreeable) and London could comfortably be changed to the name of many major cities in the Western world – increasingly, perhaps, any major city. However, these standards might be less relevant in relatively monocultural Helsinki, capital of Finland. This latter point highlights how population diversity may strongly affect notions of expert teaching.

There is perhaps an inevitable tension for all teachers (not just excellent ones) between working for the nation state and its claims for a particular identity and adopting a truly global and inclusive approach to educate young people to see the world as a place full of diverse but equal communities. This point supports the major argument of this book that there cannot be a superordinate model of expert teaching: diversity of models is a healthy and necessary global phenomenon from which systems can learn and introduce innovation and change. So does the London model offer ideas for New York, Sydney, Paris, Beijing, Dubai . . . ? The answer, we argue, is 'yes', but it is not a matter of cut and paste, it is adaptation. It is perhaps noteworthy too that the London model sought to celebrate and also retain London teachers, a notoriously difficult thing to manage in urban schools that have all the challenges of 'difficult' students, poverty, dysfunctional parents – the list is endless.

London (and other English cities) have also tried the US-inspired 'Teach First' scheme (see www.teachfirst.org.uk), which gives 'very clever' graduates six weeks' training and asks them to devote two years of their lives to working in a tough urban setting before going off to work for a big corporation or similar high-flying job (see graduates.teachfirst.org.uk). As this is not an 'expert teacher' model, we cite it here as another example of the kind of political initiative that, in our view, is more of a distraction for the profession and the public. They are high profile in a media sense, politicians trumpet their success with little evidence and they rarely last long enough to be evaluated in any serious depth, so whatever merits such a scheme may have are not captured and disseminated.

England developed a rather similar model called Fast Track, designed to develop future leaders of education; it began in 2001 and was scrapped in 2007. Again, it was not a model of expert teaching, but it was interesting for its emphasis on accelerated development and the fact that it was predicated on a necessary grounding in the classroom but also the proper rewarding of such teachers and their being offered high-level challenges throughout their first five years, including their training year. One of the authors of this book (Goodwyn) worked directly on this scheme as a provider (that is, offering fast-track places at his university) and as an assessor of candidates (a requirement to be a provider). It was a scheme with much to recommend it but it was cut long before its efficacy could be judged and it is now hard even to trace, especially as there was so little time for the academic community to provide any independent research (see Jones, 2010 for a small-scale study).

Overall, it is clear that expert teacher schemes need very considerable investment to set them up and must have sufficient life to provide any credible evidence of their impact if they are to address the complexities of teaching in any way. If the scheme is really only about retention, then after even a modest three years there would be some evidence to show whether or not it was working and whether the uptake meant that teachers were attracted by the model. Earlier, the 'Excellent Teacher' scheme in England was cited as a model that totally failed to attract teachers, whereas the Advanced Skills Teacher became a substantive element of the teaching profession: it attracted excellent candidates and they committed themselves to the scheme for the long term (Goodwyn and Fuller, 2011).

One of the key questions in the conceptualisation of models of expert teaching is how 'classroom only' is their focus or how much is the idea of the 'extended professional', especially its more ethical dimensions, addressed. The latter is extraordinarily difficult to assess and even more to 'measure' – at least given our very limited research base and statistical evidence. We argue in the final chapter that such 'measurement' is a chimera but that it is possible to *evaluate* these dimensions, based on human judgement and interpretation. It may be that sophisticated measures can be developed when expert teaching is better understood and has substantial investment and when schemes have built in sound modes of evaluation based on credible and independent academic evidence. The next section explores some models that are conceptualised to integrate some of the less measurable dimensions of expert teaching. The Scottish Chartered Teacher scheme (abolished in 2012) deserves special attention as one of the more developed schemes in the world in this sense.

Chartered teachers as a sophisticated model

We believe that one of the more imaginative and holistic approaches to expert teacher status has been the development of models using the term 'chartered'. This term is widely used in well-established and typically top-tier professions, some with a long history of using the term – for example, chartered accountants in England have used the term since 1854; other professions include engineering, architecture, management, marketing, financial analysts, physiotherapists and many more. In England this has a long history (see below) linked to being granted a Royal Charter. The point is that these sectors consider chartered status as a mark of the top professionals in that field. To become chartered will typically include many years of practice, undertaking further qualification beyond degree level and maintaining a record of continuing professional development. Once achieved, chartered status has considerable prestige attached to it and comes with a code of conduct allowing clients/the public to put their trust in such individuals, knowing that the professional body they represent will insist on high standards and remove the status if it is abused. Finally, the status usually comes with significant material gain: being an accountant is one thing, being chartered allows for much higher fees.

Essentially then, chartered status is the most desirable designation in many top professions. When one considers titles used in teaching such as Advanced Skills, Highly Accomplished, Leading, Outstanding and so on, they seem rather simplistic and narrow in scope. Bringing the term 'chartered' into teaching imports a degree of kudos, one familiar to the public and politicians and, potentially at least, providing some credibility to the profession itself, implying comparability with other, well-established and well-paid, professions. There are several examples; the London version has been briefly considered, but without claiming a great deal for its status. The Scottish model is the most developed version: quotations below come from the website of the General Teaching Council for Scotland (www.gtcs.org.uk).

The opening premise adopts the same approach as many other designations:

> **What are the benefits of Chartered Teacher status?**
>
> Experienced teachers have faced a difficult choice: to gain further rewards and respect for their professionalism, they have to move away from the classroom into a management post. However, by gaining Chartered Teacher status, with CPD advantage, you will:
>
> - increase your earning power
> - enhance you professional recognition and career progression
> - gain membership of the City and Guilds of London Institute (MCGI): a qualification comparable to a Master's degree
> - remain a classroom-based professional.
>
> By obtaining Chartered Teacher status, you can gain the respect and financial rewards appropriate for an experienced professional and you will gain additional knowledge, skills and abilities that will enable you to enhance the quality of learning experiences and achievements of the students you teach.

However, the standards for Chartered status went much further than some others and clearly articulate an extended professional model, including the idea of professional *action*:

> **The Standard**
>
> The Standard consists of four key components:
>
> - Professional values and personal commitments;
> - Professional knowledge and understanding;
> - Professional and personal attributes; and
> - Professional action.
>
> *(Scottish Government website)*

The stress is very much on the teacher as a caring, imaginative human being; this contrasts quite sharply with the AST:

> ***Professional Values and Personal Commitments***
>
> The Chartered Teacher, having developed beyond the basic requirements of the Standard for Full Registration, *should demonstrate four central professional values and personal commitments:*
>
> - *Effectiveness in promoting learning in the classroom*
>   Since teaching is about promoting learning, the Chartered Teacher must be strongly motivated to be effective in securing the well-being and educational progress of learners.

- *Critical self-evaluation and development*

  No matter how effective the Chartered Teacher may be, there is a commitment to enhanced performance. Practice is subject to regular review and there is a continuing search for new and improved ways of supporting pupils' learning through discussion with others and by reading and research.
- *Collaboration and influence*

  The Chartered Teacher will be committed to influencing and having a leading impact in team and school development, and to contributing to the professional development of colleagues and new entrants to the profession. As a member of a wider professional community, he or she will be committed to influencing the development of teaching and learning, and to strengthening partnerships with other professional groups, parents and other agencies.
- *Educational and social values*

  The Chartered Teacher is committed to core educational and social values, such as concern for truth, personal responsibility, equality, social justice and inclusion, and to pupils' personal, social, moral and cultural development.

The characteristics that these teachers must demonstrate very closely map Hattie's, but they also emphasise that the teacher is not just a reflective practitioner but also a deeply informed professional with a real awareness of research and publications:

> ***Professional Knowledge and Understanding***
>
> The Chartered Teacher *should demonstrate through his or her work a critical understanding of:*
>
> - current approaches to teaching and learning
> - current research on teaching and learning
> - changing social and cultural contexts of education
> - the school curriculum, its knowledge base, and how the curriculum relates to life in the community, including citizenship and the world of work
> - educational assessment and its interpretation
> - responses to pupil differences and to pupils experiencing barriers to learning
> - principles and practices of social justice, inclusion, equality and democracy, and strategies to counter discrimination
> - education and the promotion of personal well-being, and community and environmental development
> - teachers as co-educators with parents and other professionals
> - the nature of professionalism

- current policy debates
- ICT and its importance in teaching and learning.

This standard even mentions ICT, something missing from AST and HAT. Fundamentally, the Chartered Teacher is defined both holistically and morally, with a really clear emphasis on their humanity and caring.

Both the professional and the personal are articulated:

> ***Professional and Personal Attributes***
>
> The Chartered Teacher *should be able to demonstrate a range of skills and attributes that are characteristics of all forms of professional work:*
>
> - having enthusiasm and the capacity to motivate
> - communicating effectively
> - being resourceful and positive, and adopting a problem-solving approach
> - being creative and imaginative, and having an open attitude to change
> - being systematic and well organised, focused, determined and hardworking
> - demonstrating empathy and fairness, being caring and approachable
> - showing consistent performance across all professional areas.

Finally, the emphasis is not on just gaining the status but using it in the real world of school:

> ***Professional Action***
>
> As noted earlier, these professional values and personal commitments, knowledge and understanding, and professional and personal attributes must interact and result in professional action of various kinds.
>
> The consultation process confirms support for identifying *nine forms of professional action.* These can be categorised to correspond to the four professional values and personal commitments, namely, *Effectiveness in promoting learning in the classroom; Critical reflection, self-evaluation and development; Collaboration and influence; and Educational and social values.*

One example of such action is:

> articulating a personal, independent and critical stance in relation to contrasting perspectives on educational issues, policies and developments

And the instances given are:

> undertaking critical evaluations of official educational documents, research reports, articles or books in relation to the current debates in the educational and wider community engaging with others in the critical discussion of educational policy and practice

Whereas the AST tends to be characterised as carrying out policy (the technicist delivery model), the Chartered Teacher is far more critical and independent. The short-lived Excellent Teacher did have some requirements of this kind but never became a model with any significance. Overall, for the aspiring expert teacher the Chartered model is the one that captures in some depth the qualities of 'great' teachers; it may prove to have been the best of its kind in Europe, possibly the world, and could be a prototype for long-term development. Some might argue that because it was described as being within the reach of all experienced teachers, its status may be devalued. In the end it comes down to professional credibility and the development of a robust and fair assessment system.

One aspect of chartered status in any profession is that the award comes from a professional body which is self-regulating and free from political interference. The recent example in England of the designation Advanced Skills Teacher being abolished in 2013 could not happen to chartered architects or engineers: the term belongs to them alone. As a result, some organisations in England that have a specific focus have opted for Chartered Teacher. England's somewhat convoluted constitutional history means that these bodies tend to be Royal Societies (to become a 'learned society' originally involved a royal charter – the oldest in England, established in 1660, is simply called the Royal Society; its focus being essentially the sciences, there have been further developments in disciplines such as physics and chemistry).

The Geography Association's list of requirements for teachers seeking GA Chartered status (see GA website, www.geography.org.uk) is interesting for a number of reasons:

- Honours degree in geography or related subject (60 per cent geography content) or B.Ed with geography (or 15 years' teaching experience if no relevant degree is held);
- at least six years' teaching experience;
- commitment to CPD, embedding it in your own practice, and supporting others.

This is straightforward and it naturally stresses subject knowledge but it also emphasises demonstrating working with others (see Chapter 8). It then stresses the status that is on offer:

> If you are successful in your application for Chartered status you will also become a Fellow of the Royal Geographical Society (with IBG) if you are not so already.
>
> You can use existing documentation to support your application, such as:
>
> - your Professional Development Record, which can be used as evidence for the CPD portfolio required for award of CGeog (Teacher).
> - evidence you have collected for performance management.
>
> Where did these criteria originate?

The criteria for Chartered Geographer (Teacher) were set by the Privy Council.

This is a much more ideological inflection and reminds us of Eraut's point (see above) that professions are essentially ideologies; what could be more distinguished than recognition by the Privy Council?

The Association Science Education (ASE) emphasises the skilled nature of teaching:

> Science teaching is a demanding and complex process. Skilled science teachers, knowledgeable in pedagogy, science education and science deserve professional recognition. The ASE has worked in collaboration with the Science Council to create a mechanism which recognises and celebrates high quality science teachers and science education professionals through the award of Chartered Science Teacher (CSciTeach) status.
>
> The introduction of the CSciTeach designation provides for the first time an opportunity for individuals to gain an award which accredits and values their all round expertise in science education and their commitment to updating the knowledge, skills and understanding they require. CSciTeach, as our current President, Professor Sir Gareth Roberts, noted:
>
> '. . . will provide science teachers, working in a wide range of settings, with a professional status recognising and rewarding their high quality expertise which is in turn underpinned by a commitment to CPD. Ultimately the main beneficiaries, however, will be our pupils and students.'
>
> *(Education in Science, Feb 2005) (ASE website)*

But it combines this with a direct link to other, top-tier, professions:

> **What is CSciTeach?**
>
> CSciTeach, or Chartered Science Teacher, is a chartered designation in line with other awards, such as Chartered Scientist, Chartered Engineer, Chartered Accountant or Chartered Surveyor, that recognises the professional standing of an individual working in that field. The awards are made under powers granted by the Privy Council to particular organisations and incorporated in their Royal Charters. As a chartered designation CSciTeach recognises the unique and demanding combination of skills, knowledge, understanding and expertise that are required by individuals involved in practicing and advancing science teaching and learning.
>
> Chartered Science Teachers, therefore, are professionals, teachers and educators, who are practicing and/or advancing science teaching and learning and for whom knowledge and skills in pedagogy, science education and science are essential elements in their role. They will have a critical awareness of current issues which is informed by developments in educational practice, pedagogy and scientific endeavour.

The ASE rightly stresses that this kind of teacher recognition is not susceptible to government policies and has an equivalence that might make it globally recognisable:

> **Who awards CSciTeach?**
>
> ASE awards CSciTeach. Under the terms of its Royal Charter, ASE, as a licensed body of the Science Council, is empowered to award CSciTeach to individuals who meet the requirements and to maintain a register of holders of the designation. This register in turn is a special section of the register of Chartered Scientists (CSci) which underpins the quality and equivalence of the awards. In other words it means that CSciTeach will be widely accepted alongside other chartered qualifications.

Finally, it relates the instrinsic rewards and the extrinsic and returns to the key concept of expertise:

> **What are the benefits of CSciTeach?**
>
> As CSciTeach is in its infancy the benefits relate mainly to raising the overall profile of science teaching and learning and, for individuals, to providing recognition of their expertise and commitment. In time, as with other chartered designations, it is hoped that CSciTeach will provide access to more tangible benefits and rewards. Currently CSciTeach aims to:
>
> promote high-quality science teaching and learning;
> recognise high and improving professional expertise;
> reflect best effective practice in science education;
> provide evidence of a commitment to continuing professional development.

As has been argued already, this use of 'chartered' as a term is clearly an attempt to give teaching a comparable status to, say, chartered engineers, accountants, librarians and so on. It also places the award outside the vagaries of political policy change; AST and Excellent Teacher were not a status and, chiefly defined by pay levels, they could be abolished or diminished overnight – as, indeed, they have been. Equally, the AST role did not evolve over its ten years into a realistic expectation for the majority of experienced teachers; figures in 2009 suggest about 4,500 ASTs out of about 500,000 teachers.

Scotland aimed for 5,000 Chartered Teachers within five years; this would have been a very significant proportion of the teacher population. The model was worth considering in some detail as it was arguably the most developed of its kind in Europe (Connelly and McMahon, 2007). The GTCS made it clear that the focus was on teachers staying in the classroom and achieving more recognition at the same time.

The Chartered Teacher in Scotland has been replaced by a new set of standards encapsulated as the Standard for Career-Long Professional Learning, supporting the development of teacher professional learning (GTCS, 2012). These standards retain the spirit of the Chartered Teacher but do not link to a status or designation.

An outlier model and distributed model: teachers in Finland

One Western country that has consistently excelled in PISA ratings over the years and is highly regarded across the globe as a leading education nation is Finland. Its sustained success has for a long time prompted educationalists to consider how Finland has achieved this and has encouraged other developed systems to see if they might distill the magic Finnish ingredient in order to inject it into their less successful jurisdictions. We describe Finland as an 'outlier' model because it appears to be a system that fosters expert teachers with no need for a model or a career structure. In that sense it appears to contradict the message of this book, which is that expert teacher models matter and can be adapted between systems. Our argument is that Finland is so exceptional as to be a non-generative example: it is not for copying or even adaptation. It provides a sharp contrast to most developed systems across the world, but, with its population of 5.4 million (Greater London alone has at least 8.6 million), offers no solution to their deep-seated problems.

The reasons behind Finland's success (Sahlberg, 2015) are complex, perhaps unique, not because they have an incomprehensible approach to education but because the evolved working parts of their system are, it seems, in a remarkable and harmonious relationship.

In Finland, teaching is a long-established and prestigious career. Children certainly aspire to be doctors and lawyers and to join the other high-status professions, but they are equally attracted to becoming teachers. This is in part because teachers are respected and appreciated; they are highly qualified (requiring a master's degree for full-time employment) and job selection is a challenging process with only top candidates securing a job. Even more challenging is the selection process for trainees: typically in any year only about 10 per cent of applicants secure a training place. However, it is also important to stress that selection is not determined by academic prowess alone – it is a factor but not dominant. The eventual high level of qualification by all teachers is seen as an outcome of being a good teacher. We argue that in such an outlier system, teacher expertise is part of the normal culture of all teachers and in that sense is a form of distributed intelligence that gives all teachers access to that knowledge and culture throughout their careers. We are sure that the reality of life for teachers is not quite as perfect as this sounds, but we are also clear that Finland does not need a specific model of expert teaching, certainly not in the near future. What Finland offers is a system with hugely desirable characteristics that foster expert teaching, and these can certainly be adapted by other systems, however different they may be.

The Finnish curriculum is much less obviously 'academic' than that of many comparable nations. Finnish students have the least number of class hours per week in the developed world but achieve the best results in the long term. Students in Finland sit no compulsory exams until age 17–19. Schools use teacher-based assessment, the approach is essentially descriptive and used in a formative manner to inform feedback and assessment for learning.

Very significant emphasis is put on pupil and teacher trust and well-being. This is especially pertinent here as we argue strongly for a research agenda that seeks to provide evidence for how such complex concepts as 'trust' may be properly acknowledged in models of expert teaching. Can trust be measured, or perhaps more importantly, can it be understood as a key factor in excellent teaching? A feature of the Finnish curriculum is that outdoor and practical learning opportunities and health-related physical activity sessions are a normal feature of everyday school life, enabling the maintenance of a healthy body and mind: this is hardly the stuff of hot-house achievement.

Finnish schools are truly autonomous: head teachers and teachers have considerable independence in developing and delivering their own individual curricula, adapted to their locality. Teachers are encouraged to evolve multiple pedagogic approaches rather than just 'teacher-proof' approved models, and such pedagogical freedom generates a much greater degree of creativity, teacher pro-activity and classroom-level innovation. The emphasis on individual emotional well-being for students and teachers creates a contiguous culture where all members of the school community have an aligned aspiration – that is, to learn, but also to learn together, and not for league table outcomes or to pass inspection.

The Finnish Ministry of Education's philosophy is consistently to trust the professionals, parents and communities to determine local policy and practice, and yet this translates into the highest levels of national academic success. In simple terms, high-quality teachers are appreciated and trusted and are enabled to carry out the job effectively and as they see fit. Changing political agendas are not reflected in schools or the curriculum and, as a result, what pertains is a school system that is stable yet innovative and a teacher workforce that is secure but highly motivated to improve.

The government does play its part, not by intervening but by resourcing, so, in Finland, all students receive a free education from seven years of age and until they complete their university studies. Equally, all pupils receive free school meals, resources, materials, transport and support services.

An inclusive approach means that all classes are mixed ability, with most containing two or more teachers and the emphasis on ensuring that students needing additional support receive it in the classroom rather than being segregated. The majority of teachers stay with one class for many years, moving with the students through their entire school experience and so developing deep-seated relationships.

Most schools are combined primary and secondary, so avoiding damaging transitions and providing a consistent ethos and common approach for the whole of the students' time in the institution. There is a remarkably informal culture: students address teachers by their Christian names, do not wear uniforms and are encouraged to relax in the classroom and in the school; parents normally have a teacher's personal telephone number. The teacher's 'authority' is not, therefore, as an authority figure but as 'authorised', that is given status through recognition.

The success of the Finnish system is evidenced in international league tables and may well seem remarkable to educational systems which endlessly measure standards and effectiveness through standardised data, high-stakes testing, performance tables and inspection regimes. Finnish schools seem characterised by a lack of relentless competition; instead they have a cooperative ethos that enables the sharing of best practice and focuses on teaching as a holistic activity rather than represented by a fragmented set of workers in separate silos.

In summary, Finland is remarkable and its world-class reputation is thoroughly deserved. It may not be unique as a country in the sense that some other countries are similar to it in some ways, but we know of no others that come close to it in terms of a high-quality system that all stakeholders support. It has remarkable stability and has provided solid evidence that a very good system can endure without endless reforms and innovations. In Finland the teachers are trusted to be innovative in the classroom and at school level.

In essence, then, Finland is so exceptional that it is not a model that can be copied or imitated, as least not in the first half of the twenty-first century. What we have to recognise is that while expert teaching can develop in many countries, different models will need to be tried until the best one is found for what is likely to be a much less benign culture than Finland's. We have consistently argued that systems can, and should, learn from each other; Finland offers long-term vision and aspiration but not a short-term political 'fix'. In the next two decades, all developed systems need to invest in research and development to identify and retain the best classroom teachers and to investigate how to nurture a climate of teaching and learning in which expertise can thrive.

Singapore: a centralist but teacher-centred model

We conclude this chapter on emerging models with a look at a country that might be compared to Finland in terms of size (Finland 5.4 million, Singapore 5.7), educational aspirations, relative political stability and the significant resources devoted to schools and teachers. It is also comparable in that teaching has high status and attracts some of the best graduates. However, it is equally interesting for its contrasts to Finland.

Singapore is not an open and transparent system like Finland. It makes statements such as:

> Teachers – The Heart of Quality Education
> Singapore Growing a World Class Education Service

> To sustain a high-performing education system, Singapore's educators will take on an active role in shaping the development of their profession. MOE is committed to supporting the teaching profession in developing a new Teacher Development Centre as a focal point for teacher professional development. MOE will also strengthen the career development opportunities for educators who wish to deepen their expertise in teaching.
>
> *(Ministry of Education press release, 9 Sept 2009)*

Statements like this appear, suddenly and simply, just as a press release, often accompanied by a speech. Policy documents and consultations are not the 'style' of Singapore; rather, announcements and directives are the normal discourse. Yet the rhetoric is remarkably similar to that of many other developed systems: the quotation above has the classic statement, 'growing a world class education service'. However, with Singapore such a claim has real resonance. Its students certainly perform very well in the PISA and similar tests and, more importantly for this book, its school system attracts and retains some of the best graduates. Perhaps the most striking recognition that Singapore has achieved is its starring role in the highly influential McKinsey report on how the best systems continue to improve (Mourshed, Chijioke and Barber, 2010), where it is singled out as the most consistently improving system and is used by the authors as an indicator of how the very best systems pay the most attention to teacher professional development. They state:

> Singapore provides an example of how a system shifts in emphasis as it goes through the various stages of the entire improvement journey, from poor to great, as Singapore has done over the past forty years. During this time it has decreased central guidance on teaching and learning as its system performance has risen. Singapore system leaders describe their system as having gone through three phases: 'Survival-driven' (1959–78), 'Efficiency-driven' (1979–96), and 'Ability-driven' (1997–present). Singapore's Survival phase was primarily focused on enrolment and ensuring that every child had a school seat. This resulted in schools being built at the rate of one per month and the teaching force doubling, from 10,500 in 1959 to over 19,000 by 1968. By the end of this period, Singapore had achieved near universal primary education. However, almost 30 per cent of primary school pupils did not progress to secondary school, and English language proficiency was low and educational wastage high (in terms of failing to achieve the expected standards and leaving school prematurely). The Efficiency phase focused on reducing performance variation across the school system. 'Our challenge was how to achieve above average outcomes from below average inputs,' recalls one Singaporean leader. Students were streamed into different tracks based on their aptitude, not only to reduce dropout rates, but just as importantly, to ease the burden on teachers so that they only taught classes of students with similar capability levels. Simultaneously, Singapore created the Curriculum

> Development Institute of Singapore (CDIS) in 1980 in order to develop a suite of supporting teaching materials that could be used off-the-shelf by less-experienced and less-skilled teachers. A Singaporean system leader recalls, 'For each lesson, we created the lesson plan, the teacher manual, the student workbook, and the activity or experiment or video that would open the lesson.' Each classroom in the same grade and subject level received exactly the same resources, and CDIS held workshops with teachers to explain how to use the materials effectively. Moreover, teachers had to keep a record book of their classroom activities, which were submitted to the principal every Monday. Regular student assessments enabled the Ministry of Education to monitor student outcome progress. As one system leader noted, 'We were highly prescriptive in our teaching and had a mass production mindset. . . . We were textbook-bound and examination-driven.' Through the 1980s and 1990s, Singapore raised the floor of performance in the system significantly, and narrowed the achievement gap across its ethnic groups (Exhibit 22) Singapore moved from rigid prescription to greater flexibility as it embarked on its good to great improvement journey.
>
> *(Mourshed, Chijioke and Barber, 2010)*

The report argues that this centralist, controlling model was a necessary stage for the Singaporean system at that time, making it possible for a different approach to developing teacher expertise to emerge.

> By the end of the 1980s, Singapore had introduced school formats that had greater autonomy, including establishing Independent Schools in 1988 and Autonomous Schools in 1994. By 1995, Singapore's school system was among the top-performing systems in the world, topping TIMSS rankings in both math and science that year. The Curriculum Development Institute of Singapore closed its doors in 1996 because 'it was no longer needed.' Then, in 1997, Singapore launched 'Thinking Schools, Learning Nation' (TSLN), marking the start of its Ability phase and emphasizing a shift in focus toward enabling each student to reach the maximum of his or her potential. This focus on student ability required schools to be given much greater flexibility and responsibility for how they should teach and manage their students. TSLN gave teachers greater freedom in classroom practice, and gave principals decision rights on school management matters. It introduced school clusters to create a peer-based forum for school leadership development and the sharing of effective teaching and learning practices across schools. It also changed its school inspection model, replacing the previous highly centralized model with a more collaborative one focused on self-assessment and quality assurance. Throughout the latter period, Singapore worked intensively on strengthening the caliber of its teachers and principals so that they could make the best use of their greater freedoms. It established a system that accommodated three career tracks (Leadership,

> Teaching, and Senior Specialist), narrowed recruitment into teaching to the top one-third of each graduating cohort, expanded professional development to one hundred hours per year, and creating mentorship pairings for school leaders.
>
> *(Ibid.)*

In this section the report traces the move away from a highly prescriptive approach to teaching and towards a teacher-centred approach, with a high-quality workforce that is continuously improving and a career pathway that is keeping the best teachers in the classroom and working with other teachers to improve their practice.

> More recently it has focused on strengthening the networks of Professional Learning Communities (PLCs) in schools that encourage teachers to collaborate with one other in reviewing and improving their classroom practice. In the words of one system leader, 'As the skills of our educators rose, we needed to change our approach in how we managed them. We could no longer prescribe what they did, we had to treat them like professionals who had good judgment, knew their students well, and who could make their own decisions.' Singapore's experience focuses us on a second important question about control: whether the degree of prescription and flexibility within a school system can or should vary within that system.

This move to 'treating them like professionals' and acknowledging their 'good judgement' resonates very strongly with the ethos in Finland. The report at this point in its argument comments interestingly on England:

> The answer is that it can: there are examples in our sample in which the school system has given more attention to scripting its low-performing schools while providing more flexibility to the higher performing ones. England, when on the fair to good journey in 1996, launched a literacy and numeracy program, tightening guidance over classroom practice. The system cascaded improvement targets to each school and mandated that every day every student should be given a 'literacy hour' and a 'daily maths lesson,' and provided teachers with models of literacy and numeracy instruction that they were expected to use if they could not demonstrate higher performance on their own. High-performing schools that were already exceeding minimum proficiency targets were exempt from this prescription.

This is not, in our view, accurate. During the entire period of the National Literacy Strategy schools experienced a huge degree of surveillance and inspection (Goodwyn and Fuller, 2011). It must be noted that Michael Barber is not only one of the authors of the McKinsey reports but was also the driving force behind the National Literacy Strategy (Goodwyn and Fuller, 2011). We would argue that a generation of teachers was *deskilled* by the strategy and our point is that systems can most definitely regress if they remove autonomy and individual responsibility from teachers as this leads to an erosion of professionalism across the whole system and seriously weakens its expertise.

The report also covers the way Singapore rewards and encourages its best teachers and all teachers to become increasingly expert:

> These systems recruit top-performing students into the teaching profession, and so aim to provide competitive remuneration relative to other professions. For example, in Singapore, teachers currently receive a salary that is one notch higher than that of civil servants with equivalent qualifications performing general administrative functions. In addition, top-performing teachers receive a bonus that is the equivalent of up to three months' salary.
>
> *(Mourshed, Chijioke and Barber, 2010)*

The report stresses the fundamental emphasis on professional development but also development that fits individual teachers' aspirations:

> systems undergoing the great to excellent journey seek to provide a greater number of professional development hours, but allow teachers flexibility in selecting the topics that are most relevant to their own development needs. For example, in Singapore, where teachers are encouraged to participate in one hundred hours of training each year, they are free to select the training modules that fulfill their own interests and needs.

Singapore certainly deserves praise for its relentless attention to supporting teacher development, and it continues to evolve. Its emerging career structure for teachers is now one of the most calibrated in the world. The only real source for understanding Singapore's focus on developing expert teachers is the official ministry website, often through press releases (as above) or summaries of speeches. The first quotations below indicate the attention to all teachers; later there is more focus on the higher levels of teaching:

> **Growing a World Class Education Service**
>
> To sustain a high-performing education system, Singapore's educators will take on an active role in shaping the development of their profession. MOE is committed to supporting the teaching profession in developing a new Teacher Development Centre as a focal point for teacher professional development. MOE will also strengthen the career development opportunities for educators who wish to deepen their expertise in teaching.

This is a typical example of their centralist approach, but is followed by:

> ***Nurturing a Teacher-Driven Culture of Professional Excellence***
>
> (i) Supporting the Development of Schools as Professional Learning Communities
>
> MOE will strengthen the network of Professional Learning Communities (PLCs) where teachers come together regularly to share and learn from one another. Such continuous professional dialogue and feedback are critical to driving enhancement and innovation in the classroom. PLCs will provide teachers the platform for continuous dialogue to lead and drive improvements, hone their own classroom practice and maintain their professional currency. Over time, these communities could extend across schools, to the cluster level and eventually to the national level.

The nature of the language is interesting, the almost maternal word 'nurturing' being very atypical of most political rhetoric.

> (ii) Establishing a Teacher Development Centre
>
> MOE will also support the establishment of a Teacher Development Centre (TDC) as a focal set-up for teachers to gather and work collectively towards a higher level of professional competence. For teachers, and run by teachers, the TDC will build their instructional capacity, draw out pedagogical leadership from the fraternity, as well as advance continuous learning and improvement. It will serve as a source of expertise for the PLCs, and be a key enabler in achieving the Vision for the Teaching Service – Singapore Teachers: Lead. Care. Inspire. By championing professional values and the core of practice underpinning the teaching profession, the TDC can also help to build a deep sense of pride, identity, ownership and collaborative professionalism among teachers.

More detail follows but, most unusually, the Ministry of Education did undertake a consultation with teachers to ensure that the new career structure was supported by the profession.

> MOE's Director-General of Education, Ms Ho Peng, will lead a team of educators to engage the teaching fraternity on proposals for the implementation of the TDC. In the coming months, the team will consult with teachers to explore how best the TDC can be organised to meet its aspirational goals. In particular, the consultation aims to draw out the teachers' views on how the TDC can support the continued growth of the teaching fraternity as a community of professionals.

Singapore's investment in teachers is quite remarkable, as is their development of a highly calibrated career structure for the best teachers, making it very attractive to stay in the classroom. Teachers can choose one of three tracks:

> Education Officers have a choice of three career tracks – Leadership, Senior Specialist and Teaching. MOE will further enhance career opportunities for teachers on the Teaching Track with a new apex appointment for Principal Master Teacher, the creation of a new Lead Teacher position, and appointment of more Senior Teacher positions. This will help to groom a core group of experts that will further develop the pedagogical capability of the teaching force.

Those who choose the teaching track can aspire to

> ***Apex Appointment – Principal Master Teacher***
>
> Master Teachers, as leading practitioners on the Teaching Track, are role model teachers who mentor other teachers to achieve professional excellence. As 'teachers of teachers', Master Teachers play a valuable role in curricular innovation, championing their subject discipline and driving new pedagogies to uplift teaching practices in schools.
>
> In recognition of their role, MOE will raise the apex of the Teaching Track from the current Master Teacher Level 2 to a new Superscale-grade Principal Master Teacher appointment. As the chief pedagogical experts for their subjects at the national level, Principal Master Teachers will lead the fraternity to drive teaching excellence across the education system.
>
> Master Teachers Level 1 will also take on greater responsibilities as pedagogical leaders and their job level will be raised to the equivalent of a Vice-Principal. While primarily attached to MOE Headquarters, Principal Master Teachers and Master Teachers will teach master-classes in schools, lead the professional development of their colleagues, drive curricular innovation in schools, and engage in pedagogical research and innovation.

If this were not remarkable enough, every school has a Lead Teacher:

> At the school level, MOE will introduce a new Lead Teacher position to champion a culture of teaching excellence and collaborative professionalism. Steeped in subject knowledge and pedagogical skills, the Lead Teacher will lead Senior Teachers and partner school leaders to build professional capacity within the school in the areas of subject content, pedagogy and assessment. Lead Teachers will also play a key role in developing their schools into vibrant Professional Learning Communities, and grow the teaching profession by sharing their subject expertise with other teachers within the cluster.

All of this is backed up by the creation of the Academy for Singapore Teachers and a massive programme of ongoing professional development called the Framework for Teaching, including support for gaining a higher degree:

> MOE will also provide more opportunities for Senior Teachers, Lead Teachers and Master Teachers to pursue postgraduate training in pedagogical areas and to participate in a range of overseas attachment programmes that would enable them to exchange international best practices in pedagogy and educational research.

And all this should lead to a world-class education for students:

> A quality teaching force with a strong expertise in curriculum and pedagogy and a culture of continual professional development are key to preparing students with the knowledge, skills and attributes required for the 21st-century workforce. MOE will continue in its efforts to build a quality teaching force and grow a world-class education service for our students.

Finally, this system, centralised though it be, is also very flexible:

> There will be flexibility for lateral movements across the different tracks. Education Officers can choose to move across the different career tracks, as long as they satisfy the standards and criteria of the job / career track they aspire to take on.
>
> Like any other profession, career advancement is only limited by your own performance and potential.

This system proposed in 2009 is now fully operational in Singapore, although evidence of how it is working is not officially available. The teacher growth model is symbolised by an opal and the line 'every teacher a gem'. Teachers are encouraged to see themselves as demonstrating that they are:

- A community builder
- An ethical educator
- A transformational leader
- A collaborative learner
- A competent professional.

What is striking here is that there is so much emphasis on the least measurable dimensions of teaching.

While there can be no disputing the facts of the economic investment in teachers and the creation of the teaching career infrastructure, we have no studies of the teachers themselves and how they experience this system. Singapore students always come very high in the PISA rankings but, as we continue to argue, these tables are only based on test results and measurable outcomes.

Conclusion

This chapter has attempted to capture newer forms of expert teaching such as the various Chartered models and how two very different systems, Finland and Singapore, develop the best teachers. It has also explored some issues around comparability in relation to the London model and whether certain kinds of context might help with productive comparisons. Throughout we have looked critically at international comparisons, whether PISA or the Global Teacher Status Index. Overall it is clear that many countries are grappling with the development and retention of the best teachers in the classroom, offering such teachers attractive career structures, status recognition and other roles directly related to the classroom. In the final chapter we move to considering the future.

References

ASE website: www.ase.org.uk

Barber, M. and Mourshed, M. (2007) *How the World's Best-performing School Systems Come Out On Top*. New York: McKinsey & Co.

Chartered London Teacher website: www.clt.ac.uk

Connelly, G. and McMahon, M. (2007) 'Chartered teachers: Accrediting professionalism for Scotland's teachers – a view from the inside', *Journal of In-Service Education* 33(1): 91–105.

DCSF (2009) *Standards for Teachers*. London: DCSF.

DfE (Department for Education) (2014) 'Experts to visit Shanghai to raise UK maths standards', press release, 18 February. London: DfE.

Donaldson, G. (2010) *Teaching Scotland's Future*. Edinburgh: Scottish Government. Available at: www.scotland.gov.uk/Publications/2011/01/13092132/0

Fuller, C., Goodwyn, A. and Francis-Brophy, E. (2012) 'Being an advanced skills teacher: Professional identity and status'. *Teachers and Teaching: Theory and Practice* 19(4): 463–474.

Goodwyn, A. and Fuller, C. (eds) (2011) *The Great Literacy Debate*. London: Routledge.

GTCS (General Teaching Council for Scotland) website: www.gtcs.org.uk

Jones, J. (2010) 'Leadership lessons from the Fast Track programme for teachers in England'. *Educational Management Administration & Leadership* 38: 149–163.

Mourshed, M., Chijioke, C. and Barber, M. (2010) *How the World's Most Improved Schools Systems Keep Getting Better*. New York: McKinsey & Co.

Sahlberg, P. (2015) *Finnish Lessons 2:0: What Can the World Learn From Educational Change in Finland?* (2nd edition). New York: Teachers College.

'Teach First' scheme website: www.teachfirst.org.uk

TLTP Education (2014) 'Shanghai maths teachers to share best practice', press release, 5 November: news.tltp.co.uk (accessed 21 Jan 2015, 11.30 a.m.).

Varkey Foundation (2016) 'Global Teacher Status Index'. Available at: www.varkey foundation.org/teacherindex

8

THE FUTURE OF MODELS OF EXPERT TEACHING

Politics, policy and sustainability

Andrew Goodwyn

This chapter draws out the trends and patterns across the world and offers comparisons of successful and problematic developments. It includes a review of the very latest policies and practices and makes recommendations about the future directions of the expert teacher role. It also argues for further research and new forms of research that will allow us to escape mechanistic measurements of expert teaching such as test scores. A new paradigm is needed in which expertise is understood in its cultural and historical context and the benefit of such models is clearly linked to teacher status and student well-being and self-efficacy rather than the reductive pressures of standards alone.

Policy and politics

We would argue that policy in relation to the recruitment and retention of the best teachers remains a fundamental weakness in most developed systems. In many places, using the term 'policy' is not even accurate as there has never been a considered policy, just more 'initiatives'. England is a spectacular case of constant change by successive governments and ministers, recent examples being the 2013 termination of the AST and the vague proposal for a 'Master' teacher. There is one potentially promising development, a college of teaching, which will be considered below. Scotland looked to stand out and have a really thought-through policy, but its Chartered Teacher model is defunct and its new standard (see Chapter 7), however well intentioned, has replaced a powerful concept with what is essentially an innocuous guideline.

In true federal style the US approach has been to have no central government policy but to allow the development of the independent National Board for Professional Teaching Standards (NBPTS), and it can be argued that this balance – no political policy and an independent body – is an option for many countries. Australia has had distinct state policies and no national overarching scheme until a recent development in 2012. This chapter will, amongst other things, build on Chapter 6 and review the National Board as an independent, politically neutral organisation with genuine autonomy and a sustainable future, and speculate on the promise of the migration of the HAT model to Australia.

In all instances one might argue that there should be government policy related to the long-term future and status of the teaching profession, with a focus on expert teaching. The essential practical question, 'How do you keep the best teachers wishing to continue in the classroom?', and the supplementary one, 'How do you help these teachers to disseminate their knowledge to other teachers?', are factors in every developed system. This is such a well-understood point that systems should be examining models and evaluating how they might offer solutions. There is a simplistic view that has already been explored about merely rewarding the 'highest performing' teachers, not the rest, in the belief that this approach will somehow do the trick. Our view is that this can only have disastrous consequences for morale and retention and will make teachers direct competitors with each other, with no inclination to share their best practice. Schools will be equally competitive to attract the highest performing teachers and the endless issue of 'failing schools' will be perpetuated.

Our argument is that two clear options are emerging for policy. If a central or federal government truly wishes to raise the status of the profession and attract and retain some of the best graduates, it needs to build the reputation of the teaching profession over generations, not electoral cycles. This is not a naïve view, even if it is, in a sense, looking for an ideal. The history of the last 30 years is clear in most countries, and it is one of repeated failures despite huge investment; the exceptions, such as Singapore and Finland, do not offer replicable models. England, once again, provides the perfect example, with its very expensive Fast Track scheme (discussed earlier) scrapped just as it was about to achieve some of the aims for which it was set up. It was also scrapped before any robust evaluation of its effectiveness took place, so nothing was learnt from it as an experiment – except that political interference was the villain of the piece. The observation that change is not necessarily progress comes to mind. Finland stands out as a quietly effective environment in which a combination of investment and trust of the teaching profession has created a truly remarkable professional context in which students thrive and achieve, parents are happy and teachers have high status and job satisfaction; they appear also to be the best qualified teacher workforce in the world (see Chapter 7). However, as we have argued, Finland, like Singapore, is an outlier, in this instance, which means its model of success is not easily replicable and, indeed, might be seen as something of a distraction because it is better conceptualised as 'unique'.

Raising the status of the profession has many dimensions but must begin with attracting the 'best people', whether newly graduated or changing career. 'Best people' is a deliberately broad term as there is no proven link between, for example, academic excellence and effective teaching. The art of teaching is too complex to reduce to counting qualifications and grades; however, this is no reason not to seek the 'best people' – i.e. those who combine excellent academic knowledge with excellent personal qualities suited to teaching. Essentially policymakers need to escape from the reductive notion that excellent subject knowledge, demonstrated by academic qualification, is the Holy Grail and that all other factors are minor in comparison.

Our concern in this book is with the other dimension, which may be simply expressed as 'retention' but crucially concerns retaining the best teachers *in the classroom* and developing teachers who are *leaders of teaching and learning*. We argue that government policy should be designed to facilitate the development of an expert teacher model that is supported by the teaching profession. We believe teachers should feel a pride in the outstanding practice of certain colleagues who are, in every sense, exemplary. If the profession has ownership of the model, most issues of elitism would be irrelevant. If the profession is committed to a properly and rigorously tested means of selection of these teachers, then issues of its credibility are also countered. Finally, if the opportunity is open to all but the numbers selected reflect the fact that only some teachers, at that point, meet the criteria, then the selection process itself will be respected and supported. This is where the US National Board stands out as a credible model.

It is important to make the distinction between a society like Finland and a 'credible model'. Finland's success is clearly significantly related to a political and cultural consensus within a democratic society, and we would argue this is almost certainly a unique situation. Other societies may exercise high state control, meaning they can *impose* expert models; others are in democracies but riven with endless political short-termist interference where such models (the AST, Chartered, etc.) simply come and go. The NBPTS survives within a riven democracy mostly by being outside political interference, hence it is a 'credible model' for most developed systems.

The National Board: a credible model that can speak to policymakers

The US National Board was established not by government policy but by the vision of an independent body, free from governmental interference. We have covered this history in detail in Chapter 6. Here the focus is on the future and especially the Board's attempts to influence policy, as it were, from the 'outside' and thus keep its independence. Its credibility and longevity also allow it to be a strong and respected advocate for the profession, with an increasing body of evidence, some of it research based, of the importance of its mission and impact of its certified teachers. It is an important point that one principle underlying this development was the somewhat intractable independence of the individual states, so it might be argued that the independence of the NBPTS was more of an unintended consequence than a brilliant strategy. However, after more than 25 years of reasonable success and sustainability, that does not mean it cannot now be considered as offering a credible model.

For example, this particular aspect is also of relevance to Australia, a federal nation, and is one reason why we think the relatively new Highly Accomplished and Lead Teacher model in this country has a good chance to succeed and become stable. Teacher certification remains at state level, with teachers technically only qualified to teach in one state, and one aim of the NBPTS was to certify teachers at a higher level. Essentially this has been a great success, although there is little evidence that NBPTS certification has meant more teacher mobility – which may not be of much significance.

However, the Board has increasingly acted as an advocate for 'Advancing the profession' and it states (see the website) as one of its two strategic goals, 'Promoting a vision of accomplished teaching that elevates the profession', adding the objective: 'Advancing Education Policy' by engaging 'with district, state and federal policymakers and other stakeholders to support education policy that empowers teachers and improves student learning, growth and achievement'. By working in this way the Board is following the recommendation made in the major review of its work by the National Research Council (see Chapter 6): 'The NBPTS should continue to invest in its larger mission of influencing the teaching field in broad, comprehensive ways' (NRC, 2008, pp. 261–262). We argue that this may be the best kind of model for the future – an independent body of sufficient credibility and substance to be a constant influence on policy.

The website has a direct set of comments about the Board's relationship to, first, federal and second, state policymaking.

> **Federal Policy**
>
> The National Board actively works with Congress, the U.S. Department of Education and other federal agencies to shape education policy that advances teaching and learning.
>
> This includes providing research to inform effective legislation, sharing *success stories* from National Board Certified Teachers across the country and providing testimony on important issues in education reform. Most importantly, it involves bringing the voices of accomplished teachers from the classroom to the Capitol.
>
> *(NBPTS website)*

This is a bold and emphatic claim and the use of the word 'testimony' is interesting, perhaps a more legalistic and persuasive influence on politicians for whom evidence is notoriously unconvincing. The statement also includes examples of successful engagements, and these are very well worth quoting as globally expert teacher schemes have produced little evidence of impact on the larger system.

We are arguing here that this level of detail is not 'parochial' but precise and specific. For example:

> **STEM [Science, Technology, Engineering and Maths] Master Teacher Corps**
>
> The National Board has endorsed legislation introduced by Senator Al Franken (D-MN) to fund the creation of a national STEM Master Teacher Corps as part of the reauthorization of the Elementary and Secondary Education Act (ESEA). Members of the corps would receive a $15,000 annual bonus if teaching in a high-need school or a $5,000 annual bonus if teaching in a non-high-need school. Under the bill, one of the proposed criteria for selecting members of the STEM Master Teacher Corps is achieving National Board Certification. Senator Franken originally introduced this bill in April 2011 and reintroduced it in February 2013.
>
> In July 2012, five National Board Certified Teachers and National Board President and CEO Ron Thorpe participated in a White House event announcing the Obama Administration's support for the creation of the STEM Master Teacher Corps.
>
> **College and Career Ready Classrooms Act**
>
> In March 2012, the National Board endorsed a bill by Senator Tom Harkin (D-Iowa), which would direct investments to states and districts to provide teachers with the professional development necessary to successfully implement college- and career-ready standards. The bill would also create new career pathways for teachers to serve as coaches and mentors and in other teacher leadership roles to implement instructional strategies aligned to college- and career-ready standards.
>
> *(NBPTS website)*

These are clearly very US-specific and perhaps short-term initiatives that are, in themselves, subject to political change. However, they are concrete evidence of influence at federal level.

Equally, the Board works with the numerous state policymakers to ensure that there is a connection between their federal work and their state work. They set out their approach as follows:

> **State Policy**
>
> The National Board serves as a platform to elevate the voices of National Board Certified Teachers (NBCTs) as advocates for policies that advance teaching and learning in their states and districts.
>
> As proven experts on what works in the classroom, NBCTs are frequently asked to share their ideas and opinions with state and local policymakers. The

> National Board provides support and resources to NBCT networks across the country to reach state legislators and other leaders to shape effective education policies and practices. This includes helping to connect stakeholders to create powerful coalitions, organizing stakeholder and media events that build momentum, providing research and data that demonstrate the impact of accomplished teaching and providing advocacy training to ensure that we move the needle.
>
> *(NBPTS website)*

This latter point, about the consistent and continuous advocacy of the Board to build coalitions and create connections, is especially important. All 'high-performing jurisdictions', even smaller ones such as Singapore and Finland, have considerable variety in their geographies and local constituencies. Teachers always work in specific communities, however diverse – that is, they work at a very local level whether in a metropolis or a deeply rural village or town. We focused on this point when looking at the London Chartered Teacher designation. The sustained and patient effort by NBPTS to connect the local and the national is emphasised by holding annual Hill Days – that is, days focused on Capitol Hill, the seat of power and policymaking:

> NBCT networks across the country have annual Hill Days which provide a focused opportunity to meet with legislators to provide the latest information about the positive impact that NBCTs are having as teacher leaders in and out of the classroom.
>
> - To learn about the availability of state and local funding and incentives for National Board Certification, click *here*.
> - To find out how to contact your elected officials, click *here*.
> - Also, join your local *NBCT Network* to learn more about policy activities in your area.
>
> *(NBPTS website)*

Here are some examples of NBCT advocacy activities from around the country:

- The New Mexico NBCT Network works with members of the state legislature to have new NBCTs recognized on the floor of the House and Senate. This special event highlights the growth of NBCTs in a variety of certificate areas. NBCTs from around the state are able to meet with their legislators to celebrate their achievement. The event is planned for the same weekend as the network's annual conference, which provides another opportunity for NBCTs and candidates to share ideas for the best policies and practices in their classrooms.
- In Wyoming, the Ellbogen Foundation provided an opportunity for the NBCTs from around the state to come together and develop bold new

> ideas for continuing to improve in their practice. After the summit, the NBCT Teacher Leaders developed a white paper to share with stakeholders and policy makers.
>
> *(NBPTS website)*

In summary, the National Board has an enviable history as a sustainable model for developing teacher expertise and recognising and accrediting it and remaining safe from political interference. In 2013 it reached a milestone (on its own terms) as there were finally more than 100,000 certified teachers, with some in every state. In real terms this is a small proportion of the estimated total of serving US teachers according to 2011 National Center for Educational statistics of 3.7 million state school teachers and 0.4 million in the private sector; our calculation, excluding the private sector, is that this amounts to perhaps 3 per cent. The English AST was never more than 1 per cent and the Chartered teacher model of Scotland, which aimed for a much higher proportion, has not yet had the opportunity to prove what numbers it might attract. So, although 3 per cent after 25 years is a small proportion, it is a clear piece of evidence that an independent body such as the National Board can make a sustained and increasingly important contribution to the development of high levels of teacher expertise and become an influence on state and federal policy.

In concluding this section it is important to mention that the NBPTS had a major review of its history and effectiveness (discussed in Chapter 6) conducted by a totally independent and credible institution, the National Research Council of the National Academy of Sciences, which produced a book-length report (NRC, 2008). That report could only make recommendations to a self-managing and autonomous body, leaving it to the educational wisdom and robustness of that institution to determine its way forward and act on those recommendations, one of which is that 'The NBPTS should pursue an ongoing research agenda to evaluate progress toward its goals' (NRC, 2008).

The Board is following this up, and boldly states on its website:

> More than a decade of research from across the country confirms: Students taught by Board-certified teachers learn more than students taught by other teachers. Estimates of the increase in learning are in the order of an additional one to two months of instruction. The positive impact of having a Board-certified teacher (NBCT) is even greater for minority and low-income students. This improvement in student outcomes is mirrored by NBCTs achieving stronger results on leading measures of teacher effectiveness, including robust classroom observations and value added scores. The compelling research on the effectiveness of Board certified teachers is particularly noteworthy when compared to the lack of consistent research on the effectiveness of teachers with master's degrees.
>
> *(NRC, 2008)*

In support of these claims it cites a range of research (see references below). We feel certain that this boldness is both justified and necessary. It is clearly self-promotion – but that is something the teaching profession is notoriously weak at.

The Board adds: '81% of Americans across the political spectrum believe teachers should achieve Board certification, beyond licensure, as it is in other professions' (2014 PDK/Gallup poll) (NRC, 2008). While poll research has none of the credibility of independent research, it always has some influence, especially with the media and policymakers. Overall it is clear that NBPTS is really showing the way in asserting the value of developing expert teachers and in raising the status of the profession.

Finally, one other report deserves a mention as it was chiefly written by National Board teachers but sponsored by a separate body, the Centre for Teacher Quality (CTQ). This is one of those independent think tank-style organisations, not attached to a university (although it was originally) and with a commercial aspect to its work.

Its website states:

> A high-quality public education system for all students will not be achieved without a bold brand of leadership from their teachers.
>
> CTQ's three strategies:
>
> - Cultivate: Deepening and assessing the impact of teacher leadership on learning
> - Incubate: Advancing school designs for 21st-century leadership and student learning
> - Scale: Developing and marketing a system to spread teachers' knowledge and skills as leaders of their profession
>
> *(CTQ website)*

It appears to be truly supportive of teachers and their expertise and, unusually, is not funded by a conservative foundation. The report discussed below was published in 2008 and led to further work for the CTQ with NBPTS, including the publication *The National Board for Professional Teaching Standards and the Future of a Profession*, which is also a valuable and independent review of NBPTS.

CTQ have coined a new term for leading teacher, 'teacherpreuner', which they define as 'a special brand of classroom expert who blurs the lines of distinction between those who teach in schools and those who lead them' (CTQ website). We have not added this term to our list of generally accepted descriptors but recognise why such a neat hybrid term, combining teaching with a business-orientated semantic connation, may well develop some potency.

Our main interest here is their report *Measuring What Matters: The Effects of National Board Certification on Advancing 21st Century Teaching and Learning*, which has the additional title, *A* TeacherSolutions *Report by 10 National Board Certified Teachers* (CTQ, 2008).

The report opens with the remarks:

> More so than ever before, policymakers and the public believe the fate of American public education rests with teachers. Over the last 15 years, study after study points to the powerful effects of qualified teachers and quality teaching on student achievement. However, poor children and those of color are still far less likely to be taught by good teachers – no matter how 'good' is defined. Unfortunately, little consensus exists among researchers and policymakers on how to define a qualified teacher and how to most effectively identify and reward effective teachers.
>
> *(CTQ, 2008, p. 1)*

We would certainly agree with the point about policymakers and lack of consensus. The report gives ten teachers space to undertake their own review of research and develop the case for teachers like themselves to be heard. The preface further defines the policy context:

> Many policymakers – from both sides of the political aisle – have welcomed the assessments of the National Board as a tool to professionalize teaching. Teaching has long been described as a 'semi-profession' due to its truncated training, its unenforced standards, and its ill-defined body of knowledge. While the National Board generated strong bipartisan support in its early years of development, several researchers and education think tank analysts have begun to question the cost-benefits of the assessments. The arguments for and against the return on investment often seem more political than substantive.
>
> *(CTQ, 2008, p. 7)*

The report adopts a strong and positive rhetoric that these teachers should be given much more expert status as influencers of policy:

> This outstanding team of NBCTs (see p. 51 for a list of participants) reviewed a wide range of National Board research studies and participated in webinars with a number of scholars who conducted or analyzed the research findings. They examined the pros and cons of different research methods, and they applied their own experiences to what they heard and learned – always reflecting on the intersection of large-scale empirical data, their own development as expert teachers, and the nature of the students they teach and serve. They deliberated and debated among themselves. They also reached out to colleagues – including members of the Teacher Leaders Network – to generate additional perspectives and insights.
>
> *(Ibid.)*

This report is not unique but it is special in being independent of NBPTS but having their full cooperation. It is also a rare example of expert teachers reviewing research about expert teaching. It is over fifty pages long and for the purpose of this book we limit ourselves to quoting from some of their main recommendations. They outline what they consider a major issue with current research data:

> The researchers' conclusions and policy implications were often based on limited or misguided thinking about what effective teaching looks like, and their evaluation of student attainment was nearly always confined to test scores, not authentic work products that offer multidimensional evidence of learning. It is a complicated challenge to measure teaching and its impact on students, but difficult and important work deserves equally complex and thoughtful assessment.
>
> *(CTQ, 2008, p. 16)*

They continue by developing their argument for measuring what matters in expert teaching:

> Before we can assess (and replicate) effective and engaging teaching, we need a rich and well-developed portrait of what it looks like – from everyday classroom practice to its end product, student learning. We cannot be satisfied with the limited, inadequate information about teaching quality yielded by standardized test results. In our review of the research, we were also struck by the inadequate vision of quality professional development in many of the studies that delve into the relationship between the National Board process and professional growth. We found little acknowledgement that the crucial catalyst for meaningful and sustainable professional growth is a rich description of accomplished practice.
>
> *(Ibid.)*

We heartily endorse these views and also, especially, this next point:

> We believe higher standards and expectations for student learning must be accompanied by a vibrant, detailed picture of what successful teachers know and can do to reach those goals. The existing research does not embrace, much less illuminate, this concept of exceptional, skilled teaching.
>
> *(Ibid.)*

What the report makes clear is that the work of the Board is developing some of that knowledge of exceptional teaching but that the research agenda needs to change to find new and credible ways to capture the effects of the best teaching, going well beyond – though without ignoring – simplistic measures based on test scores. The report also cites a selective and useful body of research evidence to support its conclusions; this is presented at the end of the chapter as an NBPTS reference list.

Sustainability? Strengths and weaknesses of extant and recent models

Political interference may remain the most fundamental issue in high-performing systems but the various models can be considered as displaying characteristics revealing both strengths and weaknesses. Using Hattie's work (see Chapter 3), we offer a brief summary of the major models. Hattie was very clear that his characteristics offer a profile, not a checklist.

He first synthesises the findings into five dimensions:

Expert teachers:

- A: can identify essential representations of their subject,
- B: can guide learning through classroom interactions,
- C: can monitor learning and provide feedback,
- D: can attend to affective attributes, and
- E: can influence student outcomes (Hattie, 2003).

All the models explored in this book do relate to these overarching dimensions. Some, like the AST, are highly generic and could be criticised for lack of attention to the idea of 'subject', whereas the US HAT model could be considered overly dominated by the notion of subject. The new Australian version (see below) does not copy the US subject inflection, another interesting example of global influence with local adaptation. We summarise Hattie's outline of the specific characteristics of expert teachers (Hattie, 2003, pp. 6–10); we then offer an approximate mapping onto some of the major expert teacher models.

Expert teachers:

A1 have deeper representations about teaching and learning.
A2 adopt a problem-solving stance to their work.
A3 can anticipate, plan, and improvise as required by the situation.
A4 are better decision-makers and can identify what decisions are important and which are less important decisions.

B5 are proficient at creating an optimal classroom climate for learning.
B6 have a multidimensionally complex perception of classroom situations.
B7 are more context-dependent and have high situation cognition.

C8 are more adept at monitoring student problems and assessing their level of understanding and progress, and they provide much more relevant, useful feedback.
C9 are more adept at developing and testing hypotheses about learning difficulties or instructional strategies.
C10 are more automatic.

D11 have high respect for students.
D12 are passionate about teaching and learning.

E13 engage students in learning and develop in their students' self-regulation, involvement in mastery learning, enhanced self-efficacy, and self-esteem as learners.
E14 provide appropriate challenging tasks and goals for students.
E15 have positive influences on students' achievement.
E16 enhance surface and deep learning.

Table 8.1 provides a simple overview of some of the key models discussed in the book:

TABLE 8.1

Expert teacher model	*Current status*	*Independence*	*Synergy with Hattie*
Advanced Skills Teacher, Australia	Current but potentially diminishing	State controlled	Modest
Advanced Skills Teacher, England	Terminated	Government controlled	Modest
Chartered Teacher, Scotland	Terminated	Government controlled	Modest, great emphasis on professional values
Highly Accomplished Teacher, USA	Ongoing	Independent	Strong but subject inflected
Highly Accomplished Teacher, Australia	Under development	Independent	Strong
Master Teacher, England	Proposed	Government controlled (probably)	Weak

In his work Hattie consistently differentiates between 'experienced' and 'expert' teachers, commenting:

> The manner used by the teacher to treat the students, respect them as learners and people, and demonstrate care and commitment for them are attributes of expert teachers. By having such respect, they can recognize possible barriers to learning and can seek ways to overcome these barriers. The picture drawn of experts is one of involvement and caring for the students, a willingness to be receptive to what the students need, not attempting to dominate the situation. Too often experienced teachers tended to create more physical and psychological distance between themselves and their students than do experts.
>
> *(2003, p. 8)*

He adds: 'Berliner (1988) claimed that experts' sense of responsibility played a part in their feelings as well. Expert teachers, like experts in most domains, show more emotionality about successes and failures in their work' (ibid.).

Taken together these quotations help us reflect on the lack of ways to recognise and, perhaps, evaluate the more emotional elements that are such a distinguishing feature of the expert teacher's classroom. We know that the impact of teachers on students' achievement is too often considered the gold, and only, standard of expertise. The impact of teachers on students' outcomes in high-stakes tests is too often considered the 'gold', and only, standard of expertise. We consider that other outcomes such as self-efficacy, self-regulation, willingness to be challenged are equally – perhaps even more – important as their value may last a lifetime. The problem, as Hattie makes clear, is that we have not yet discovered dependable and credible ways to capture these achievement effects and attribute them to teacher effects.

A credible and sustainable model? Australia's Highly Accomplished Teacher scheme

It fits very well with the spirit of this book to conclude with a look at a relatively new model that illustrates many of the best elements of the systematic development of an expert teaching designation. This Australian initiative began its development in 2011 and was established by 2013. Like the National Board in the USA, it has an independent agency overseeing it and stems from a federal system that had various versions of the AST and now seeks to create a supra-federal form of certification so that teachers have a portable accreditation, making them recognised and employable anywhere in the country. The scheme is too new to be offered as robust and well tried but is well worth reviewing for its strengths and long-term potential. All references are to the excellent website (www.aitsl.edu.au) of the Australian Institute for Teaching and School Leadership (AITSL). AITSL as a body is a public company with its own constitution and an independent board of directors: it stresses that it is not a government department. The website outlines the nature of its work and already contains a wealth of information and many supportive resources for teachers. This book has looked at numerous models and standards and this section will not exhaustively document what is still a very new development; instead, it will outline the main features of the model and why it appears to have a robust future.

As a preamble it is important to state that Australia has been experimenting with expert teacher models for about thirty years in some states (see Chapter 5). The term Advanced Skills Teacher was coined there and later co-opted by England; we think it an entirely healthy development that the Australian government has funded the development of a new model and has adapted the successful US Highly Accomplished Teacher approach. It has similarities but many distinct differences. The most obvious difference is that certification is by level of accomplishment and there is no subject or phase specialism.

A particularly impressive element is that the new model has widespread support across the educational and political sectors and 17 different pilots were carried out in 2011 to test out various aspects of the proposals before they were implemented. This piloting approach was also a feature of the development of the US HAT model and contrasts to, for example, the AST designation in England, which was simply launched full scale. The pilot studies in Australia were small-scale but highly focused. Three of the studies were focused on parents and the community, helping AITSL ensure that the standards and concept made sense to parents and would be welcome in communities. We believe this dimension is very important for addressing the need to raise the status of teaching in the public's understanding.

The standards are organised into 'Domains of Teaching', 'Professional Knowledge', 'Professional Practice' and 'Professional Engagement'. Within each domain are focus area descriptors, seven in total, which are broken down into the standards. Professional Knowledge has two descriptors: 'Know students and how they learn' and 'Know the content and how to teach it'. Professional Practice has three: 'Plan for and implement effective teaching and learning', 'Create and maintain supportive and safe learning environments' and 'Assess, provide feedback and report on student learning'. Professional Engagement has two: 'Engage in professional learning' and 'Engage professionally with colleagues, parents/carers and the community'. There is a clear and elegant simplicity about these statements, although there might be some anxiety should they be seen as oversimplifying the complexity of teaching.

However, there are very helpful elaborations of the rationale for each domain worth quoting in full:

> The Standards are grouped into three domains of teaching; Professional Knowledge, Professional Practice and Professional Engagement. In practice, teaching draws on aspects of all three domains.
>
> **Professional Knowledge**
>
> Teachers draw on a body of professional knowledge and research to respond to the needs of their students within their educational contexts.
>
> Teachers know their students well, including their diverse linguistic, cultural and religious backgrounds. They know how the experiences that students bring to their classroom affect their continued learning. They know how to structure their lessons to meet the physical, social and intellectual development and characteristics of their students.
>
> Teachers know the content of their subjects and curriculum. They know and understand the fundamental concepts, structure and enquiry processes relevant to programs they teach. Teachers understand what constitutes effective, developmentally appropriate strategies in their learning and teaching programs and use this knowledge to make the content meaningful to students.
>
> Through their teaching practice, teachers develop students' literacy and numeracy within their subject areas. They are also able to use Information and Communication Technology to contextualise and expand their students' modes and breadth of learning.
>
> *(AITSL website)*

This is an excellently simple definition without *over*simplifying, equally comprehensible to both teachers and to parents and other stakeholders. The last paragraph ensures that teachers see their contribution to the broad learning objectives of their school and to the lives of their students in a twenty-first-century economy.

> **Professional Practice**
>
> Teachers are able to make learning engaging and valued. They are able to create and maintain safe, inclusive and challenging learning environments and implement fair and equitable behaviour management plans. They use sophisticated communication techniques.
>
> Teachers have a repertoire of effective teaching strategies and use them to implement well-designed teaching programs and lessons. They regularly evaluate all aspects of their teaching practice to ensure they are meeting the learning needs of their students. They interpret and use student assessment data to diagnose barriers to learning and to challenge students to improve their performance.
>
> They operate effectively at all stages of the teaching and learning cycle, including planning for learning and assessment, developing learning programs, teaching, assessing, providing feedback on student learning and reporting to parents/carers.
>
> *(Ibid.)*

The emphasis here is on achieving a balance between understanding students' needs and challenging them to ensure their intellectual development as well as their well-being and self-esteem. It is particularly welcome that student data is to be used 'to diagnose barriers to learning' rather than to reductively demonstrate teacher performance.

> **Professional Engagement**
>
> Teachers model effective learning. They identify their own learning needs and analyse, evaluate and expand their professional learning, both collegially and individually.
>
> Teachers demonstrate respect and professionalism in all their interactions with students, colleagues, parents/carers and the community. They are sensitive to the needs of parents/carers and can communicate effectively with them about their children's learning.
>
> Teachers value opportunities to engage with their school communities within and beyond the classroom to enrich the educational context for students. They understand the links between school, home and community in the social and intellectual development of their students.
>
> *(Ibid.)*

There is an admirable emphasis here on the role of teachers that goes beyond the classroom but always reflects on the status of teachers. Recent research (Goodwyn, 2013) suggests that the teaching profession may need to display its expertise more publically, to make the complexity and challenge of teaching more explicit. This is different from the emphasis in paragraph two, which states that teachers 'are sensitive to the needs of parents/carers and can communicate effectively with them about their children's learning', which can be seen as the traditional role of interacting with parents within the school setting. The emphasis in paragraph three is on a much more ambassadorial, proactive role within the community. This gives Highly Accomplished and Lead teachers much higher-profile opportunities to raise the status of the teaching profession in their local communities.

There are four levels (Graduate, Proficient, Highly Accomplished and Lead), all with detailed descriptors too long to quote. However, the opening statement of each gives a good idea of how the hierarchy operates.

> **Career stages**
>
> The four career stages (Graduate, Proficient, Highly Accomplished and Lead) in the Standards provide benchmarks to recognise the professional growth of teachers throughout their careers. The descriptors across the four career stages represent increasing levels of knowledge, practice and professional engagement for teachers. Progression through the stages describes a growing understanding, applied with increasing sophistication across a broader and more complex range of situations.
>
> ***Graduate teachers***
>
> Graduate teachers have completed a qualification that meets the requirements of a nationally accredited program of initial teacher education. The award of this qualification means that they have met the Graduate Standards. On successful completion of their initial teacher education, graduate teachers possess the requisite knowledge and skills to plan for and manage learning programs for students. They demonstrate knowledge and understanding of the implications for learning of students' physical, cultural, social, linguistic and intellectual characteristics. They understand principles of inclusion and strategies for differentiating teaching to meet the specific learning needs of students across the full range of abilities.
>
> *(Ibid.)*

We feel this sets the bar at an appropriately high level as it stresses that novice teachers should have been trained to a high professional level and be fully competent when they begin their teaching careers. The proficient level fits well with ideas embedded in, for instance, the Dreyfus model as a clear expectation of progress to be made by all teachers – which also, in a sense, defines an acceptable minimum for all experienced teachers.

> ***Proficient teachers***
>
> Proficient teachers meet the requirements for full registration through demonstrating achievement of the seven Standards at this level.
>
> *(Ibid.)*

The next two levels offer the really exciting prospect of an increasing number of teachers becoming leaders of learning.

> ***Highly Accomplished teachers***
>
> Highly Accomplished teachers are recognised as highly effective, skilled classroom practitioners and routinely work independently and collaboratively to improve their own practice and the practice of colleagues. They are knowledgeable and active members of the school.
>
> *(Ibid.)*

The emphasis here on being highly effective but also collaborative is especially powerful. The accreditation process (see below) strongly accentuates the need to demonstrate collegiality and a commitment to the development of other teachers; this is an important dynamic for the development of the profession in any country.

> ***Lead teachers***
>
> Lead teachers are recognised and respected by colleagues, parents/carers and community members as exemplary teachers. They have demonstrated consistent and innovative teaching practice over time. Inside and outside the school they initiate and lead activities that focus on improving educational opportunities for all students. They establish inclusive learning environments, meeting the needs of students from different linguistic, cultural, religious and socio-economic backgrounds. They continue to seek ways to improve their own practice and to share their experience with colleagues.
>
> *(Ibid.)*

These lead teachers should exemplify all the qualities of the Highly Accomplished teacher but with the addition of being consistently innovative and connecting with the community, not just parents. We feel that innovation and respect are very importantly connected and that this is one of the most dynamic elements in this new model of expert teaching. Such teachers are ambassadors for a model of teaching that is always developing, constantly evaluating and never complacent and in a position to communicate these dynamics to parents and the wider community. This is where this model demonstrates the spirit of places like Finland and Singapore without borrowing their approaches.

This logically leads to each standard having four levels; one example will suffice to indicate how this works.

Know students and how they learn

Physical, social and intellectual development and characteristics of students

> Graduate level: Demonstrate knowledge and understanding of physical, social and intellectual development and characteristics of students and how these may affect learning.
>
> Proficient level: Use teaching strategies based on knowledge of students' physical, social and intellectual development and characteristics to improve student learning.
>
> Highly Accomplished level: Select from a flexible and effective repertoire of teaching strategies to suit the physical, social and intellectual development and characteristics of students.
>
> Lead teacher level: Lead colleagues to select and develop teaching strategies to improve student learning using knowledge of the physical, social and intellectual development and characteristics of students.
>
> (*Ibid.*)

These levels demonstrate both a consistency across each one and a demonstrably higher level of skill that can be made evident in practice. Levels in some other models tend just to add in modifiers like 'very' to differentiate levels; these level descriptors are clearer and more robust.

The certification process (see *Guide to the Certification of Highly Accomplished and Lead Teachers*, AITSL, 2013) is similar to that of the AST model in England, involving assessment by an external assessor who has been appropriately trained and who visits and observes the candidate; the latter will also have prepared a portfolio of evidence and have references from a range of professional peers. As a process it is nothing like as long or detailed as the US HAT model but it will be available to far more teachers and there is no cost to the candidate. The Lead teacher assessment is slightly more complex but not more onerous. The process is also very sensibly designed to fit with existing school practices of annual appraisal and so on. For example:

> Certification will benefit all those involved in the process, including teachers, school leaders and education systems. The recognition and certification of excellence aims to encourage teachers to engage in a process aimed at developing ongoing, collaborative, learning professionals who strive to reflect upon and improve practice. It involves significant reflection on current classroom practice and the wider school influence of the teacher, and comprehensive feedback on strengths and areas for improvement.
>
> It is important that where possible and appropriate, certification processes fit with other arrangements in which teachers are involved. The process of certification aligns with other processes that teachers are required to undertake including observations of practice, annual performance reviews against

> performance and development goals, processes to maintain registration/accreditation as a teacher, and alignment to school plans and school-wide development.
>
> *(AITSL, 2013)*

The five principles that inform the certification of Highly Accomplished and Lead teachers are equally clear and concise:

> **Standards-based**
>
> Certification is awarded against the *Australian Professional Standards for Teachers*. It represents an assessment against the Standards, independent of any use it might then be put to by teachers, their employers, or others. It is not proposed to limit the number of teachers who can be certified as Highly Accomplished and Lead teachers, provided they meet the Standards.
>
> **Student-improvement focused**
>
> Certification recognises those teachers who are highly effective in improving student outcomes. Evidence of student outcomes is central to the certification process. Student outcomes are broadly defined and include student learning, engagement in learning and wellbeing.
>
> **Development driven**
>
> Certification is part of a wider career development approach that includes professional learning, performance assessment and development. Participation in the certification process should be a positive experience for participants and provide useful feedback that further enhances development and learning, including for those teachers who do not achieve certification.
>
> **Credible**
>
> Certification is credible when assessments of teacher performance are based on rigorous, valid, reliable, fair and transparent measures and processes. The evaluation of teacher practice will be based on consistent application and moderation of these processes by trained assessors, and multiple methods and sources of evidence. Consistency of judgements will be maintained across the diverse contexts where teachers work, so that context does not disadvantage any applicant.
>
> **Evidence-based**
>
> Certification must be built on nationally and internationally recognised best practice and contribute to the development of evidence about what works

> in promoting and recognising teacher quality. The operation of the certification process will be evaluated and the results used to further improve it.
>
> *(Ibid.)*

This model is a true example of global adaptation, drawing on a number of other tried models but also innovative and locally inflected. It is currently free from short-term political interference and so offers a fresh opportunity to develop a robust national system of expert teacher recognition and development. It also has a built-in evaluation process that will be extremely important and perhaps offer real opportunities for independent research that can finally address some of the serious gaps in our knowledge of what characterises expert teaching and how it can better be described and measured. The final section of the book will consider areas for further research.

Future development and research

Perhaps the weakest element in the development of successful models of expert teaching is the lack of compelling, especially longitudinal, research. It is particularly notable that the well funded, and comprehensive, evaluation of the National Board's Accomplished Teacher model mainly concluded that it could not arrive at proper conclusions or recommendations. Though stating that accomplished teachers did make a difference to student achievement, they found statistical evidence very hard to come by; there was also too much variation between states for meaningful national-level conclusions. They pointed out that much more research is needed – suggesting, in fact, a rich vein for future research. One recommendation was that researchers should 'Investigate the effects of the [certification] process on the candidates using pretest/posttest and longitudinal designs – to permit comparisons between successful and unsuccessful candidates' (NRC, 2008, p. 8).

To our knowledge, no research producing useful data about the effects of HAT certification or any other scheme yet exists. Our research on Advanced Skills Teachers in England could only report on ASTs' own perceptions of how becoming an AST had improved their own teaching. It is also important to recognise that AST status could be achieved after a two-day assessment procedure, whereas the HAT is a year-long process with far more elements than the AST model. The Chartered Teacher was much more comparable to the HAT but was discontinued too soon to provide any robust data about teacher change. As for what happens to unsuccessful candidates in any of these schemes – why they were unsuccessful and whether they try again and so on – this is an area that has been completely neglected.

The report frequently comments on how little 'hard' evidence could be found about a relationship between certification and clearly improved test scores and they 'recommend research on the effects of Board certification on teachers' practices; these studies should utilize both quantitative and qualitative methods to examine a variety of measures of teachers' practice and of student outcomes' (NRC, 2008, p. 8).

This is probably the Holy Grail for politicians, so might lead to greater investment in expert teacher schemes. We continue to argue that student outcomes need to be broadly interpreted, to be much more sophisticated than just test scores or equivalents. The HAT scheme is unusual in offering so many different certifications across age phases and specialisms but it does mean that research could be conducted to '[s]tudy the relationships between board certification and student outcomes across the various stages of the board certifications' (NRC, 2008, p. 8).

In other countries this might have to be undertaken with a simpler design, perhaps comparing elementary certified teachers with secondary or comparing some of the subject associations' Chartered schemes in England in relation to teacher change and student outcomes.

The report is adamant that there is far too little robust data on how certified teachers make a difference, especially to students (see Chapter 8 of the report). It also concludes that the kinds of difference such teachers may make may not really manifest themselves in the very narrow range of skills captured by student test scores (ibid., p. 194), for example 'higher order thinking skills and enthusiasm for learning'.

We need further meta-analytical research, but Hattie's work has shown the way, making a strong case for understanding what the best teaching looks like and so offering ways for assessing, recognising and developing it. What evaluations there have been of models of expert teaching, such as of the National Board, raise more questions than they answer. Some recent reports have had some success in bringing certain of the values of expert teaching to the attention of politicians, but their large claims rest on a rather selective research base. It is worth referring here to the development of the field of expertise studies and the Cambridge handbook quoted in Chapter 1, which contains only the briefest section on teaching, reminding us that teaching is a recent entrant to the field.

The current obsession in so many systems with measuring all teacher competence through narrow tests of student achievement is, in our view, counterproductive to the development of a highly effective and confident teaching profession. It also has severe negative implications for teacher morale and teacher retention. It seems increasingly clear that vitally important areas of teacher effectiveness are currently neglected in most models of performance management. These areas are essentially those related to teacher values and to relationships with students. These dimensions do appear in expert teacher models, though with extraordinary variations; the new Australian model is promisingly explicit about these dimensions and may offer real opportunities for fundamental research.

We argue that investment is needed to enhance our understanding of the very important role these areas play in expert teaching. They are often side-lined because they seem so difficult to measure, but this, paradoxically, may be their strength. Their importance cannot be reduced to numbers – or at least we have not found a way yet to do so. If such numbers were accurate and based on sound evidence there would be nothing wrong in rating a teacher's capability to, for example, form positive relationships with students. Much more important in the medium term is research that spotlights the essential role of relationship building in good teaching, which can then be extended to the way expert teachers excel in this respect.

We have consistently argued that diverse models of expert teaching are both organic to systems and cultures and mutually beneficial in offering different innovations that can be adapted to local circumstances. What we lack is substantial investment in research that would reveal not only what expert teaching looks like but, more importantly, what are some of its benefits that we cannot currently accurately assess. For example, there is almost no research about the perceptions of parents and the community with regard to expert teacher designations – how such perceptions might relate to the status of the profession, for instance. Similarly, it would be useful to know the views of teachers about whatever model their system has developed and how they feel about its importance or negative impact. Such research would have to be based on a substantial and well-established model (like the National Board) and conducted over time to even out results. It would also need to be fiercely independent and not subject to any political agenda.

We have finally reached a time when international comparative research is a realistic possibility. We do not see this as like PISA or its equivalents, where the creation of a league table is the divisive outcome. It is interesting that at the time of writing, and discussed above, there has been an attempt to create an international league table of teacher status in 25 countries; this is the Global Teacher Status Index, based on research by the GEMS organisation. We have expressed our doubts about both the motives and the methodology for this 'innovation', not least whether its recent addition of the equivalent of a Nobel prize for teaching may not make the whole idea a glamorous gimmick. We have stressed throughout the book that a diversity of models of expert teaching is far more useful than searching for a model that might work anywhere. The Global Index, we suggest, tells us much more about societal and cultural differences in attitudes towards teaching than anything else. Such an index is more likely to catch the eye of politicians and the media than become a meaningful instrument for understanding changes to teacher status around the world. One of the impressive elements of the AITSL model is the foregrounding of teacher engagement with the community. Recent research (Goodwyn, 2013) suggests that the AST model was successful in raising the status of the best teachers in the profession but did not gain sufficient public recognition – and that this was a missed opportunity.

Rather than international league tables, we want research to give us a deeper understanding of what counts as expert teaching in different cultures and contexts, to make comparisons and contrasts about expert teachers that lead to new insights into innovative and creative pedagogies. Such research should lead to fresh ideas in many systems. The adaptation of the USA's Highly Accomplished Teacher model by Australia shows a commendable desire to refresh the Advanced Skills Teacher concept with a much more credible model of teacher assessment and certification. At a time when England has terminated the Advanced Skills Teacher and considered introducing a very dubious Master Teacher standard and Scotland has abandoned the Chartered Teacher, it is good to see the US model thriving and the new Australian model offering real promise.

England has been much discussed in this book, with very reasonable reference to its obsession with constant politically motivated change, which has led to an unstable teaching profession and arbitrary decisions such as the abolition of the General Teaching Council and the demise of the Advanced Skills Teacher. So it is encouraging to conclude this section with a glimmer of hope. There has been much discussion about the relative vacuum created by both these changes and what might be a way forward. One proposal, which appears to have political backing, is to create a new and independent body called the College of Teaching (CoT) (we might devote much space to whether this is the right name, not least because there already is a College of Teachers). However, discussion of a body that has yet to be truly established would be premature. On its website it boldly asserts:

> The College of Teaching will be the new independent chartered professional body for the teaching profession. The College will be committed to the improvement of education through the support of teacher development and recognition of excellence in teaching. It will be led by teachers, enabling the teaching profession to take responsibility for its professional destiny, set its own aspirational standards and help teachers to challenge themselves to be ever better for those they serve.
>
> The proposals for the new College of Teaching have been developed through extensive consultation with the teaching profession and have gained widespread support across the profession and with related stakeholder groups.
>
> *(CoT website)*

We entirely welcome such a development and it is clear that the profession in England needs such reform. However, a body of this sort will need not only substantial funding to get started, which will almost certainly have to come from government, but also significant income for a sustainable future. A survey conducted in late 2014 under the banner of 'Claim your College' (see CoT website) produced a very positive response from teachers. However, qualitative research by Goodwyn in 2014 and 2015 found both strong support for the idea and deep cynicism about it becoming a reality. The research found that senior leaders looked back on the GTC as mostly an irrelevance and had deep doubts about any possibility of the college having true independence. On the other hand, the majority deeply regretted the passing of the AST and hoped that a new national body might create a new model of expert teaching. So England may be emerging from a period of endless turbulence around the profession, full of noisy rhetoric supporting a world-class profession while policies actually undermined both the status of the profession and teaching as a career: a sustainable and independent body even more powerful than the NBPTS might emerge, but we suggest that it would need a similar period of 25 years to fulfil that potential.

Conclusions but rather more aspirations

We have reached an important moment in the history and development of models of expert teaching. Many systems now have such models or are exploring their potential. We have established there is no globally apposite model that every system should adopt – indeed, we are clear that all models should be fit for local purpose but remain open to learning from other models, adapting continually and aware of developments elsewhere that allow for 'testing'.

It is also an interesting moment in the development of expertise studies per se. Understandings of human expertise have advanced enormously in the twentieth century. Despite this, we note that some areas of expertise are much more precisely defined and are domains where research can offer relatively conclusive outcomes: chess, for example. Teaching will never be chess and chess will never be teaching. The classroom, the tutorial room, the lecture hall, the Virtual Learning Environment, a discussion board, a Skype tutorial – whatever spaces are devoted to the act of teaching and learning will remain, almost certainly, problematically unstructured domains with infinite and bewildering numbers of variables. However, the study of these domains could not be more important if we are to enable all students to flourish and all teachers to develop expertise.

We argue that teaching has to insist on its place as a top-tier profession, and part of that process has to involve identifying and celebrating the very best expert teachers. The teachers in each system must, within reason, 'own' the model. We believe this is true of any standards-based structure, any performance management system, but most certainly in any model of expert teaching designed to add status to the whole profession and select exemplary teachers. All such models must be free from political interference if they are to have any chance of long-term credibility and sustainability. The concept of the expert teacher is now well established and set to play an important part in the improvement of students' lives far into the future.

References

46th Annual PDK/Gallup Poll, October 2014, p. 50, http://pdkintl.org/noindex/PDKGallupPoll_Oct2014.pdf

AITSL (Australian Institute for Teaching and School Leadership): www.aitsl.edu.au

AITSL (2013) *Guide to the Certification of Highly Accomplished and Lead Teachers*. Carlton South: Education Services Australia/SCSEEC.

College of Teaching (CoT) website: www.collegeofteachers.ac.uk

CTQ (Center for Teacher Quality) (2008) *Measuring What Matters: The Effects of National Board Certification on Advancing 21st Century Teaching and Learning*. Carrboro, NC: Center for Teacher Quality.

Goodwyn, A. (2013) 'Head teachers view of Expert teachers: Do they see the Advanced Skills Teacher as an innovation benefitting the profession?' Paper given at the European Educational Research Association, Istanbul (September).

Goodwyn, A. (2014) 'Head teachers view of Expert teachers: Do they see the Advanced Skills Teacher as an innovation benefitting the profession?' Paper presented to the British Educational Research Association, University of London (September).

Goodwyn, A. (2015) 'Has the Advanced Skills Teacher role been an advance for the profession? The views of principals and other senior leaders'. Paper presented at the American Educational Research Association Conference, Chicago (April).

Hattie, J. (2003) *Teachers Make a Difference: What is the Research Evidence?* Auckland: University of Auckland.

National Board for Professional Teaching Standards (NBPTS): www.nbpts.org

NRC (National Research Council) (2008) *Assessing Accomplished Teaching: Advanced-Level Certification Programs*. Washington, DC: The National Academies Press.

References for NBPTS from the CTQ report

Salvador, S.K. and Baxter, A. (2010) 'National Board Certification; Impact on teacher effectiveness'. Charlotte-Mecklenburg Schools, Center for Research and Evaluation, Office of Accountability.

Strategic Data Project (2012) 'SDP Human Capital Diagnostic: Los Angeles Unified School District'. Center for Education Policy Research, Harvard University.

Strategic Data Project (2012a) 'Learning about teacher effectiveness: SDP Human Capital Diagnostic: Gwinnett County Public Schools'. Center for Education Policy Research, Harvard University.

Vandervoort, L. G., Amrein-Beardsley, A. and Berliner, D. C. (2004) 'National Board Certified Teachers and their students' achievement', *Education Policy Analysis Archives*, 12(46).

Varkey Foundation (2016) www.varkeyfoundation.org/teacherindex

INDEX